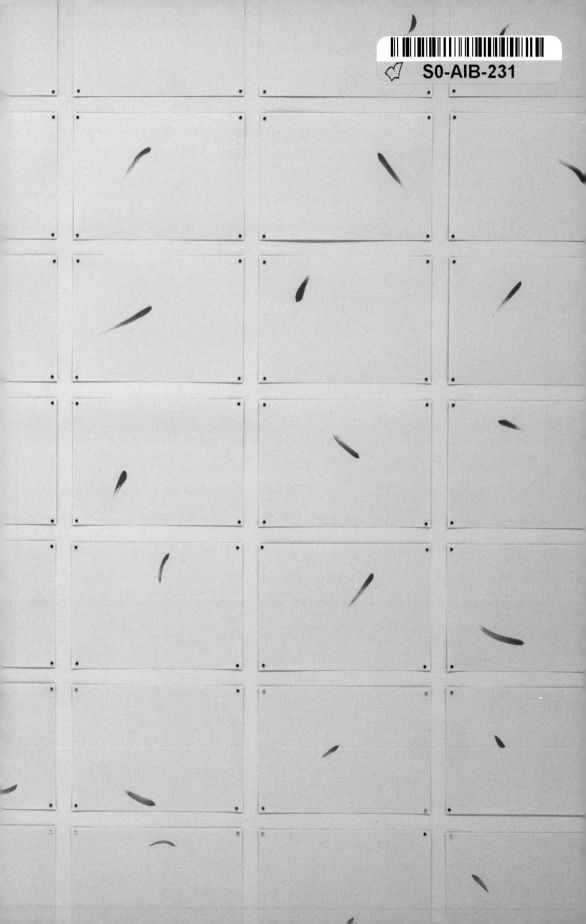

A House Called Tomorrow

A House Called Tomorrow

Fifty Years of Poetry from Copper Canyon Press

EDITED BY MICHAEL WIEGERS

COPPER CANYON PRESS

PORT TOWNSEND, WASHINGTON

Cover art: Erika Blumenfeld. Detail of *Encyclopedia of Trajectories: Untitled Meteor (2017.07.30—04:39:24 UTC—Perseids—Camera 14A)*, 2017, 10.25 × 14.25 inches, single-stroke drawing with finely ground 23.75 karat gold suspended in gum Arabic on 140-pound Arches Aquarelle hot-pressed watercolor paper. www.erikablumenfeld.com

Endpapers: Erika Blumenfeld. Installation view of 49 drawings from *Encyclopedia of Trajectories,* 2017–2018. Each drawing is 10.25 × 14.25 inches with finely ground 23.75 karat gold suspended in gum Arabic on 140-pound Arches Aquarelle hot-pressed watercolor paper. Installed in the Main Studio at the Robert Rauschenberg Foundation Residency, Captiva, Florida, January–February 2018. (Photo: Erika Blumenfeld)

Copper Canyon Press is in residence at Fort Worden State Park in Port Townsend, Washington, under the auspices of Centrum. Centrum is a gathering place for artists and creative thinkers from around the world, students of all ages and backgrounds, and audiences seeking extraordinary cultural enrichment.

LIBRARY OF CONGRESS CATALOGING-IN-PUBLICATION DATA

Names: Wiegers, Michael, editor.
Title: A house called tomorrow : fifty years of poetry from Copper Canyon
    Press / edited by Michael Wiegers.
Description: Port Townsend, Washington : Copper Canyon Press, [2023] |
    Includes indexes. | Summary: "This is an anthology that celebrates 50
    years of Copper Canyon Press publications, one extraordinary poem at a
    time. Since its founding in 1972, Copper Canyon has been entirely
    dedicated to publishing poetry books; here Editor in Chief Michael
    Wiegers invites Press staff and board—past and present—to help curate a
    retrospective"—Provided by publisher.
Identifiers: LCCN 2022036244 (print) | LCCN 2022036245 (ebook) |
    ISBN 9781556596629 (paperback) | ISBN 9781619322684 (epub)
Subjects: LCSH: Poetry—Collections. | Copper Canyon Press. |
    American poetry—21st century. | American poetry—20th century. |
    Poetry, Modern—21st century—Translations into English. |
    Poetry, Modern—20th century—Translations into English. | LCGFT: Poetry.
Classification: LCC PN6101 .H665 2023 (print) | LCC PN6101 (ebook) |
    DDC 811/.508—dc23/eng/20220922
LC record available at https://lccn.loc.gov/2022036244
LC ebook record available at https://lccn.loc.gov/2022036245

ISBN 9781556596704 (hardcover)

9 8 7 6 5 4 3 2 first printing

COPPER CANYON PRESS

Post Office Box 271
Port Townsend, Washington 98368
www.coppercanyonpress.org

in memory of J. Patrick Lannan Jr.

What we need is more people who specialize in the impossible.

THEODORE ROETHKE

Acknowledgments

The editor would like to thank all the Copper Canyon Press staff, current and former, who have made this work possible. I cannot name you all, and some of you are already defining the next fifty years. I would like to particularly thank Thatcher Bailey, Joseph Bednarik, David Brewster, Valerie Brewster, David Caligiuri, Angela Garbes, Sam Hamill, Claretta Holsey, Mary Jane Knecht, George Knotek, Phil Kovacevich, Alison Lockhart, Walter Parsons, John Pierce, Jessica Roeder, Tonaya Rosenberg, Tree Swenson, and Bill True: you have been mentors, guides, and friends, offering unbridled encouragement, imagination, and a shared passion for the work of Copper Canyon Press. I also want to thank Ella Wiegers, who loves trading stories with her dad about all the poets who have passed through our house and lives.

I am grateful as well to the members of Copper Canyon Press's board of directors, past and present. Currently we are blessed by the presence of

Anne Barker, President
Zeinab Agha
Donna Bellew
Emily Bennett
Jeffrey Bishop
John Branch
Rozlyn Anderson Flood
Mimi Gardner Gates
Mark Hamilton
Paul Neutz
Joseph Roberts
Jill Ruckelshaus
Kim Brown Seely
Ira Silverberg
Rick Simonson
Byron Springer
Dan Wagoner
Jonathan Wright

Contents

1980–1989

1990–1999

2010–2019

Preface

And so poetry is not a shopping list, a casual disquisition on
the colors of the sky, a soporific daydream, or bumpersticker
sloganeering. Poetry is a political action undertaken for the sake
of information, the faith, the exorcism, and the lyrical invention,
that telling the truth makes possible. Poetry means taking
control of the language of your life. Good poems can interdict
a suicide, rescue a love affair, and build a revolution in which
speaking and listening to somebody becomes the first and last
purpose to every social encounter.

June Jordan

Across the room from my desk at Copper Canyon Press, a floor-to-ceiling wall
of shelves contains all the books that we've published over the past fifty years. I
see this wall itself as a metaphor full of metaphors. It's a shared vision made up
of many visions, a voice made up of many voices. As at any library or bookstore,
the community of books gathered there is an invitation to the next book that will
arrive and change this community. That wall of books sets forth the possibility that
poetry is unified by its differences and is even made possible by the uncertainty of
which new book will join the group.

For nearly as long as poetry has been written, we seem to have argued over what
poetry actually is. At Copper Canyon we address this argument every day in the
books we edit and publish. I believe this is not an intellectual argument but rather
an elusive evolution toward empathy and connection. For centuries, definitions of
poetry have been driven by its very elusiveness, so whenever we attempt the question
of poetry, we approach an appreciation of the individual voice of the poet. As the
following pages demonstrate, styles and gestures may seem similar from poet to
poet, yet there is no singularity to what constitutes this art form. For all the different
styles, aesthetics, opinions, and assertions, we engage in common experiences
whenever we read or hear a poem.

A year before I joined Copper Canyon Press as its managing editor, I was
enthralled by the press's nascent efforts to revive the poetry of Hayden Carruth,
via his *Collected Shorter Poems, 1946–1991*. In that book, Carruth's poem "The

Impossible Indispensability of the Ars Poetica" wrestled with what poetry is and is not. It jumped out at me, and for the past thirty years, it has served as a guiding model for me to consider. And that expanding wall of books in my office has also guided me, as it has guided what appears in this book. I've always treasured and shared Carruth's assertion that "What a poem is / Is never to be known, for which I have learned to be grateful." The work of a poem transforms thought and feeling; it embraces mystery, uncertainty, and doubt as it walks a tightrope between expression and the architecture of being a made, considered thing. So often I have heard people express that they are intimidated by poetry, or that they don't understand it. Many believe poetry is a puzzle to be solved or a machine that builds meaning—an object that is available to few. A poem isn't just a sculpture made of words, nor is it just an expression of one poet's thoughts or feelings. It isn't simply an assemblage of a writer's scribbled opinions and urgencies, their explorations and assertions. Rather than say what poetry *is not,* I prefer to consider all the varieties of what it can be, from the well-hidden syntactical marks buried deep in Stone Age caves to the effectively marketed poems of younger poets who encourage us toward a future. A poem is often an invitation, a wide-open opportunity to join in an experience or idea. As I hope this book demonstrates, poetry is no one thing, yet is all these things, offering infinite possibilities.

Meanwhile, whereas a poem is expansive in its possibilities, a book *is* an object with physical limitations. It is a made thing that, when done well, assists the work of those sometimes undefinable poems. And even though many multiplicities come together in a poetry book, poetry books are finally objects that begin and end in solitude. They start with the poet alone with a blank page or an overwhelming screen and are later liberated by the reader, also alone under a lamp or the sun. That sacred bond between reader and writer is a communion that profoundly honors the individual who is reading or writing the book. Astonishingly, this book you are holding—like so many books over the course of history—has passed through many other readers and writers. This book is a vehicle passing through the traditions, imaginations, and intellects of poets, as well as through their lips, tongues, ears, eyes, fingertips, influences, and gestures. Whether you are a reader discovering Copper Canyon Press for the first time or have known the Press for years and are now revisiting a community of poets via this book, I want to welcome you and thank you for joining and extending this tradition. At Copper Canyon Press we believe in you, dear reader, just as we believe in the poets whose work is included here. Everyone possesses the ability to recognize poetry and be moved by a poem's capacity to express the unsayable, and to thereby unlock our sometimes unrecognizable selves. Every time one of my colleagues brings forth a book idea or new poem, and whenever some poet advocates for another poet or a poem they love, or when one book alludes to another, each is participating in a desire to be part of making change, celebrating individuals in community. With each poem we read, I believe, we are changed. From its inception, Copper Canyon has existed in a sort of tension between the desire for change and the acknowledgment of progressive traditions. As you read these pages, you are joining us in a belief that change is possible and essential.

The etymological roots of *publishing* are in the Latin *publicare:* to make public. *Poetry* has its roots in the Greek verb for "creating" or "making" (*poiesis*). Alongside the tension between tradition and change, Copper Canyon has navigated another tension, between individuals and audiences. As a nonprofit publisher, we slalom through an art form that by its nature resists commodification. Poetry often celebrates singular (and sometimes contrarian) voices, while the marketplace assigns value and importance based on sales data and review attention. Copper Canyon Press has grown from its roots by embracing poetry and publishing simultaneously—starting with its first book, Gerald Costanzo's *Badlands,* published in 1973. The tension between poetry and the marketplace is wincingly obvious in the crude handmade design of that first book; traditions were being necessarily questioned. The conditions in the United States at the time of that first publication were obviously different from conditions now, fifty years later. *Roe v. Wade* had just become settled law; the Watergate trials began, and Richard Nixon entered his second term as president; the US war in Vietnam was scraping to an end; the Environmental Protection Agency was in its infancy with efforts to promote clean air and water alongside the foundation of the Endangered Species Act; members of the American Indian Movement occupied the Pine Ridge Reservation at Wounded Knee and, in 1977, Leonard Peltier was imprisoned; the World Trade Center opened in New York; the first cell phone call was made. In 1973, Donald Trump was sued by the Justice Department for discrimination and then he countersued. There was no Google, no Amazon, no Apple.

Back in 1973 technological changes encouraged a do-it-yourself sense of independence, bringing options that enabled a growing desire to subvert homogenization and monopolization within the publishing industry. Energized by civil and cultural unrest and catalyzed by the era's countercultural fashions and passions to make art, a clutch of young poets, literature students, and letterpress printers (including Jim Gautney, Sam Hamill, Emily Karle, Bill O'Daly, Tree Swenson, and Tina Wolfe) decided to simultaneously embrace publishing—a very tradition-bound industry—while also rejecting and ignoring some of publishing's accepted traditions. Soon after, the founders of the press were encouraged by Bill

Ransom and Joe Wheeler to bring their nascent publishing enterprise to Port Townsend, Washington, to be in residence with Centrum. Here they started publishing their friends alongside other young poets they met through Centrum's Port Townsend Writers Conference, where they taught letterpress printing workshops. Letterpress printing, at the time a recently discarded technology (and therefore inexpensive), made it possible to create an alternative to cheap mass-market paperbacks, to provide a response to those "best-seller" books that reinforced the dominant culture yet somehow found their way to remainder tables and pulping facilities. Copper Canyon Press even provided space and equipment for Scott Walker to start Graywolf Press.

Then, as now, young writers wanted change, wanted something different, and wanted to be heard. Poets, writers, and translators managed to subvert an industry—and a larger literary culture—by utilizing the gleanings cast off as uneconomical. Today, passionate DIY poets and readers take readily to social media in order to be heard or employ print-on-demand technology to start their own presses. The desire to publish, to make a voice heard to a *public,* is as persistent as the great undying pool of poetry. Some are even turning once again to antique letterpress equipment found online in a dance between tradition and innovation. Poets continue to be among the most eloquent citizens responding to our shared challenges and the desire to hold humanity accountable.

It is equally obvious that, despite whatever successes were achieved over the past five decades, many notable injustices have persisted stubbornly. As poets remind us, we clearly have much more work to do. Books by poets who were just starting their paths fifty years ago—poets such as Arthur Sze, June Jordan, Ted Kooser, and C.D. Wright—continue to encourage a fierce and persistent beauty. When the Press was founded, Jericho Brown, Ocean Vuong, Sherwin Bitsui, Natalie Diaz, and Alex Dimitrov had yet to be born. Thankfully, with each passing day, new poets follow, in turn building the tradition alongside poets such as Paisley Rekdal, Mark Bibbins, Deborah Landau, Victoria Chang, and Matthew Zapruder. As this book shows, Copper Canyon Press advocates on behalf of new voices taking up the age-old desire to confront the inequities of society and celebrates poets who seek to redeem language and, through it, human behavior.

This interplay of new generations responding to current conditions and to the traditions that precede them, which is a collaborative acknowledgment of literary history alongside the unending and upending desire to "make it new," seems to me to be central to the work of poets. I'm reminded of David Budbill:

Two hundred years ago Issa heard the morning birds
singing sutras to this suffering world.

I heard them too, this morning, which must mean,

since we will always have a suffering world,
we must also always have a song.

I like to think that the interplay between tradition and change is essential as
well to the work of literary publishers charged with a role in the stewardship
of written culture. When James Laughlin founded New Directions in 1936, he
started publishing the great Modernists who would remake American literature.
In the midfifties, almost twenty years before Copper Canyon was conceived,
City Lights Books introduced readers to the Beats via its Pocket Poets series and
remade the landscape of poetry. Earlier, Jonathan Williams started the Jargon
Society and championed the Black Mountain poets—that same year, Barney
Rosset bought Grove Press, through which he would go on to independently
fight censorship and obscenity laws on behalf of the avant garde, on behalf of the
entire country. Poetry was central to their efforts to elevate BIPOC, queer, and
countercultural voices. Copper Canyon, Graywolf, Coffee House, Milkweed, and
our many cousin presses—independent publishers founded in honor of expansive
and varying modes of literary expression—have tried to improve upon the past,
joining a tradition that goes back to the invention of the first metal type during
the Goryeo Dynasty (and Sejong's subsequent creation of hangul in Korea), and
to Gutenberg's use of cast type, oil-based inks, and a wooden press that would
lead to the European Renaissance a generation later. The promise of independent
publishers is to change and educate minds, to challenge their times, and to alter
the course of history by revivifying culture. Hayden Carruth's poem "California,"
dedicated to Adrienne Rich, applies equally to poetry and publishing:

                                    Tolstoi said
        the purpose of poetry is to provoke
        feeling in the reader, to "infect" the reader,
        he said,—and so to induce a change,
        a change of conscience
        that may lead to a change in the world, that will
        lead to a change in the world!
        How can poetry be written by people who want no change?

Every time I consider that twenty-six letters (in English) can carry so many of the emotions, ideas, intellectual intensities, and whimsical, self-creating curiosities that make us who we are, I am again amazed. That poets are able to bend those letters to and around the breath and heartbeat transforms my amazement into astonishment and gratitude. I share with C.D. Wright a belief in words: "My relationship to the word is anything but scientific; it is a matter of faith on my part, that the word endows material substance, by setting the thing named apart from all else. *Horse,* then, unhorses what is not horse."

*

Within these pages you will find poems recommended by poets, former and current staff, board members, interns, and donors. Their stories and their love of particular poems are at the heart of Copper Canyon Press.

As I began contemplating this anthology, I recognized that nearly every poem I encountered had a memorable personal story. I would read an Arthur Sze poem and remember the excitement I felt the first time I read *Archipelago,* or remember walking along the acequia near his home. I'd read a C.D. Wright poem and immediately hear her voice in my ear a few days before she passed away, or I'd remember the utterly strange thrill of reading *Deepstep Come Shining* for the first time, and later the story of the Hummingbird Lady who eventually graced its cover. How deeply I miss C.D. A Hayden Carruth poem would bring me to the gentle, painfully sweet note he sent upon the birth of my daughter, or to the night when in the midst of a panic attack he tried to escape from the scene of a New School reading, and how afterward I took him to dinner to unwind at the Minetta Tavern. I recall the tears gathering the first time I read Mark Bibbins's *13th Balloon*—a book that evoked in me the response I've had so many times, that it might be the best manuscript I'd ever read. I recall delicate conversations with poets such as Jericho Brown, Deborah Landau, and Victoria Chang, who invited me into their books, and how my best response was "yes, and more please," suggesting that they add more poems. I recall telling Alberto Ríos that he might have *two* books inside the manuscript he first sent to me; Ted Kooser and John Balaban, *separately,* sending me Natalie Diaz's first manuscript of *When My Brother Was an Aztec.* I remember how, when we first met, Natalie was a little surprised to learn that I'd already read her book. I recall Janeen Armstrong, then our new shipping manager, admitting that she had been looking at manuscript submissions alongside the intern crew she managed, and urging me to pay attention to Alison

Rollins. Or the conversation I had while editing Shirley Kaufman's *Threshold,* when she told me about Taha Muhammad Ali, whose poems were quoted in her book. After my initial attempt to publish a US edition of Taha's book was met with rejection, I persevered, and we published *So What.* I remember the hilarious stories he told when we first met and his asking me whether to read his new poem "Revenge" at the Geraldine R. Dodge Poetry Festival. I also recall how his poems lured the editor Alison Lockhart to come from South Africa to work with us—a relationship that continues still. I remember reading Ocean Vuong's first-book manuscript and how my colleague Elaina Ellis, fresh from hearing him read, lavished smitten praise upon his poems. I consider a road trip to visit Jim Harrison with my colleague Joseph Bednarik, a fierce advocate of Harrison, and Joseph's spot-on imitations of the larger-than-life poet. These stories are my own—they are seemingly endless and could fill up many pages.

There was never just one person who made and grew the Press and its nearly 700 published books. Copper Canyon Press has always been a compilation of many voices, a richness of multiple stories waiting to leap from any of us. And yet, alongside all this abundance, the "small press" intimacy and independence remain. C.D. Wright would often address the reader of her poems and essays, within her poems and essays: "Dear reader." The first time I read those two words I was struck by how I, an unknown reader, was being invited into the substance and thinking of her poems. I felt as though I were being asked to join in collaboration and conversation with the poet—and not to simply consume her work. In editing this anthology, I decided I wanted to be guided by such invitation and collaboration. In telling the story of Copper Canyon Press, I believe it would be false—and predictable—to choose all the poems myself, so I turned to the many people who have sustained Copper Canyon over fifty years. I asked our poets, as well as current and former colleagues, interns, board members, and industry colleagues, to recommend their favorite poems for *A House Called Tomorrow* (a title that arrived at the passionate suggestion of our finance manager, Julie Johnson). I also asked for stories about why these choices were important to them, contributions to the growing narrative that is the Press. Nearly two hundred people responded. You'll find a list of those who suggested poems at the back of this book.

The poetry community—poets, booksellers, teachers—has long offered manuscript recommendations. I wanted to turn the tables somewhat and invite others into the process of choosing from among abundance. Nonetheless, further choices had to be made. I discovered that several poets were overrepresented, several poems were duplicated, and still others were too long to accommodate within the limit of page counts. As is my editorial practice, I've tried to balance the Press's tradition alongside the newborn enthusiasm of my CCP colleagues and poets. Since many of the submitted suggestions came from recent books, and because we had already published *The Gift of Tongues* to celebrate the first formative years of the Press, I've favored selections from the subsequent twenty-five years. I'd originally hoped to include all the stories that accompanied the poem recommendations but had to let go of that idea so that the book didn't become unwieldy. (I apologize to those whose suggestions were omitted, but stay tuned. Your stories, along with your poem suggestions, will be appearing elsewhere.)

With this editorial strategy, I've found myself energized yet again by the Copper Canyon community. Through your recommendations, I've rediscovered poems I may have forgotten over the years, or I have returned to them with matured eyes, reading them in entirely new ways. Once again I find myself incredibly grateful for what is being given to Copper Canyon Press by so many hands, minds, and hearts.

I've always believed that books will last and sustain us and are perfect object partners to the bodily voice and breath. However, when I recently culled the decaying library at the home of the great poet W.S. Merwin and his wife Paula, I recognized the fragility of books as they fell apart in my hands. Each day as I hear about new iterations of book banning in schools and in libraries I'm reminded of the capacity of books to challenge society. The dissemination of literature has long been perceived as a threat to the powerful because it honors individuals unrecognized by power. As I stand in horrified consideration of the devastation of libraries and other cultural institutions in our current wars and climate collapse, I start to wonder what books can withstand. What can they offer that allows humanity to not only survive but thrive? I find solace in the courageous and wise voices of poets within these pages and the pages of other books, and also in the responses we regularly receive at the Press from our beloved readers. I am continually encouraged and energized by the passion of all my colleagues at Copper Canyon Press who have made books possible over so many years. As Theodore Roethke would say, they "specialize in the impossible." Copper Canyon Press's best years are ahead of it, and we have the potential to play a vital role in how poetry is perceived, read, and written in this century. You, dear reader, are a part of this tradition as you hold this book, and you are a part of the future promise of Copper Canyon Press. Your act of reading this book honors the many voices that are great within us. At the end of the anthropocentric world, there will be a last uttered word, and that word will be a poem, just as there was a first poem at language's beginning, at the moment when we started expressing sorrow or joy, astonishment or curiosity. I am not alone in trusting the alchemy of alphabets to transform a poem from something spoken and heard to something held. Dear reader, the great pool of poetry is inexhaustible.

MICHAEL WIEGERS

About the Cover Art

Ut pictura poesis.

Horace

Erika Blumenfeld is a multidisciplinary artist who is the current artist in residence at the National Aeronautics and Space Administration (NASA). Erika was first introduced to us by friends at Lannan Foundation, and Copper Canyon Press has in turn introduced her work to poets whose book covers feature her art. As we were considering ideas for the cover of this anthology, I recalled visiting her studio several years ago, where she showed me and the poet Lisa Olstein her stunning project *Encyclopedia of Trajectories,* which charts and translates meteors into hand-drawn flashes of gold, one of the precious metals brought to earth via meteor strikes during the earth's formation. Blumenfeld first studies NASA recordings of meteors entering our atmosphere and then humanizes those celestial events by using a traditional ink brush to "perform" a single stroke of 24 karat gold onto paper. To quote her project description:

> The *Encyclopedia of Trajectories* project is a quest to activate the long-held knowledge, both scientific and cultural, that we are deeply connected to the universe across its 13.8 billion years. The material composing our bodies shares cosmic origins with the material composing the planets, asteroids and comets in our solar system. Scientifically, this material, having derived from distant stars across time, threads back to the primordial material that emerged moments after our universe burst into being. Culturally, our star gazing has filled us with wonder across all civilizations, sparking art and architecture, philosophy and science, mythology, folklore as well as navigation and place-making. The *Encyclopedia of Trajectories* project intends to study the notion of an embodied relationship with the stars and began with an inquiry into how, in our human form, we can comprehend the immensity of our cosmic heritage—that we are, in our very chemistry, of and from the stars.

To investigate this embodied relationship, I've been drawing every shooting star that occurred over a one-year period. Shooting stars evoke both the wonder of the cosmos and also our longing to have a connection with it, evidenced by the fact that we have, since at least the time of Ptolemy, sent our deepest wishes to them in hopes they might hear us.

The "meteor events" that Blumenfeld studies write their own unique patterns in the darkness—creating bursts of light and motion akin to the poems we are celebrating during our golden anniversary. Poems and entire mythologies have been drawn from the stars, just as Blumenfeld translates the night sky's ineffable moments into single gestures, drawn into a grand community of stars and constellations.

Highlights: A Copper Canyon Press Timeline

1970s

Publishes forty-nine books and letterpress chapbooks, by poets such as:

- Gary Snyder
- Sam Hamill
- W.M. Ransom
- James Masao Mitsui
- Robert Hedin
- Richard Hugo
- Kim Stafford
- Kenneth Rexroth
- David Lee
- Ezra Pound
- Robert Wrigley
- William O'Daly
- Olga Broumas
- Primus St. John
- George Hitchcock
- Thomas McGrath

Switches from letterpress printing to out-of-house offset printing

1972: Copper Canyon Press is founded in Denver, Colorado

1973: Publishes its first book, Gerald Costanzo's *Badlands: First Poems*

1974: Moves to Port Townsend, Washington; in residence with Centrum at Fort Worden State Park

1974: Graywolf Press starts in Copper Canyon Press's headquarters building

1980s

Publishes sixty-two books, including collections by:

- Barry Lopez
- Pablo Neruda
- Carolyn Forché
- Robert Bringhurst
- Jaan Kaplinski
- Cold Mountain, translated by Red Pine
- James Laughlin
- Carolyn Kizer
- Vicente Aleixandre, translated by Lewis Hyde and others
- Denise Levertov
- William Stafford
- Jim Heynen

1983: Publishes Red Pine's *The Collected Songs of Cold Mountain,* his first book of translations from the Chinese

1984: Publishes Pablo Neruda's *Still Another Day,* the first in a series of translations of the poet's work

1985: Signs distribution agreement as one of the original publishers represented by Consortium Book Sales and Distribution

1989: Thomas McGrath wins the Lenore Marshall Award for *Selected Poems: 1938–1988,* the first major award for a Copper Canyon Press book

1990s

Publishes 83 books

1990: Establishes nonprofit status

1990: Creates its first board of directors, whose initial members include Rick Simonson, Joe Wheeler, Denise Levertov, and Charles Johnson

1991: Publishes Pablo Neruda's *The Book of Questions,* the first Copper Canyon Press book to sell more than twenty thousand copies

1992: First grant from Lannan Foundation, for Hayden Carruth's *Collected Shorter Poems*

1992: Hayden Carruth wins the National Book Critics Circle Award and the Ruth Lilly Award for *Collected Shorter Poems;* the book is also a finalist for the National Book Award

1992: *Poetry: The Unsayable Said,* a national branding and marketing campaign, is launched through the support of a multiyear grant from Lila Wallace–Reader's Digest Foundation

1992: Receives major multiyear grant from Mellon Foundation to help with organizational development, stabilization, and succession planning

1993: Publishes W.S. Merwin's *The Second Four Books of Poems,* the first of many collections by Merwin

1993: Publishes Lucille Clifton's *Book of Light*

1993: Establishes iconic *shih* as pressmark/logo

1995: Publishes *Archipelago* by Arthur Sze

1995: Hayden Carruth First Book Award series launches, with Erin Belieu's *Infanta* named the winner

1996: Hayden Carruth wins National Book Award for *Scrambled Eggs & Whiskey*

1997: John Balaban nominated for National Book Award for *Locusts at the Edge of Summer: New and Selected Poems*

1998: Publishes Jim Harrison's *The Shape of the Journey,* starting a long relationship with the novelist and poet

1998: W.S. Merwin wins the Ruth Lilly Award

1998: Begins copublishing relationship with *The American Poetry Review* and the Honickman First Book Award, with Joshua Beckman's *Things Are Happening*

2000S

Publishes 192 books

2000: In a speech during the first postwar presidential visit to Vietnam, Bill Clinton cites *Spring Essence,* a translation by John Balaban, as an example of American cultural diplomacy, giving copies to Vietnamese leadership

2002: Madeline DeFrees wins the Lenore Marshall Award for *Blue Dusk*

2002: Ruth Stone wins National Book Award for *In the Next Galaxy;* Alberto Ríos is nominated the same year for *The Smallest Muscle in the Human Body*

2004: Publishes Ben Lerner's debut collection, *The Lichtenberg Figures*

2004: Ted Kooser named US Poet Laureate; *Delights & Shadows* becomes first Copper Canyon book to sell more than 100,000 copies

2004: Sam Hamill leaves Copper Canyon Press

2004: C.D. Wright wins a MacArthur Award for Poetry

2005: Ted Kooser wins the Pulitzer Prize for *Delights & Shadows*

2005: Begins publishing original work by W.S. Merwin, starting with *Migration: New & Selected Poems,* after reissuing several of his early books that were out of print

2005: W.S. Merwin wins the National Book Award for *Migration*

2006: After several transitions in the Press's leadership, a management team is formed to direct the Press

2009: Heather McHugh receives MacArthur Award for Poetry

2009: C.D. Wright wins 2009 Griffin Poetry Prize

2010S

Publishes 180 books

2010: W.S. Merwin named US Poet Laureate

2010: Acquires the backlist of Ausable Press (forty-nine poetry titles including work by Laura Kasischke, James Richardson, Eric Pankey, and Linton Kwesi Johnson)

2010: C.D. Wright wins National Book Critics Circle Award and Lenore Marshall Award for *One With Others*

2010: C.D. Wright and James Richardson are both finalists for the National Book Award

2011: Through a grant from the Paul Allen Foundation, develops industry-standard open-source coding protocol to create bespoke poetry e-books

2011: Laura Kasischke wins National Book Critics Circle Award for *Space, in Chains*

2012: Publishes *When My Brother Was an Aztec,* the first book by eventual Pulitzer Prize winner Natalie Diaz

2014: Publishes Jericho Brown's *The New Testament*

2015: Ben Lerner receives a MacArthur Award for Poetry

2016: Publishes Ocean Vuong's first book, *Night Sky with Exit Wounds,* which wins T.S. Eliot Prize

2019: Arthur Sze wins the 2019 National Book Award for *Sight Lines;* Jericho Brown's *The Tradition* is a finalist for the National Book Award

2020S

Publishes seventy books between 2020 and 2023

2020: Jericho Brown wins the Pulitzer Prize in Poetry for *The Tradition*

2022: Copper Canyon Press Publishing Fellowship begins

2022: Arthur Sze wins the Ruth Lilly Award

2023: Changes logo/pressmark

A House Called Tomorrow

1973–1979

GERALD COSTANZO

from *Badlands: First Poems,* 1973

Everything You Own

Sometimes I think you're
from the South. You speak

with that drawl. You move
slowly as if taken by heat.

There are burning desires,
strange elevations you

never overcome. Everything
you own is in your

pockets. I see you in the
drugstore down on Main,

sipping soda, spitting
tobacco, mopping your brow.

You could tell me what this
country needs.

ROBERT HEDIN

from *Snow Country*, 1975

Transcanadian

At this speed, my friend, our origins are groundless.
We are nearing the eve of a great festival,
The festival of wind.
Already you can see this road weakening.
Soon it will breathe
And lift away to dry its feathers in the air.
On both sides the fields of rape seed and sunflowers
Are revolting against their rows.
Soon they will scatter wildly like pheasants.
Now is the time, my friend, to test our souls.
We must let them forage for themselves,
But first—unbuckle your skin.
It is out here, in the darkness
Between two shimmering cities,
That we have, perhaps for the last time, chance
Neither to be shut nor open,
But to let our souls speak and carry our bodies like capes.

W.M. RANSOM

from *Waving Arms at the Blind,* 1975

Pastime Café

The eyes in this place droop
thick puckers under the eyes
folds under necks droop
jowls and the plants in the windows
droop plants in the pictures on the walls
droop cigars in racks
bowling trophies, unmatched silver droops
this table and its cracked vinyl chairs
droop warm salads, year-old crackers
droop my tired hands droop
Eddy Arnold droops from the jukebox
I wake up away from you again
and my whole body droops.

GLADYS CARDIFF

from *To Frighten a Storm,* 1976

Combing

Bending, I bow my head
and lay my hands upon
her hair, combing, and think
how women do this for
each other. My daughter's hair
curls against the comb,
wet and fragrant—orange
parings. Her face, downcast,
is quiet for one so young.

I take her place. Beneath
my mother's hands I feel
the braids drawn up tight
as piano wires and singing,
vinegar-rinsed. Sitting
before the oven I hear
the orange coils tick
the early hour before school.

She combed her grandmother
Mathilda's hair using
a comb made out of bone.
Mathilda rocked her oak wood
chair, her face downcast,
intent on tearing rags
in strips to braid a cotton
rug from bits of orange
and brown. A simple act
preparing hair. Something
women do for each other,
plaiting the generations.

RICHARD HUGO

from *Duwamish Head,* 1976

Neighbor

The drunk who lives across the street from us
fell in our garden, on the beet patch
yesterday. So polite. Pardon me,
he said. He had to be helped up and held,
steered home and put to bed, declaring
we got to have another drink and smile.

I admit my envy. xxxviii found him in salal
and flat on his face in lettuce, and bent
and snoring by that thick stump full of rain
we used to sail destroyers on.
And I've carried him home so often
stone to the rain and me, and cheerful.

I try to guess what's in that dim warm mind.
Does he think about horizoned firs
black against the light, thirty years
ago, and the good girl—what's her name—
believing, or think about the dog
he beat to death that day in Carbonado?

I hear he's dead, and wait now on my porch.
He must be in his shack. The wagon's
due to come and take him where they take
late alcoholics, probably called Farm's End.
I plan my frown, certain he'll be carried out
bleeding from the corners of his grin.

T.E. JAY

from *River Dogs,* 1976

Fir

He eats rain
and the shared light
of a single star.

The far-rooted wind
blesses and terrifies him
    in turn.

His slow fire burns greener
than a great cat's eye.
Blind as the sky,
he never sleeps
but his dreams
can make it snow.

KENNETH REXROTH

from *The Silver Swan: Poems Written in Kyoto, 1974–75,* 1976

"As the full moon rises"

As the full moon rises
The swan sings
In sleep
On the lake of the mind

GEORGE HITCHCOCK

from *The Piano Beneath the Skin,* 1978

Solitaire

all that winter you were gone
the skylarks went on crutches
I woke up every dawn
to crows quarreling in ditches

I'd been there before I knew
that landscape of demented kings
I'd seen the courtiers in blue
masks and idiot posturings

when you're nailed to a scar
you don't think much of fine words
the jugglers at the bazaar
or the man who eats swords

the world's deceptive—too many
crafty smiling bones
eyes masquerading in money
and loquacious spoons

so I said goodbye to the foxtrot
and to badminton in the park
I shuffle the deck and deal out
snowflakes in the dark

DAVID LEE

from *The Porcine Legacy*, 1978

For Jan, with Love

1

John he comes to my house
pulls his beat-up truck in my drive
and honks
Dave John sez Dave my red sow
she got pigs stuck and my big hands they won't go
and I gotta get them pigs out
or that fucker she's gonna die
and I sez John goddam
we'll be right down and John sez Jan
he yells JAN where's Jan she's got little hands
she can get in there and pull them pigs
and I sez Jan and he sez Jan and Jan comes
what? Jan sez and John sez tell Jan Dave
and I sez Jan John's red sow's got pigs
stuck and his hand's too big and won't go
and he's gotta get them pigs out
or that fucker's gonna die (John he turns
his head and lights a cigarette)
(he don't say fuck to no woman)
and Jan she sez well let's go
and we get in John's beat-up damn truck
and go to pull John's pigs

2

John's red sow she doesn't weigh
a hundred and sixty pounds
but he bred her to his biggest boar
and had to put haybales by her sides
so the boar wouldn't break

her back because Carl bet five dollars
he couldn't and John he bet
five she could and John he won
but Carl enjoyed watching anyway

   3

John's red sow was laying
on her side hurting bad
and we could see she had a pig
right there but it wouldn't come she
was too small and John sez see
and I sez I see that pig's gotta come out
or that fucker's gonna die
and Jan puts vaseline on her hands
and sez hold her legs and I hold her legs
and Jan goes in after the pig
and John gets out of the pen and goes
somewheres else

Jan she pulls like hell pretty soon
the pig come big damn big little pig
dead and I give Jan more vaseline and she goes
back in to see about any more
and John's red sow pushes hard on Jan's arm
up to her elbow inside and Jan sez
there's more help me and I help
another pig damn big damn dead comes
and John's red sow she seems better
and we hope that's all

   4

John's red sow won't go
out of labor so we stay all night
and John brings coffee and smokes
and flashlight batteries and finally Jan
can feel another pig but John's red sow's
swole up tight and she can't grab hold

but only touch so I push her side
and she grunts and screams and shits all over Jan's arm
and Jan sez I got it help me and I help
and we pull for a goddam hour and pull
the pig's head off

and I sez oh my god we gotta get that pig now
or that fucker's gonna die for sure
and John sez what happened? and Jan
gives him a baby pig's head in his hand
and John goes somewheres else again
while Jan goes back fast inside
grabbing hard and John's red sow
hurts bad and Jan sez I got something help me
and I help and we start taking that pig out
piece by piece

    5

Goddam you bitch don't you die
Jan yells when John's red sow don't help no more
and we work and the sun comes up
and finally we get the last piece of pig out
and give John's red sow a big shot of penicillin
her ass swole up like a football
but she don't labor and John sez
is that all? and Jan wipes her bloody arms
on a rag and sez yes and John climbs in
the pen and sez how's my red sow?
and we look and go home and go to bed
because John's red sow that fucker she died

ROBERT WRIGLEY

from *The Sinking of Clay City*, 1979

The Sinking of Clay City

When the last mine closed
and its timbers turned pliable as treesap,
the town began to tilt, to slide
back into its past like a wave.

Old men, caught by the musk
of seeping gas, arrived at the mainshafts
hours before dawn. Their soft hands
turned the air like handles on new picks.

Here and there a house split,
a cracked wishbone,
and another disappeared like crawlspace
behind a landslide.

So the townspeople descended the sloping entrances,
found them filled with a green
noxious water. Each drank a little
and forgot about the sun.

Some dug at rusted beercans
or poked at a drowned rat, more patient
than dedicated archaeologists,
and waited for their other lives to join them.

1980–1989

BARRY LOPEZ

from *Desert Reservation,* 1980

Desert Reservation

I'd heard so much good
about this place,
how the animals were cared for
in special exhibits. But

when I arrived I saw even
prairie dogs had gone crazy in
the viewing pits; Javelina had no mud to
squat in, to cool down; Otter was
exposed on every side, even in his den.
Wolf paced like a mustang,
tongue lolling and crazy-eyed,
unable to see anyone who looked like
he did—only Deer, dozing opposite in
a chain-link pen.

Signs explain
the animals are good because
they kill animals who like oats
or corn too much.

Skunk has sprayed himself out,
with people rapping on his glass
box. Badger's gone to sleep
under a red light and children ask
if he's dead in there (dreaming of dead
silence). And
Cougar stares like a clubbed fish
into one steel corner all morning, figuring.

Only Coyote doesn't seem to care, asleep under a
creosote bush, waiting it out.

Even the birds are walled up here,
held steady in chicken-wire cages for
the staring, for souvenir photos.
And this, on the bars for Eagle:

> *The bald eagle was*
> *taken as a fledgling*
> *from a nest in New*
> *Mexico by an*
> *Indian. He planned on*
> *pulling feathers for cer-*
> *emonial headdresses*
> *every year. The*
> *federal government seized*
> *the bird and turned*
> *it over to the*
> *Desert Reserve*
> *for safekeeping.*

Bear walks in his own
pee, smells concrete
and his own shit all day long.
He wipes his nose on the wall,
trying to kill it.

At night when management is gone,
only the night watch left,
the animals begin keening: now
voices of Wood Duck and
Turtle, of Kit Fox and everyone else,
Bear too, lift up like the bellowing
of stars and kick the walls.

14 miles away, in Tucson, are movie houses,
cold beers and roads out of town,
but they say animals know how to pass the time
well enough. And after a few beers
they'd be just like Indians—
get drunk, fall down and spoil it all.

DENISE LEVERTOV

from *Wanderer's Daysong*, 1981

Poet and Person

I send my messages ahead of me.
You read them, they speak to you
in siren tongues, ears of flame
spring from your heads to take them.

When I arrive, you love me,
for I sing those messages you've
learned by heart, and bring,
as housegifts, new ones. You hear

yourselves in them,
self after self. Your solitudes
utter their runes, your own
voices begin to rise in your throats.

But soon you love me less.
I brought with me
too much, too many laden coffers,
the panoply of residence,

improper to a visit.
Silks and furs, my enormous wings,
my crutches, and my spare crutches,
my desire to please, and worse—

my desire to judge what is right.

I take up
so much space.
You are living on what you can find,
you don't want charity, and you can't
support lingering guests.

When I leave, I leave
alone, as I came.

WILLIAM STAFFORD

from *Sometimes Like a Legend,* 1981

British Columbia

After the border, it was trees all the way to
the end. When we talked to a native and
looked at his expression turned away, it was
trees. It was trees when anyone asked us
where we had been: land and land and land,
mountain by mountain, and everywhere.

We came to a lake so sudden that it
held a sharp outline in it, upside down:
the opposite shore offered us in the water.
And we waded in trees, drowned in them, held
there in the sky. I will never find enough
of the open again. I walk with my
family, carefully anonymous, hidden in trees.

ROBERT SUND

from *The Hides of White Horses Shedding Rain,* 1981

Considering Poverty and Homelessness

homage to Bashō

I cannot go back now,
    for what I have not done.
Of what is done,
take—and be kind.
    I am building a voice for my grief.
Alone, on foot,
if years from now I have learned anything,
    I will wander back.
Dust will rise up
on a dry winter road
where no one has walked before.

RICHARD SHELTON

from *A Kind of Glory,* 1982

Promises

When America closes for the night
and the last ferryboat leaves Port Townsend,
those of us left behind
cannot remember where it is going.

Low tide hesitates, gathers its strength
and begins to return, bringing driftwood,
seaweed torn up by the roots
and a little light to help us
find our way home. If we were drunker
or younger, we think we might sprawl here
on the beach all night, listening
to the sea's absolute authority
and to foghorns calling each other
like lost and lovesick whales.

But we are no longer boys
who can sleep where we fall and wake
to begin a new journey. We have made
many promises and kept some.
We have wives who are not waiting up
for us but whose eyes will open
no matter how quietly we open the door,
and close again when we close it,
having seen in that moment everything,
understood everything, and forgiven nothing.

CAROLYN KIZER

from *Mermaids in the Basement: Poems for Women*, 1984

Bitch

Now, when he and I meet, after all these years,
I say to the bitch inside me, don't start growling.
He isn't a trespasser anymore,
Just an old acquaintance tipping his hat.
My voice says, "Nice to see you,"
As the bitch starts to bark hysterically.
He isn't an enemy now,
Where are your manners, I say, as I say,
"How are the children? They must be growing up."
At a kind word from him, a look like the old days,
The bitch changes her tone: she begins to whimper.
She wants to snuggle up to him, to cringe.
Down, girl! Keep your distance
Or I'll give you a taste of the choke-chain.
"Fine, I'm just fine," I tell him.
She slobbers and grovels.
After all, I am her mistress. She is basically loyal.
It's just that she remembers how she came running
Each evening, when she heard his step;
How she lay at his feet and looked up adoringly
Though he was absorbed in his paper;
Or, bored with her devotion, ordered her to the kitchen
Until he was ready to play.
But the small careless kindnesses
When he'd had a good day, or a couple of drinks,
Come back to her now, seem more important
Than the casual cruelties, the ultimate dismissal.
"It's nice to see you are doing so well," I say.
He couldn't have taken you with him;
You were too demonstrative, too clumsy,
Not like the well-groomed pets of his new friends.

"Give my regards to your wife," I say. You gag
As I drag you off by the scruff,
Saying, "Goodbye! Goodbye! Nice to have seen you again."

PABLO NERUDA

from *Still Another Day,* 1984, 2005
Translated from the Spanish by William O'Daly

VI

Pardon me, if when I want
to tell the story of my life
it's the land I talk about.
This is the land.
It grows in your blood
and you grow.
If it dies in your blood
you die out.

VICENTE ALEIXANDRE

from *A Longing for the Light,* 1985, 2007
Edited by Lewis Hyde; translated from the Spanish by Robert Bly,
Lewis Hyde, Stephen Kessler, David Pritchard, David Unger, and others

Who I Write For

I

Historians and newsmen and people who are just curious ask me, Who am I writing for?

I'm not writing for the gentleman in the stuffy coat, or for his offended moustache, not even for the warning finger he raises in the sad ripples of music.

Not for the lady hidden in her carriage (her lorgnette sending its cold light through the windowpanes).

Perhaps I write for people who don't read my poems. That woman who dashes down the street as if she had to open the doors for the sunrise.

Or that old fellow nodding on a bench in the little park while the setting sun takes him with love, wraps him up and dissolves him, gently, in its light.

For everyone who doesn't read my writing, all the people who don't care about me (though they care for me, without knowing).

The little girl who glances my way as she passes, my companion on this adventure, living in the world.

And the old woman who sat in her doorway and watched life and bore many lives and many weary hands.

I write for the man who's in love. For the man who walks by with his pain in his eyes. The man who listened to him. The man who looked away as he walked by. The man who finally collapsed when he asked his question and no one listened.

I write for all of them. I write, mostly, for the people who don't read me. Each one
and the whole crowd. For the breasts and the mouths and the ears, the ears
that don't listen, but keep
my words alive.

II

But I also write for the murderer. For the man who shut his eyes and threw himself
at somebody's heart and ate death instead of food and got up crazy.

For the man who puffed himself up into a tower of rage and then collapsed on the
world.

For the dead woman and the dead children and dying men.

For the person who quietly turned on the gas and destroyed the whole city and the
sun rose on a pile of bodies.

For the innocent girl with her smile, her heart, her sweet medallion (and a
plundering army went through there).

And for the plundering army that charged into the sea and sank.

And for the waters, for the infinite sea.

No, not infinite. For the finite sea that has boundaries almost like our own, like a
breathing lung.

(At this point a little boy comes in, jumps in the water, and the sea, the heart of
the sea, is in his pulse!)

And for the last look, the hopelessly limited Last Look, in whose arms someone
falls asleep.

Everyone's asleep. The murderer and the innocent victim, the boss and the baby,
the damp and the dead, the dried-up old fig and the wild, bristling hair.

For the bully and the bullied, the good and the sad,
the voice with no substance
and all the substance of the world.

For you, the man with nothing that will turn into a god, who reads these words
without desire.

For you and everything alive inside of you,
I write, and write.

LH

JAAN KAPLINSKI

from *The Wandering Border,* 1987
    Translated from the Estonian by the author with Sam Hamill
    and Riina Tamm

The East-West Border

The East-West border is always wandering,
sometimes eastward, sometimes west,
and we do not know exactly where it is just now:
in Gaugamela, in the Urals, or maybe in ourselves,
so that one ear, one eye, one nostril, one hand, one foot,
one lung and one testicle or one ovary
is on the one, another on the other side. Only the heart,
only the heart is always on one side:
if we are looking northward, in the West;
if we are looking southward, in the East;
and the mouth doesn't know on behalf of which or both
it has to speak.

JAMES LAUGHLIN

from *The Owl of Minerva,* 1987

I Know How Every Poet

feels about his new poem
(and usually every poem)

it's the best he ever
wrote and better than

anybody else's rush it
off to a magazine the

presses are waiting they
say there are a hundred

thousand poets writing
in the USA (maybe more)

and if each one writes
at least one poem a week

that's a lot of diffused
satisfaction but Horace

was smarter he put his
new poems in a trunk

and left them there for
seven years or so he said

but I don't believe him.

JEAN JOUBERT

from *Black Iris,* 1988
   Translated from the French by Denise Levertov

Brilliant Sky

Never between the branches has the sky
burned with such brilliance, as if
it were offering all of its light to me,
to say—what? what urgent mystery
strains at that transparent mouth?
No leaf, no rustle . . . It's in winter,
in cold emptiness and silence, that the air
suddenly arches itself like this into infinity,
and glitters.
                This evening, far from here,
a friend is entering his death,
he knows it, he walks
under bare trees alone,
perhaps for the last time. So much love,
so much struggle, spent and worn thin.
But when he looks up, suddenly the sky
is arrayed in this same vertiginous clarity.

THOMAS MCGRATH

from *Selected Poems: 1938–1988,* 1988

Praises

The vegetables please us with their modes and virtues.
The demure heart

Of the lettuce inside its circular court, baroque ear
Of quiet under its rustling house of lace, pleases
Us.
     And the bold strength of the celery, its green Hispanic
¡Shout! Its exclamatory confetti.
And the analogue that is Onion:

Ptolemaic astronomy and tearful allegory, the Platonic circles
Of His inexhaustible soul!
O and the straightforwardness

In the labyrinth of Cabbage, the infallible rectitude of Homegrown Mushroom
Under its cone of silence like a papal hat—
     All these
Please us.
     And the syllabus of the corn,
that wampum,

its golden

Roads leading out of the wigwams of its silky and youthful smoke;
The nobility of the dill, cool in its silences and cathedrals;
Tomatoes five-alarm fires in their musky barrios, peas
Asleep in their cartridge clips,
beetsblood,

colonies of the imperial

Cauliflower, and the buddha-like seeds of the pepper
Turning their prayerwheels in the green gloom of their caves.
All these we praise: they please us all ways: these smallest virtues.
All these earth-given:
and the heaven-flung fruit also . . .

As instance

Banana which continually makes angelic ears out of sour
Purses, or the winy abacus of the holy grape on its cross

Of alcohol, or the peach with its fur like a young girl's—
All these we praise: the winter in the flesh of the apple, and the sun
Domesticated under the orange's rind.
                              We praise
By the skin of our teeth, Persimmon, and Pawpaw's constant
Affair with gravity, and the proletariat of the pomegranate
Inside its leathery city.
                        And let us praise all these
As they please us: skin, flesh, flower, and the flowering
Bones of their seeds: from which come orchards: bees: honey:
Flowers, love's language, love, heart's ease, poems, praise.

THOMAS MCGRATH

from *Selected Poems: 1938–1988*, 1988

Something Is Dying Here

In a hundred places in North Dakota
Tame locomotives are sleeping
Inside the barricades of bourgeois flowers:
Zinnias, petunias, johnny-jump-ups—
Their once wild fur warming the public squares.

Something is dying here.
                    And perhaps I, too—
My brain already full of the cloudy lignite of eternity . . .

I invoke an image of my strength.
                              Nothing will come.
Oh—a homing lion perhaps
                    made entirely of tame bees;
Or the chalice of an old storage battery, loaded
With the rancid electricity of the nineteen thirties
Cloud harps iconographic blood
Rusting in the burnt church of my flesh . . .

But nothing goes forward:
The locomotive never strays out of the flower corral
The mustang is inventing barbwire the bulls
Have put rings in their noses . . .

The dead here
Will leave behind a ring of autobodies,
Weather-eaten bones of cars where the stand-off failed—

   Strangers: go tell among the Companions:
   These dead weren't put down by Cheyennes or Red Chinese:
   The poison of their own sweet country has brought them here.

OLGA BROUMAS

from *Perpetua,* 1989

Touched

         Cold
December nights I'd go
and lie down in the shallows
and breathe the brackish tide till light

broke me from dream. Days I kept busy
with fractured angels' client masquerades.
One had a tumor
recently removed, the scar

a zipper down his skull, his neck
a corset laced with suture.
I held, and did my tricks, two
palms, ten fingers, each a mouth

suctioning off the untold harm
parsed with the body's violent grief
at being cut. Later a woman
whose teenage children passed on in a crash

let me massage her deathmask
belly till the stretch
marks gleamed again, pearls
on a blushing rise. A nurse of women HIV

positives in the City
came, her strong young body filled
my hands. Fear grips her only
late at night, at home, her job

a risk on TV. It was calm, my palm
on her belly and her heart

said Breathe. I did. Her smile
could feed. Nights I'd go down

again and lie down on the gritty
shale and breathe the earth's salt
tears till the sun
stole me from sleep and when you

died I didn't
weep nor dream but knew you
like a god breathe in
each healing we begin.

1990–1999

MARVIN BELL

from *Iris of Creation,* 1990

Poem After Carlos Drummond de Andrade

"It's life, Carlos."

It's life that is hard: walking, sleeping, eating, loving, working and
    dying are easy.
It's life that suddenly fills both ears with the sound of that
    symphony that forces your pulse to race and swells your
    heart near to bursting.
It's life, not listening, that stretches your neck and opens your eyes
    and brings you into the worst weather of the winter to
    arrive once more at the house where love seemed to be in
    the air.

And it's life, just life, that makes you breathe deeply, in the air that
    is filled with wood smoke and the dust of the factory,
    because you hurried, and now your lungs heave and fall
    with the nervous excitement of a leaf in spring breezes,
    though it is winter and you are swallowing the dirt of
    the town.
It isn't death when you suffer, it isn't death when you miss each
    other and hurt for it, when you complain that isn't death,
    when you fight with those you love, when you
    misunderstand, when one line in a letter or one remark in
    person ties one of you in knots, when the end seems near,
    when you think you will die, when you wish you were
    already dead—none of that is death.
It's life, after all, that brings you a pain in the foot and a pain in the
    hand, a sore throat, a broken heart, a cracked back, a torn
    gut, a hole in your abdomen, an irritated stomach, a
    swollen gland, a growth, a fever, a cough, a hiccup, a
    sneeze, a bursting blood vessel in the temple.
It's life, not nerve ends, that puts the heartache on a pedestal and
    worships it.

It's life, and you can't escape it. It's life, and you asked for it. It's life,
     and you won't be consumed by passion, you won't be
     destroyed by self-destruction, you won't avoid it by
     abstinence, you won't manage it by moderation, because
     it's life—life everywhere, life at all times—and so you
     won't be consumed by passion: you will be consumed
     by life.

It's life that will consume you in the end, but in the meantime . . .
It's life that will eat you alive, but for now . . .
It's life that calls you to the street where the wood smoke hangs,
     and the bare hint of a whisper of your name, but before
     you go . . .

Too late: Life got its tentacles around you, its hooks into your heart,
     and suddenly you come awake as if for the first time, and
     you are standing in a part of the town where the air is
     sweet—your face flushed, your chest thumping, your
     stomach a planet, your heart a planet, your every organ a
     separate planet, all of it of a piece though the pieces turn
     separately, O silent indications of the inevitable, as among
     the natural restraints of winter and good sense, life blows
     you apart in her arms.

PABLO NERUDA

from *The Yellow Heart*, 1990, 2002
Translated from the Spanish by William O'Daly

Love Song

I love you, I love you, is my song
and here my silliness begins.

I love you, I love you my lung,
I love you, I love you my wild grapevine,
and if love is like wine:
you are my predilection
from your hands to your feet:
you are the wineglass of hereafter
and my bottle of destiny.

I love you forward and backwards,
and I don't have the tone or timbre
to sing you my song,
my endless song.

On my violin that sings out of tune
my violin declares,
I love you, I love you my double bass,
my sweet woman, dark and clear,
my heart, my teeth,
my light and my spoon,
my salt of the dim week,
my clear windowpane moon.

JOHN BALABAN

from *Words for My Daughter,* 1991

Words for My Daughter

About eight of us were nailing up forts
in the mulberry grove behind Reds's house
when his mother started screeching and
all of us froze except Reds—fourteen, huge
as a hippo—who sprang out of the tree so fast
the branch nearly bobbed me off. So fast,
he hit the ground running, hammer in hand,
and seconds after he got in the house
we heard thumps like someone beating a tire
off a rim   his dad's howls the screen door
banging open   Saw   Reds barreling out
through the tall weeds towards the highway
the father stumbling after his fat son
who never looked back across the thick swale
of teazel and black-eyed susans until it was safe
to yell fuck you at the skinny drunk
stamping around barefoot and holding his ribs.

Another time, the Connelly kid came home to find
his alcoholic mother getting raped by the milkman.
Bobby broke a milkbottle and jabbed the guy
humping on his mom. I think it really happened
because none of us would loosely mention that
wraith of a woman who slippered around her house
and never talked to anyone, not even her kids.
Once a girl ran past my porch
with a dart in her back, her open mouth
pumping like a guppy's, her eyes wild.
Later that summer, or maybe the next,
the kids hung her brother from an oak.
Before they hoisted him, yowling and heavy

on the clothesline, they made him claw the creekbank
and eat worms. I don't know why his neck didn't snap.

Reds had another nickname you couldn't say
or he'd beat you up: "Honeybun."
His dad called him that when Reds was little.

*

So, these were my playmates. I love them still
for their justice and valor and desperate loves
twisted in shapes of hammer and shard.
I want you to know about their pain
and about the pain they could loose on others.
If you're reading this, I hope you will think,
Well, my Dad had it rough as a kid, so what?
If you're reading this, you can read the news
and you know that children suffer worse.

*

Worse for me is a cloud of memories
still drifting off the South China Sea,
like the 9-year-old boy, naked and lacerated,
thrashing in his pee on a steel operating table
and yelling "*Dau. Dau,*" while I, trying to translate
in the mayhem of Tet for surgeons who didn't know
who this boy was or what happened to him, kept asking
"Where? Where's the pain?" until a surgeon
said "Forget it. His ears are blown."

*

I remember your first Hallowe'en
when I held you on my chest and rocked you,
so small your toes didn't touch my lap
as I smelled your fragrant peony head
and cried because I was so happy and because
I heard, in no metaphorical way, the awful chorus

of Soeur Anicet's orphans writhing in their cribs.
Then the doorbell rang and a tiny Green Beret
was saying trick-or-treat and I thought *oh oh*
but remembered it was Hallowe'en and where I was.
I smiled at the evil midget, his map-light and night
paint, his toy knife for slitting throats, said,
"How ya doin', soldier?" and, still holding you asleep
in my arms, gave him a Mars Bar. To his father
waiting outside in fatigues I hissed, "You shit,"
and saw us, child, in a pose I know too well.

I want you to know the worst and be free from it.
I want you to know the worst and still find good.

Day by day, as you play nearby or laugh
with the ladies at Peoples Bank as we go around town
and I find myself beaming like a fool,
I suspect I am here less for your protection
than you are here for mine, as if you were sent
to call me back into our helpless tribe.

PABLO NERUDA

from *The Book of Questions,* 1991, 2001
Translated from the Spanish by William O'Daly

VI

Why does the hat of night
fly so full of holes?

What does old ash say
when it passes near the fire?

Why do clouds cry so much,
growing happier and happier?

For whom do the pistils of the sun burn
in the shadow of the eclipse?

How many bees are there in a day?

STEPHEN BERG

from *New & Selected Poems,* 1992

On This Side of the River

to Millie

> *Simply trust:*
> *don't the petals also flutter down*
> *just like that?*
>
> Issa

I undress and lie down next to you in bed
and throw one of my legs across yours, I wait
until you are completely lost
then slide my head on the pillow with yours.
Your hair gets caught in my teeth.
I stretch a little to rub my head against yours, so
gently neither of us can feel it,
my breath goes and returns with yours.
There is a moon. Clouds streak its face.
At this late hour by the river the cherry trees stand alone,
black tongueless sentinels
that report nothing.
Wind shakes the flowers that hang over the water,
on the other side families sit down to eat.
I know it.
Not one petal has been torn loose,
and I lie here with my hands on you, not moving,
seeing us today under the trees
sitting with our legs crossed facing each other, talking,
and try to remember what we said.
Get up. I want you to explain
what no couple has ever understood—
the silence, our two skins, the fact that one dies first.
One angry face the color of the

blossoms flashes up and leaves.
The moon pours in. I begin telling you about
my life like the cabdriver in the story
who plows all night through Moscow desperate
for someone to listen to him and winds up at dawn
standing under a streetlamp, snow chilling his mouth,
telling his horse how terrible life is because his
five-year-old son died yesterday, and not one passenger would listen,
pulling the nag's ear down to his mouth, whispering deep
into it his unbearable story.

HAYDEN CARRUTH

from *Collected Shorter Poems, 1946–1991*, 1992

The Impossible Indispensability of the Ars Poetica

But of course the poem is not an assertion. Do you see? When I wrote
That all my poems over the long years before I met you made you come true,
And that the poems for you since then have made you in yourself become
     more true,
I did not mean that the poems created or invented you. How many have
     foundered
In that sargasso! No, what I have been trying to say
Is that neither of the quaint immemorial views of poetry is adequate for us.
A poem is not an expression, nor is it an object. Yet it somewhat partakes of both.
     What a poem is
Is never to be known, for which I have learned to be grateful. But the aspect in
     which I see my own
Is as the act of love. The poem is a gift, a bestowal.
The poem is for us what instinct is for animals, a continuing and chiefly
     unthought corroboration of essence
(Though thought, ours and the animals', is still useful).
Why otherwise is the earliest always the most important, the formative? The Iliad,
     the Odyssey, the book of Genesis,
These were acts of love, I mean deeply felt gestures, which continuously bestow
     upon us
What we are. And if I do not know which poem of mine
Was my earliest gift to you,
Except that it had to have been written about someone else,
Nevertheless it was the gesture accruing value to you, your essence, while you were
     still a child, and thereafter
Across all these years. And see, see how much
Has come from that first sonnet after our loving began, the one
That was a kiss, a gift, a bestowal. This is the paradigm of fecundity. I think the
     poem is not
Transparent, as some have said, nor a looking-glass, as some have also said,
Yet it has almost the quality of disappearance

In its cage of visibility. It disperses among the words. It is a fluidity, a vapor, of love.
This, the instinctual, is what caused me to write "Do you see?" instead of "Don't you
see?" in the first line
Of this poem, this loving treatise, which is what gives away the poem
And gives it all to you.

HAYDEN CARRUTH

from *Collected Shorter Poems, 1946–1991,* 1992

On Being Asked to Write a Poem Against the War in Vietnam

Well I have and in fact
more than one and I'll
tell you this too

I wrote one against
Algeria that nightmare
and another against

Korea and another
against the one
I was in

and I don't remember
how many against
the three

when I was a boy
Abyssinia Spain and
Harlan County

and not one
breath was restored
to one

shattered throat
mans womans or childs
not one not

one
but death went on and on
never looking aside

except now and then like a child
with a furtive half-smile
to make sure I was noticing.

DAVID ROMTVEDT

from *A Flower Whose Name I Do Not Know,* 1992

Kiev, the Ukraine, Nuclear Accident

In the world we've made
a cloud approaches Wyoming,
a radioactive cloud born in fire,
a graphite fire in a nuclear power plant
gone wrong. The fire will not stop.

For three days it has been raining.
In Oregon people are advised not to drink rainwater.
And in Washington and Idaho. Here in Buffalo, Wyoming,
our town water comes from Clear Creek flowing
down out of the Bighorn Mountains
and through the center of town,
beside the Busy Bee Café,
under the bridge on Main Street.
The rain falls, the water flows.
All the water that can makes its way
to the creek out of which we drink.

I sigh and with that sigh I am a child
standing face up in a heavy rain—
southern Arizona, the dark sky, the water tumbling
from the foreign clouds and sluicing along
a gutterless street. My eyes are closed
so I feel the drops pelt my eyelids.
My mouth is open as wide as I can open it,
tongue hanging out. The rain pounds
on my tongue but does not hurt.

I love this feeling and, as my mouth fills,
I swallow—cool water on what, thirty minutes before,
was another hot day. I let my arms rise
away from my sides and I begin to turn,

to spin in place like the blades of a propeller,
or those seeds with wings that come down from the trees
like eggbeaters upside down, or a ballet dancer
I have never seen. The water flies off
the ends of my fingers as it continues
to strike my tongue. Around and around
until I am so dizzy I fall and lie on my back,
eyes still closed, mouth still open. My mother
comes out in the yard to watch the rain.
She speaks to me and I look at her.
She smiles. Then she lies down next to me.
Side by side on our backs we both close our eyes,
open our mouths and drink the rain
that goes on falling.

LUCILLE CLIFTON

from *The Book of Light*, 1993

brothers

> *(being a conversation in eight poems between an aged Lucifer and God,*
> *though only Lucifer is heard. The time is long after.)*

I

invitation

come coil with me
here in creation's bed
among the twigs and ribbons
of the past. i have grown old
remembering this garden,
the hum of the great cats
moving into language, the sweet
fume of the man's rib
as it rose up and began to walk.
it was all glory then,
the winged creatures leaping
like angels, the oceans claiming
their own. let us rest here a time
like two old brothers
who watched it happen and wondered
what it meant.

2

how great Thou art

listen, You are beyond
even Your own understanding.
that rib and rain and clay

in all its pride,
its unsteady dominion,
is not what You believed
You were,
but it is what You are;
in Your own image as some
lexicographer supposed.
the face, both he and she,
the odd ambition, the desire
to reach beyond the stars
is You. all You, all You
the loneliness, the perfect
imperfection.

   3

   as for myself

less snake than angel
less angel than man
how come i to this
serpent's understanding?
watching creation from
a hood of leaves
i have foreseen the evening
of the world.
as sure as she,
the breast of Yourself
separated out and made to bear,
as sure as her returning,
i too am blessed with
the one gift you cherish;
to feel the living move in me
and to be unafraid.

4

in my own defense

what could i choose
but to slide along behind them,
they whose only sin
was being their father's children?
as they stood with their backs
to the garden,
a new and terrible luster
burning their eyes,
only You could have called
their ineffable names,
only in their fever
could they have failed to hear.

5

the road led from delight

into delight. into the sharp
edge of seasons, into the sweet
puff of bread baking, the warm
vale of sheet and sweat after love,
the tinny newborn cry of calf
and cormorant and humankind.
and pain, of course,
always there was some bleeding,
but forbid me not
my meditation on the outer world
before the rest of it, before
the bruising of his heel, my head,
and so forth.

6

"The silence of God is God."

Carolyn Forché

tell me, tell us why
in the confusion of a mountain
of babies stacked like cordwood,
of limbs walking away from each other,
of tongues bitten through
by the language of assault,
tell me, tell us why
You neither raised Your hand
nor turned away, tell us why
You watched the excommunication of
that world and You said nothing.

7

still there is mercy, there is grace

how otherwise
could i have come to this
marble spinning in space
propelled by the great
thumb of the universe?
how otherwise
could the two roads
of this tongue
converge into a single
certitude?
how otherwise
could i, a sleek old
traveler,
curl one day safe and still
beside You
at Your feet, perhaps,
but, amen, Yours.

8

". . . . . is God."

so.
having no need to speak
You sent Your tongue
splintered into angels.
even i,
with my little piece of it
have said too much.
to ask You to explain
is to deny You.
before the word
You were.
You kiss my brother mouth.
the rest is silence.

LUCILLE CLIFTON

from *The Book of Light*, 1993

"won't you celebrate with me"

won't you celebrate with me
what i have shaped into
a kind of life? i had no model.
born in babylon
both nonwhite and woman
what did i see to be except myself?
i made it up
here on this bridge between
starshine and clay,
my one hand holding tight
my other hand; come celebrate
with me that everyday
something has tried to kill me
and has failed.

W.S. MERWIN

from *The Second Four Books of Poems,* 1993

Separation

Your absence has gone through me
Like thread through a needle.
Everything I do is stitched with its color.

W.S. MERWIN

from *The Second Four Books of Poems*, 1993

The River of Bees

In a dream I returned to the river of bees
Five orange trees by the bridge and
Beside two mills my house
Into whose courtyard a blind man followed
The goats and stood singing
Of what was older

Soon it will be fifteen years

He was old he will have fallen into his eyes

I took my eyes
A long way to the calendars
Room after room asking how shall I live

One of the ends is made of streets
One man processions carry through it
Empty bottles their
Image of hope
It was offered to me by name

Once once and once
In the same city I was born
Asking what shall I say

He will have fallen into his mouth
Men think they are better than grass

I return to his voice rising like a forkful of hay

He was old he is not real nothing is real
Nor the noise of death drawing water

We are the echo of the future

On the door it says what to do to survive
But we were not born to survive
Only to live

W.S. MERWIN

from *The Second Four Books of Poems,* 1993

The Room

I think all this is somewhere in myself
The cold room unlit before dawn
Containing a stillness such as attends death
And from a corner the sounds of a small bird trying
From time to time to fly a few beats in the dark
You would say it was dying it is immortal

W.S. MERWIN

from *The Second Four Books of Poems*, 1993

The Birds on the Morning of Going

If I can say yes I
must say it to this
and now
trying to remember what the present
can bless with
which I know

from all other ages how little has come to me
that is breath
and nothing that is you

now I can see
I have been carrying this
fear
a blue thing
the length of my life asking *Is this
its place*
bringing it here

to the singing
of these brightening birds
they are neither dead nor unborn

a life opens it opens it is
breaking
does it find occasions for
every grief of its childhood
before it will have
done

oh my love here even the night turns back

T'AO CH'IEN

from *The Selected Poems T'ao Ch'ien*, 1993
Translated from the Chinese by David Hinton

Thinking of Impoverished Ancients

1

Ten thousand things, and yet nothing
without refuge but lone cloud. Into dusk—

vanishing into empty skies, into dusk,
when will last light ever grace it again?

Flushed dawn sky breaking through last
night's fog, birds take flight together:

they venture carefully from the woods,
and wing home again well before evening.

Hoarding strength and guarding life apart,
how could anyone avoid hunger and cold?

If there's no one left who understands,
then that's that: what would you mourn?

2

Bitter cold. The year ending like this,
I sun on the front porch, my coat closed.

There's nothing left of our south garden,
and dead limbs fill orchards to the north.

I try the ricejar: not a grain. I peer
inside the stove: no sign even of smoke.

It's late afternoon, classics piled nearby,
but I can't read in peace. This idle life—

it's not like Confucius in Ch'en, people
half-starved, but they're angry here, too,

and say so. Is there any solace? All those
ancients living this same enlightened life?

MARVIN BELL

from *The Book of the Dead Man,* 1994

The Book of the Dead Man (#1)

1. *About the Dead Man*

The dead man thinks he is alive when he sees blood in his stool.
Seeing blood in his stool, the dead man thinks he is alive.
He thinks himself alive because he has no future.
Isn't that the way it always was, the way of life?
Now, as in life, he can call to people who will not answer.
Life looks like a white desert, a blaze of today in which nothing distinct can
    be made out, seen.
To the dead man, guilt and fear are indistinguishable.
The dead man cannot make out the spider at the center of its web.
He cannot see the eyelets in his shoes and so wears them unlaced.
He reads the large type and skips the fine print.
His vision surrounds a single tree, lost as he is in a forest.
From his porcelain living quarters, he looks out at a fiery plain.
His face is pressed against a frameless window.
Unable to look inside, unwilling to look outside, the man who is dead is like a
    useless gift in its box waiting.
It will have its yearly anniversary, but it would be wrong to call it a holiday.

2. *More About the Dead Man*

The dead man can balance a glass of water on his head without trembling.
He awaits the autopsy on the body discovered on the beach beneath the cliff.
Whatever passes through the dead man's mouth is expressed.
Everything that enters his mouth comes out of it.
He is willing to be diagnosed, as long as it won't disturb his future.
Stretched out, he snaps back like elastic.
Rolled over, he is still right-side-up.
When there is no good or bad, no useful or useless, no up, no down, no right
    way, no perfection, then okay it's not necessary that there be direction: up
    is down.

The dead man has the rest of his life to wait for color.

He finally has a bird's-eye view of the white-hot sun.

He finally has a complete sentence, from his head to his feet.

He is, say, America, but he will soon be, say, Europe.

It will be necessary merely to cross the ocean and pop up in the new land, and the
    dead man doesn't need to swim.

It's the next best thing to talking to people in person.

CYRUS CASSELLS

from *Soul Make a Path Through Shouting*, 1994

Sung from a Hospice

Still craving a robust
Tenderness and justice,
I will go on living
With all I have seen:
Young men lusterless;
Against my blind cheek—
Blessed be the frangible
And dying,
The irreplaceable dead—
In my crestfallen arms:
With breath,
Then without it,
With flesh,
Then freed of it—

And the indurate man I heard
Condemn the stricken,
While my cousin was dying,
If he had walked these wards,
Armorless, open
To the imperiled,
Surely he would have gleaned
To sit in judgment
Is to sit in hell—

Lesions, elegies,
Disconnected phones—

Rain, nimble rain,
Be anodyne,
Anoint me
When I say outright:
In the plague time, my heart

Was tested,
My living soul
Struck like a tower bell,
Once, twice,
Four times in a single season.

SU TUNG-P'O

from *Selected Poems of Su Tung-p'o*, 1994
Translated from the Chinese by Burton Watson

Who Says a Painting Must Look Like Life?

*Written on paintings of flowering branches by Secretary Wang
of Yen-ling: two poems.*

Who says a painting must look like life?
He sees only with children's eyes.
Who says a poem must stick to the theme?
Poetry is certainly lost on him.
Poetry and painting share a single goal—
clean freshness and effortless skill.
Pien Luan's sparrows live on paper;
Chao Ch'ang's flowers breathe with soul.
But what are they beside these scrolls,
bold sketches, with spirit in every stroke?
Who'd think one dot of red
could call up a whole unbounded spring!

DAVID BOTTOMS

from *Armored Hearts: Selected & New Poems,* 1995

Shooting Rats at the Bibb County Dump

Loaded on beer and whiskey, we ride
to the dump in carloads
to turn our headlights across the wasted field,
freeze the startled eyes of rats against mounds of rubbish.

Shot in the head, they jump only once, lie still
like dead beer cans.
Shot in the gut or rump, they writhe and try to burrow
into garbage, hide in old truck tires,
rusty oil drums, cardboard boxes scattered across the mounds,
or else drag themselves on forelegs across our beams of light
toward the darkness at the edge of the dump.

It's the light they believe kills.
We drink and load again, let them crawl
for all they're worth into the darkness we're headed for.

THOMAS CENTOLELLA

from *Lights & Mysteries,* 1995

Joy

When it comes back to teach you
or you come back to learn
how half alive you've been,
how your own ignorance and arrogance
have kept you deprived—
when it comes back to you
or you yourself return,
joy is simple, unassuming.
Red tulips on their green stems.
Early spring vegetables, bright in the pan.
The primary colors of a child's painting,
the first lessons, all over again.

ARTHUR SZE

from *Archipelago,* 1995

In Your Honor

In your honor, a man presents a sea bass
tied to a black-lacquered dish by green-spun seaweed.

"Ah" is heard throughout the room:
you are unsure what is about to happen.

You might look through a telescope at the full
bright moon against deep black space,

see from the Bay of Dew to the Sea of Nectar,
but this beauty of naming is a subterfuge.

What are the thoughts of hunters driving
home on a Sunday afternoon empty-handed?

Their conception of honor may coincide
with your conception of cruelty? The slant

of light as sun declines is a knife
separating will and act into infinitely thin

and lucid slices. You look at the sea bass's eye,
clear and luminous. The gills appear to move

ever so slightly. The sea bass smells
of dream, but this is no dream. "Ah,

such delicacy" is heard throughout the room,
and the sea bass suddenly flaps. It

bleeds and flaps, bleeds and flaps as
the host slices slice after slice of glistening sashimi.

HAYDEN CARRUTH

from *Scrambled Eggs & Whiskey: Poems 1991–1995,* 1996

Auburn Poem

A book I was reading this morning
by Milan Kundera contains this: "In the algebra
of love a child is the symbol of the magical

sum of two beings." And now that child
is thirty-nine years old; she is suffering
from a cancer which we are told is incurable

and will become fatal. You have been married
for thirty years to another man, and I
have been married to three other women

and have lived with six whom I did not
marry—a disgrace but there it is, done
and irrevocable. We are old. You are

sixty-nine and I am seventy. It would be
sentimental folly to say I can see in you,
or you in me, the lineaments of our

loving youth. Yet it is true. Your voice
especially takes me back. We are here
because our daughter, whom we conceived

one fine April night in Chicago long ago,
is crucially vulnerable. We meet in agony,
in wordless despair. We meet after years

of separation and mildly affectionate
unconcern. But it's true, true, this child
who is a mature, afflicted woman

with children of her own, is still a symbol
of that magical sum we were, and in this
wretchedness, without word or touch or hidden

glance, I hold myself out to you, and I know
I am accepted without word or touch or hidden
glance. This, so late, the crisis of our lives.

HAYDEN CARRUTH

from *Scrambled Eggs & Whiskey: Poems 1991–1995,* 1996

California

for Adrienne Rich

To come again into the place of revolutionary
thought after years in the wilderness
of complacency and hard-eyed greed
and brutality
is extraordinary. A.'s kitchen
in Santa Cruz
isn't greatly different from her kitchen in
West Barnet in the old days,
small interesting ornaments here and there,
many good things to eat—
and how ideas flew from stove to table,
from corner to corner. In Santa Cruz
after twenty-odd years it was the same. Tolstoi said
the purpose of poetry is to provoke
feeling in the reader, to "infect" the reader,
he said,—and so to induce a change,
a change of conscience
that may lead to a change in the world, that will
lead to a change in the world!
How can poetry be written by people who want no change?

To be reconciled after so long,
in sunshine, among Latino voices. A. showed me
where earthquake two years ago had changed Santa Cruz
and how the people were rebuilding, making it better. Had she
been frightened? Of course. Would she move away?
Never. Here earth itself gives us the paradigm.
And the great ocean hurling its might always thunderously against
the land at Half Moon Bay is our measure

of flux and courage
and eternity.

We drove among hills, redwood and eucalyptus,
dense growth, the richness and ramifying intricacy
of the world's loveliness, and asked
what would be left
for our grandchildren, already born, when they are
as old as we? No longer do we
need an insane president to end us
by pushing a button. People
need only go on living as they are, without change,
the complacent and hard-eyed
everywhere. At the airport
after dark
among hard lights
with the massive proportions of human energy
surrounding them, two old people
embraced in love of the injured and poor, of poetry,
of the world in its still remaining remote possibilities,
which were themselves.

SHIRLEY KAUFMAN

from Roots in the Air: New & Selected Poems, 1996

Mothers, Daughters

Through every night we hate,
preparing the next day's
war. She bangs the door.
Her face laps up my own
despair, the sour, brown eyes,
the heavy hair she won't
tie back. She's cruel,
as if my private meanness
found a way to punish us.

We gnaw at each other's
skulls. Give me what's mine.
I'd haul her back, choking
myself in her, herself
in me. There is a book
called *Poisons* on her shelf.
Her room stinks with incense,
animal turds, hamsters
she strokes like silk. They
exercise on the bathroom
floor, and two drop through
the furnace vent. The whole
house smells of the accident,
the hot skins, the small
flesh rotting. Six days
we turn the gas up then
to fry the dead. I'd fry
her head if I could until
she cried love, love me!

All she won't let me do.
Her stringy figure in

the windowed room shares
its thin bones with no one.
Only her shadow on the glass
waits like an older sister.
Now she stalks, leans forward,
concentrates merely on getting
from here to there. Her feet
are bare. I hear her breathe
where I can't get in. If I
break through to her, she will
drive nails into my tongue.

ANNA SWIR

from *Talking to My Body,* 1996
Translated from the Polish by Czesław Miłosz and Leonard Nathan

There Is a Light in Me

Whether in daytime or in nighttime
I always carry inside
a light.
In the middle of noise and turmoil
I carry silence.
Always
I carry light and silence.

ANNA SWIR

from *Talking to My Body,* 1996
Translated from the Polish by Czesław Miłosz and Leonard Nathan

Virginity

One must be brave to live through
a day. What remains
is nothing but the pleasure of longing—very precious.

Longing
purifies as does flying, strengthens as does an effort,
it fashions the soul
as work
fashions the belly.

It is like an athlete, like a runner
who will never
stop running. And this
gives him endurance.

Longing
is nourishing for the strong.
It is like a window
on a high tower, through which
blows the wind of strength.

Longing,
Virginity of happiness.

JAMES GALVIN

from *Resurrection Update: Collected Poems 1975–1997*, 1997

Meteorology

The heart is such a big awkward girl,
I think it's a paper cup of gasoline.
The floor dozes off when I walk across it,
And the windows turn opaque
When they are sure no one is around.

At night when no one sees them
Lovers write each other's names
With black volcanic stones
On the white salt flats.
There were slamming doors and flowers,

A cup of milk left on the stove too long.
There was all the wind in Wyoming.
No one saw anything.
We were not evil enough to make decisions,
But able to let things happen

Evil enough.
We are learning that weather
Is always merciless—
Even if you don't mean weather—
Even the best days.

THOMAS MCGRATH

from *Letter to an Imaginary Friend,* 1997

from Part Two

With a terrible signal-to-noise ratio—is it information
Comes through all that clatter or a mere random conformity
To a known Code?
                Minimax
                        bobbery
                                palaver
                                            —you can reduce shortfall
Only so much—finally . . .
                      it is necessary to act.
                                  Even
When the information is incomplete . . .
                          —That's all right:
I'll cut for sign—and don't leave the gate open
                            I'll
Catch my own snipes.
                The village is *not* asleep, it is only
Siesta . . .

          A poor fisherman hanged in a net
Puts all heaven in a sweat . . .
                  The ratio of signal
To noise improves. I read you loud and clear. Over.

"—get out in the stream and *sing*.
                  It's a branch assignment,
                              a job
For the revolutionary fraction in the Amalgamated Union of False Magicians,
Kind of boring, from within . . ."
                  Insurrectionary
                      ancestral voices . . .
                          —coming now—
Ghosts wreathed with invincible wampum—

                                            "Hey buddy

What you doing there in the dark?"
                          —How should I know?
                                       What I'm doing

Ain't nobody
         nowhere
             never
                done before.

W.S. MERWIN

from *Flower & Hand: Poems 1977–1983*, 1997

Berryman

I will tell you what he told me
in the years just after the war
as we then called
the second world war

don't lose your arrogance yet he said
you can do that when you're older
lose it too soon and you may
merely replace it with vanity

just one time he suggested
changing the usual order
of the same words in a line of verse
why point out a thing twice

he suggested I pray to the Muse
get down on my knees and pray
right there in the corner and he
said he meant it literally

it was in the days before the beard
and the drink but he was deep
in tides of his own through which he sailed
chin sideways and head tilted like a tacking sloop

he was far older than the dates allowed for
much older than I was he was in his thirties
he snapped down his nose with an accent
I think he had affected in England

as for publishing he advised me
to paper my wall with rejection slips

his lips and the bones of his long fingers trembled
with the vehemence of his views about poetry

he said the great presence
that permitted everything and transmuted it
in poetry was passion
passion was genius and he praised movement and invention

I had hardly begun to read
I asked how can you ever be sure
that what you write is really
any good at all and he said you can't

you can't you can never be sure
you die without knowing
whether anything you wrote was any good
if you have to be sure don't write

JIM HARRISON

from *The Shape of the Journey: New and Collected Poems,* 1998

I

to D.G.

This matted and glossy photo of Yesenin
bought at a Leningrad newsstand—permanently
tilted on my desk: he doesn't stare at me
he stares at nothing; the difference between
a plane crash and a noose adds up to nothing.
And what can I do with heroes with my brain fixed
on so few of them? Again nothing. Regard his flat
magazine eyes with my half-cocked own, both
of us seeing nothing. In the vodka was nothing
and Isadora was nothing, the pistol waved
in New York was nothing, and that plank bridge
near your village home in Ryazan covered seven feet
of nothing, the clumsy noose that swung the tilted
body was nothing but a noose, a law of gravity
this seeking for the ground, a few feet of nothing
between shoes and the floor a light-year away.
So this is a song of Yesenin's noose that came
to nothing, but did a good job as we say back home
where there's nothing but snow. But I stood under
your balcony in St. Petersburg, yes St. Petersburg!
a crazed tourist with so much nothing in my heart
it wanted to implode. And I walked down to the Neva
embankment with a fine sleet falling and there was
finally something, a great river vastly flowing, flat
as your eyes; something to marry to my nothing heart
other than the poems you hurled into nothing those
years before the articulate noose.

TIMOTHY LIU

from *Say Goodnight*, 1998

Vespers

So many want to be blessed.
I only want to kneel in a quiet room.
To love what we have or not exist
at all. Nothing to help me sleep.
Only a scrap of paper slipped
into my hand: *Your body an ocean,*
a song without end. Votive candles
flickering in the dark that made us
larger than life: hip-thrust,
back-arch, mouth-grip, you on top
till we collapsed in the coiled
springs that came to rest. A chair
where you once sat. A bowl of fruit
neither one of us would touch.

from *Configurations: New & Selected Poems 1958–1998*, 1998

Darwin's Dream

Unseen at forest edge
in morning light,
Darwin watches the parade
of little animals marching
up out of sea
waters so green,
and he's pleased
by sight
of their lunar rhythm.

Darwin says look,
the little beasts
with their lovely moony eyes
parading up from sea-womb.

Watching them scatter,
Darwin counts them going
south and east, west and north,
ranks breaking, rhythm shattered,
as they trot off in new rhythm,

into dark forest after dark forest
following scent of sea
in each leaf of each tree.

JOSEPH STROUD

from *Below Cold Mountain*, 1998

Ezra Under the Constellation of the Dragon

And what shall I raise against my righteousness,
what put down anger, take from the root of my heart
vanity? I have wept and I have raved in the temple
the cottonwood makes of leaves, knelt down within
the day, death's other kingdom, and still the earth
would have of me, & the night come down in points of fire.

JOSEPH STROUD

from *Below Cold Mountain*, 1998

Provenance

I want to tell you the story of that winter
in Madrid where I lived in a room
with no windows, where I lived
with the death of my father, carrying it
everywhere through the streets,
as if it were an object, a book written
in a luminous language I could not read.
Every day I left my room and wandered
across the great plazas of that city,
boulevards crowded with people and cars.
There was nowhere I wanted to go.
Sometimes I would come to myself
inside a cathedral under the vaulted
ceiling of the transept, I would find
myself sobbing, transfixed in the light
slanting through the rose window
scattering jewels across the cold
marble floor. At this distance now
the grief is not important, nor the sadness
I felt day after day wandering the maze
of medieval streets, wandering the rooms
of the Prado, going from painting
to painting, looking into Velázquez,
into Bosch, Brueghel, looking for something
that would help, that would frame
my spirit, focus sorrow into some
kind of belief that wasn't fantasy
or false, for I was tired of deception,
the lies of words, even the Gypsy violin,
its lament with the *puñal* inside
seemed indulgent, posturing.
I don't mean to say these didn't

move me, I was an easy mark,
anything could well up in me—
rainshine on the cobblestone streets,
a bowl of tripe soup in a peasant café.
In my world at that time there was
no scale, nothing with which
to measure, I could no longer
discern value—the mongrel eating
scraps of garbage in the alley
was equal to *Guernica* in all its
massive outrage. When I looked
in the paintings mostly what I saw
were questions. In the paradise
panel of *The Garden of Earthly Delights*
why does Bosch show a lion
disemboweling a deer? Or that man
in hell crucified on the strings of a harp?
In his *Allegory of the Seven Deadly Sins:*
Gluttony, Lust, Sloth, Wrath, Envy, Avarice,
Pride—of which am *I* most guilty?
Why in Juan de Flanders' *Resurrection*
of Lazarus is the face of Christ so sad
in bringing the body back to life?
Every day I returned to my room,
to my cave where I could not look out
at the world, where I was forced into
the one place I did not want to be. In
the Cranach painting—behind Venus
with her fantastic hat, her cryptic look,
behind Cupid holding a honeycomb, whimpering
with bee stings—far off in the background,
that cliff rising above the sea, that small hut
on top—is that Cold Mountain, is that where
the poet made his way out of our world?
My father had little use for poems, less use
for the future. If he had anything
to show me by his life, it was to live
here. Even in a room without windows.
One day in the Prado, in the Hall

of the Muses, a group of men
in expensive suits, severe looking,
men of importance, with a purpose,
moved down the hallway toward me,
and I was swept aside, politely,
firmly. As they passed I glimpsed
in their midst a woman, in a simple
black dress with pearls, serene, speaking
to no one, and then she and the men
were gone. *Who was that?* I asked,
and a guard answered: *The Queen.*
The Queen. In my attempt to follow
to see which painting she would choose,
I got lost in one of the Goya rooms
and found myself before one of his
dark paintings, one from his last years
when the world held no more illusions,
where love was examined in a ruthless,
savage anger. In this painting
a woman stood next to Death, her beauty,
her elegance, her pearls and shining hair
meant nothing in His presence,
and He was looking out from the painting,
looking into me, and Death took my hand
and made me look, and I saw my own face
streaming with tears, and the day
took on the shape of a crouching beast,
and my father's voice called out in wonder
or warning, and every moment
I held on made it that much harder
to let go, and Death demanded
that I let go. Then the moment
disappeared, like a pale horse, like
a ghost horse disappearing deep inside
Goya's painting. I left the Prado.
I walked by the *Palacio Real* with its
2,000 rooms, one for every kind
of desire. I came upon the *Rastro,*
the great open-air bazaar, a flea market

for the planet, where everything in the world
that has been cast aside, rejected, lost,
might be found, where I found Cervantes,
an old, dusty copy of *Don Quixote,*
and where I discovered an old mirror,
and looking into it found my father's face
in my face looking back at me,
and behind us a Brueghel world
crowded with the clamor of the market,
people busy with their lives, hunting,
searching for what's missing. How casual
they seemed, in no hurry, as if they had all
of time, no frenzy, no worry,
as the Castilian sun made its slow
arch over us, the same sun
that lanced the fish on crushed ice
in the market stalls, fish with open mouths,
glazed stares, lapped against each other
like scales, by the dozens, the *Madrileños*
gaping over them, reading them
like some sacred text, like some kind
of psalm or prophecy as they made
their choice, and had it wrapped in paper,
then disappeared into the crowd.
And that is all. I wanted to tell you
the story of that winter in Madrid
where I lived in a room with no windows
at the beginning of my life without my father.
When the fascist officials asked Picasso
about *Guernica:* "Are you responsible
for this painting?" He looked back
at them, and answered slowly: "No.
You are." What should I answer
when asked about this poem?
I wanted to tell you the story of that winter
in Madrid, where my father kept dying, again
and again, inside of me, and I kept
bringing him back, holding him for as long
as I could. I never knew how much

I loved him. I didn't know that grief
would give him back to me, over
and over, I didn't know that those
cobbled streets would someday
lead to here, to this quietude,
this blessing, to my father
within me.

DAVID BUDBILL

from *Moment to Moment: Poems of a Mountain Recluse,* 1999

What Issa Heard

Two hundred years ago Issa heard the morning birds
singing sutras to this suffering world.

I heard them too, this morning, which must mean,

since we will always have a suffering world,
we must also always have a song.

DANA LEVIN

from *In the Surgical Theatre,* 1999

The Nurse

There are so many now, perched on the headboard, opening and closing
      their wings like moths. The kidney
is failing, and so many are arriving, alighting on the blanket, the pillow,
      falling around
the comatose patient, settling in drifts against the paper gown.
      You've been seeing this,
you've been watching them gather, you've told no one how the buzzing
      keeps growing
around the bed. Now they crowd like a sea around the body,
      listing and pushing,
the pulse of their wings lifting the current, you can feel it,
      the wind,
on the hairs of your arms, making the lamp sway,
      ruffling the chart
at the foot of the bed, they are hanging from tubes,
      perched on the monitor,
pressing and pressing with a rising hum, you can hear it,
      the whirring,
the din of their waiting, as they rustle and jostle
      and launch with a roar,
a roar of angels swarming over the body, burrowing headfirst
      into every pore—

PRIMUS ST. JOHN

from *Communion: Poems 1976–1998*, 1999

The Fountain

There is always some fountain
Where the water that's really pouring—
Is our lives.
When I hear it,
I believe in all of the storms—
Where it came from.
Then I make believe
I am one of those mossbacked prophets
Who stick on stone and wait
For everything—quietly.

"We are all pouring toward the same conviction,"
I hear the fountain say,
"But we believe that, separately,"
So I believe it all—
The whole thing's that mindless,
And today is spring.

KAREN SWENSON

from *A Daughter's Latitude: New & Selected Poems,* 1999

Sparrows

Where roof-ends rise up into dragons
in the temple quiet of Bangkok
frantic wings are sold in small cages
by women to earn a few baht.

To free wings, to befriend the flight
of even sparrows, earns Buddhist merit
and freedom for the self
trapped in repetitive cages of flesh.

Universal as dowdy sparrows,
in this gilded glitter of temples,
our ideals hover wings in sunlight
to be caged once again in the dark.

2000–2009

from *One Above & One Below,* 2000

High Lonesome

Sick now for months, I wake
to the cold glaze of a night sweat,

a metabolic stone
tossed into a mossy river.

       The dream keeps me
             company,

faithful as a sunflower, the same
crenulated eye staring
from its chronic bed where
the moon greases the far wall.

In the dark, I hear the snow
counting to itself,
three mississippi, four mississippi . . .

       The dream listens, too,

old acquaintance,
paid nursemaid nodding in the corner,
the friend you no longer have
to speak with
      to make yourself known.

    *

Welcome, genius loci, djinn fruit
weathering my salted field,

           welcome home.

    *

I am setting off with my father
in the cab of the 7 Up company truck,
his shotgun navigator,
working the route from Lisco to Lodgepole.

August smoked brown at the edges,
a dust-colored moth crushed
beneath the plate glass of the plains'
vaporous sky,
                    and I
am perched high on the black
bench seat, thighs pinking
against the burning
vinyl, the chrome radio knobs
in the shape of miniature crowns
too scalding to turn.

          We're working the morning route
from Lisco to Lodgepole,

picking up the empties
for my grandfather, bringing the bottomless
box of stale candy bars and chewing gum
for the gas-station vending machines—
                              and I smell the sugary,
acid stink rising
from the wood-slatted truck bed,
and hear the glass-rattle bell
the green bottles will make when
my father loads them,

the green, glass-rattle bell chattering
thirty miles back to Sidney.

          *

Virus makes me plural, the whole
unveiled, an archipelago—

each organ cut off from the old continent,
new islands populated by marsupials
for whom we have no names.

Their ringed tails switch in the bloodstream.

    *

My geography
       is defined by those places
       I was told never to go—

       by the lure of the train tracks
       stretched out next to the bottling plant,

where the brown bulls and rattlers
drape themselves along the hot rails,
listless, scorched ribbons,
their coils half-hidden in chin-high scrub.

       Not far away,
someone's aunt stands out
of the sun, hugging the shady rim
at the plant's front entry, below the old ad
for Kickapoo Joy Juice, the cartoon Indians
poxed where the paint has flecked away.

       Usually my father's
younger sister, not paying us any mind,
wearing her discontented face, diamond-
chip earrings, and a shiny summer dress
with quarter-sized spots of perspiration
daubed like perfume under each arm.

    *

       The reapers' house
was the only house
visible beyond the tracks,
where it leaned like a paper lantern

from a rise
in the unplowed field.
                    You could see the white tarps
laid out in a clearing beyond the front
porch, a cinder block pinning
each edge, the tarps smoothing over
the misshapen packages drying
stiffly below them.

Even then I understood their business—

even then I knew, everything is parts.

            *

            Now,
at the side of the highway, comes
the brown-haired girl
with her shoulder blades jutting
out like two pink wishbones,
the brown-haired girl carrying
the white plastic bucket, half-full, and
                            her father bending
over the bloated cow's carcass
down at the edge of the field,
its hard rubber belly hairless
and puckered like a dry lemon peel;
                        her father sawing
with his long-handled knife,
slipping it between
                    the fat and the skin—

        *

        Sometimes,
she appeared
on the old breezeway, a flock
of smaller kids
wandering out after her.

And sometimes
it was just her,
the brown-haired girl, her face
following the celebratory alarm
my cousins would make,
flinging handfuls of dust
as the iron rails began to mutter,
the train's pulse humming through us,
the measure for how soon
our freight would come.

COLD MOUNTAIN (HAN SHAN)

from *The Collected Songs of Cold Mountain,* 2000
Translated from the Chinese by Red Pine

16

People ask the way to Cold Mountain
but roads don't reach Cold Mountain
in summer the ice doesn't melt
and the morning fog is too dense
how did someone like me arrive
our minds are not the same
if they were the same
you would be here

205

My true home is on Cold Mountain
perched among cliffs beyond the reach of trouble
images leave no trace when they vanish
I roam the whole universe from here
lights and shadows flash across my mind
not one dharma appears before me
since I found the magic pearl
I can go anywhere everywhere is perfect

HỒ XUÂN HƯƠNG

from *Spring Essence: The Poetry of Hồ Xuân Hường*, 2000
Translated from the Nôm by John Balaban

On a Portrait of Two Beauties

How old are these two, anyway?
Big and little sister, equally lovely.

In 100 years, smooth as two sheets of paper.
In 1,000, they still will glow like springtime.

Will the plum tree ever know the wind and moon?
Will reed and willow accept their dull fates?

Why not portray the other pleasures? Blame
the artist, gifted, but a bit dim about love.

IKKYŪ

from *Crow with No Mouth: Ikkyū, Fifteenth Century Zen Master,* 2000
Versions by Stephen Berg, after the Japanese

from *Crow with No Mouth*

even before trees rocks I was nothing
when I'm dead nowhere I'll be nothing

*

if there's nowhere to rest at the end
how can I get lost on the way?

*

one of you saved my satori paper I know it piece by piece you
pasted it back together now watch me burn it once and for all

*

this soul torch I hold up lights the sky
think of those nights freezing staring into the river

*

my monk friend has a weird endearing habit
he weaves sandals and leaves them secretly by the roadside

*

rain drips from the roof lip
loneliness sounds like that

*

passion's red thread is infinite
like the earth always under me

RICHARD JONES

from *The Blessing: New and Selected Poems,* 2000

The Novel

I

For two days I've been crying,
from Paris to Rome, from Rome to Palermo,
weeping and sobbing here on the train
over a nineteenth-century novel.
Some paragraphs are so beautiful
I lean my head against the window
while villages fly past
like books I'll never open.
When I come to the last few sentences
of an exquisitely painful chapter,
I drop the novel in my lap
or crush it to my chest
and cover my face with my hands,
trembling and shaking.

People on the train
don't know what to do with me
or why I rock back and forth
clutching my book and sniffling.
From Paris to Rome,
the French hated me for crying.
They blew smoke in my face
and cursed me in their beautiful language.
But now, along the Amalfi Coast,
beside blue waters and grottoes,
the great hearts of the Italians
take pity—
they offer me water,
offer me wine.
We open the window and smoke together

until I compose myself.
These are my five angels—
a baker from Napoli,
a nun,
young Rafael the fisherman,
and an old married couple,
young lovers once,
now shrunk to the size of children.
The baker from Napoli speaks for them all,
asking what troubles me.
The five Italians lean forward.
For a long moment I'm silent,
looking down at the novel
that is the story of my life,
a secret between the author and me.
I am the hero,
and though I am brave,
indefatigable, loyal, intrepid,
I cannot bear to hear it all again.
My story is blessed with moments of joy,
but they are brief
and flicker like distant stars.
The author knows
truth is tragic.
Relentless, tireless, devoid of sympathy,
he talks and talks
like the heartbeat of time
while I grow weaker and weaker,
no longer a hero,
but a boy again,
weeping when my mother falls ill in the castle,
weeping when Fabiana, my little sister,
is abducted by thieves and gypsies
and forced to dance naked
before a fire in the camp of the hussars.

The Italians are waiting.
I look up at the luggage rack,
suitcases and plastic bags

piled precariously over their heads.
I look out the window at blue doors and green doors
of whitewashed houses built on the edges of cliffs
here at the foot of the famous volcano.
When I finally lean forward, I whisper,
slowly, so they will understand,
"My wife died,
and my child,
horribly,
in an accident,
in America, America,
an accident in America,
my wife and child,
morto, morto."
The Italians lean back,
overcome, delighted,
crossing themselves,
everyone talking at once.
My confession makes them happy,
makes them hungry.
They bring out sandwiches,
pears, olives, and cheese.
We feast all afternoon
until sated and sleepy,
until they all lean back in their worn red seats
and the baker, with his hands, asks,
"And now?"
I tell them I'll retreat
to an island to rest,
recover, renew my life
again. I tell this
in broken Italian
and simple French,
using only the present tense and infinitives.
I employ words I remember
from German and Spanish,
I speak English when the story
becomes complex and difficult
though the words themselves

are plain and simple.
My five angels understand best
when I make wild and mysterious gestures
with my hands, when I beat my fist
against the coffin of my heart
or fall silent,
and they have only to look in my face
to see how far I've come,
to see my heart is broken.

2

As the sun goes down,
I tell them a story,
make them swear never to repeat it,
telling the story only in English
to emphasize feeling over fact.
"I saw something very strange
today in Rome," I tell them.
"I was passing the time between trains
in the gardens of the Villa Borghese,
sitting on a bench, eating ice cream.
A man walked toward me down the gravel path
near the stalls of the *carabinieri*.
Smartly dressed, handsome, he seemed
carefree, tossing keys in his left hand
and humming under the linden trees.
A moment later a woman rushed through the gate,
running toward him,
awkwardly carrying her coat
as her shoulder bag bounced and knocked against her.
She was screaming; he ignored her
and kept walking.
I thought perhaps that he had said something to her
on the street before entering the garden
or had been forward on a crowded bus,
that she came now for revenge,
to defend her honor,
that he would feign innocence,

swear he'd never touched her.
When the woman caught the man,
she dropped her coat and bag,
spun him around
and beat him with her fists,
scratching his face,
clawing his eyes.
And the man did nothing
except close his eyes
and hold on to his broken glasses,
absorbing the blows like a saint,
like a martyr.
It was then I realized
he loved her,
she was his wife,
that she too must have loved him very much
to attack him this way in a public park.
She beat him until there was no good in it,
until he turned away
and, his back to her, began to weep.
She stepped back, yelling,
hurling questions at the wall of his back.
He turned. Unable to meet her eyes,
he said something so softly
only she could hear.
Then she took a step forward,
wanting to hit him again,
raised her fists,
but fury had left her
and the man walked away
down the path in sorrow.
She followed,
but not before she bent to pick up
the keys he had dropped in the dirt,
the keys he would have forgotten
and lost
had she not been there."

I ask the Italians if they understand.
No one says a word. Now,
I tell them, I will finish the story,
this parable, this little novel,
reminding them of their vow
never to repeat it.

"The man and woman walked to the stables
where they studied the horses of the *carabinieri*.
The proud horses—usually aloof and haughty—
returned the lovers' gaze with patient brown eyes,
tossing their heads sympathetically
like priests.
          And though I had no right
to follow the lovers with my ice cream and notebook,
though the lovers' novel was written in Italian,
I eavesdropped as the horses spoke,
as horses in Italian novels sometimes do,
forgiving the man his infidelity,
the woman her inability to forgive.
The horse-priests said,
La passione è difficile,
and offered themselves
as models of discipline.
The horses said their lives were a novel
full of grain and wind and sweat.
They told of men in blue uniforms
who arrive with the light each dawn
to wash and brush them,
bringing fresh straw.
The horses said they love each day,
galloping through the woods
or walking slowly by the villa's open windows
so their riders can admire the lovely sculptures,
the horrible *Rape of Persephone*,
the terrible *Apollo and Daphne*.
The horses said they don't understand
the human love
of stories in marble and bronze.

They understand only
that each day as they enter the woods
with light falling through trees,
with leaves under their hooves,
their hearts become so full they think
if they don't die right then
they will surely live forever.
And when the horses fell silent
and bent their heads to the sweet water
flowing fresh down the long wooden trough,
the lovers turned away,
perhaps toward home,
where they would make love,
touching each other gently and with respect,
then with increasing passion and need,
healing each other simply
with their love."

In the compartment,
the baker, nun, fisherman,
and tiny old couple
listen to each word,
leaning forward when I whisper,
nodding at a word they understand—
carabinieri, Bernini.
But I am finished talking;
I will say nothing more in English.
But they don't know that yet,
and watch me and wait to see if the story continues.
When I finally lower my head,
open my book,
and continue reading,
they don't wait for my tears;
they argue over the meaning of my story,
yelling at one another,
waving hands, interpreting,
translating, revising, editing, embellishing,
digressing
into the mystery

of lives they have observed,
adding their own emotions
and personal histories
as if they've comprehended everything I've said
and no longer need to consult me,
talking among themselves now
as if I had disappeared.

3

Just before midnight,
we take turns in the WC
with our toothbrushes and our washcloths.
When the coach lights go out,
the nun vows to watch over me
as I finish my book by flashlight,
but she's a tired angel
and falls asleep in a minute.
The old couple curl
on their seat like two cats—
they're that small.
The baker snorts and snores,
hands on his belly,
face white as flour in the moonlight.
But Rafael, the fisherman,
is too young to sleep.
He stands outside in the corridor,
admiring the moon and moonlit water,
thinking,

I will tell my friends
what I heard and saw on my journey.
I will sit in my uncle's café
and my cousin will bring wine and glasses.
We'll drink to the moon
bathing the rocky coast of our village
and to spells the moon casts on fish
we catch in our nets at dawn.
I will tell my friends about the strange American

and how fine it is to stay up all night
admiring the moon,
admiring the moonlit water.
And I will tell them how,
when the entire train was dreaming
except for the American
hidden behind his book and flashlight,
I saw an old man in the next compartment
sitting across from his daughter,
admiring her as she slept,
tenderly, secretly watching her,
biting his knuckle now and then,
so astonished was he by her beauty.

STEPHEN KUUSISTO

from *Only Bread, Only Light,* 2000

Elegy for Ted Berrigan

When I heard you read, I was only twenty,
But I knew you were a fool.
It was your weakened vanity
That did it—none of the "cool"

Poets in my required reading
Ever filled their work
With Pepsi or fucking
Or the weather in New York.

Neruda made a science of tears,
Yeats had his vision.
Roethke danced from ear to ear,
While Rilke served a mission.

Their poems were philosophy:
A rage for "God" or order
Lurked in each apostrophe.
Poetry was "harder"—

A crystal, the center
Of static divination.
By reading, one could enter
The drama of creation.

You were vulnerability—
It was gloomy being broke today;
I am in love with poetry;
Love, why do you always take my heart away?

I didn't know then
That there'd be days like this—

Weeks . . . months when
Making an honest list

Is all that finally matters.
(There's no art in being real;
Who can change it later?)
At twenty, I was pure dismissal.

I didn't want to hear
Your frail, lovely voice
Reciting pills and fear.
I thought you'd made a choice;

I thought that poets had command
Of verse—I praised conviction
And luck. I thought I had a hand
In my own destination.

CORAL BRACHO

from *Reversible Monuments: Contemporary Mexican Poetry,* 2001
Edited by Mónica de la Torre and Michael Wiegers; translated
from the Spanish

The Allure of Forms

Blissful dance. Scream
of the shadows in light.
Night that pours its animal shrill
into the morning's joy.
There it ramifies,
bursts, intertwines itself. It blossoms
on its clearest edge. It's the allure of forms
in their steep nearness, their engulfed
proximity. Rivers become entangled with, yet do not merge,
an obscure lightning, an arborescent
flame. Fauna
sliding between the blazes.
It's the pleasure of opposites: the scattered pondering,
the swarming and resonant jungle.

MdlT

MADELINE DEFREES

from *Blue Dusk: New & Selected Poems, 1951–2001*, 2001

To Marilyn Monroe Whose Favorite Color Was White

When you wriggled onto the silver screen, Marilyn—
honey blonde or platinum—I was a nun. I
found you too late in your satin sleep. Now, three
decades past, I grieve from that ancient
cloister, the alabaster body, my beautiful buried
sister. Convent movies had to be clean as
bleach. Even your titles

                      went wrong: *All About Eve.*
The Seven Year Itch. The Asphalt Jungle.
Some Like It Hot. How to Marry a Millionaire.
Sex was a bullet I dodged, that shot on the subway
grate! Skirts lifted to seventh
heaven, you scared me all right, as you scared your
jealous husband.

                Yet Joe was your friend in the end
as I hope to be. Bride at sixteen like you, given
another name, I was cast with the world's invisible
millionaire. We didn't know who we were,
Norma Jean, too young to care. Even now I imagine
you posed—a pinup everywhere woman who did it
for fifty dollars. I resent

                    the photographer smirking
away with the loot: the generous milky
breasts and bottom, pout of a wounded child. Too bad,
the bad life fate guaranteed you:
dashing absent father, unmarried mother who
had to be locked away. Say *cheese,* Marilyn. Open
those pearly gates,

               come back with me to my former
marmoreal splendor: the lily-pad I escaped

that was never my passion. Ivory walls, skulls in
our heads all day. Snowy sheets and colorless
towels. Chaste linens framing the parchment faces.
It was color I missed most of all,
white sister. I hated the pallor. I want you to play

this part over. I want to barge in as your crazy
mother stealing the scene: capsules
washed down the drain in a lethal river. The beauty
startled awake in the last act from that
white sleep history promised.

NORMAN DUBIE

from *The Mercy Seat Seat: Collected & New Poems 1967–2001,* 2001

Of Politics, & Art

for Allen

Here, on the farthest point of the peninsula
The winter storm
Off the Atlantic shook the schoolhouse.
Mrs. Whitimore, dying
Of tuberculosis, said it would be after dark
Before the snowplow and bus would reach us.

She read to us from Melville.

How in an almost calamitous moment
Of sea hunting
Some men in an open boat suddenly found themselves
At the still and protected center
Of a great herd of whales
Where all the females floated on their sides
While their young nursed there. The cold frightened whalers
Just stared into what they allowed
Was the ecstatic lapidary pond of a nursing cow's
One visible eyeball.
And they were at peace with themselves.

Today I listened to a woman say
That Melville *might*
Be taught in the next decade. Another woman asked, "And why not?"
The first responded, "Because there are
No women in his one novel."

And Mrs. Whitimore was now reading from the Psalms.
Coughing into her handkerchief. Snow above the windows.
There was a blue light on her face, breasts, and arms.
Sometimes a whole civilization can be dying

Peacefully in one young woman, in a small heated room
With thirty children
Rapt, confident and listening to the pure
God-rendering voice of a storm.

ROLF JACOBSEN

from *The Roads Have Come to an End Now: Selected and Last Poems of Rolf Jacobsen,* 2001
    Translated from the Norwegian by Robert Bly, Roger Greenwald, and Robert Hedin

Antenna-Forest

Up on the city's roofs are great plains.
The silence crawled there when no room was left for it on the streets.
Now the forest follows.
It has to be where the silence lives.
Tree after tree in strange groves.
They can barely manage since the floor is too hard.
It's a sparse forest, one branch to the east
and one to the west. Until it resembles crosses. A forest
of crosses. And the wind asks
—Who rests here
in these deep graves?

          RH

ROLF JACOBSEN

from *The Roads Have Come to an End Now: Selected and Last Poems of Rolf Jacobsen*, 2001
   Translated from the Norwegian by Robert Bly, Roger Greenwald, and Robert Hedin

Sunflower

What sower walked over earth,
which hands sowed
our inward seeds of fire?
They went out from his fists like rainbow curves
to frozen earth, young loam, hot sand,
they will sleep there
greedily, and drink up our lives
and explode it into pieces
for the sake of a sunflower that you haven't seen
or a thistle head or a chrysanthemum.

Let the young rain of tears come.
Let the calm hands of grief come.
It's not all as evil as you think.

RB

REBECCA SEIFERLE

from *Bitters,* 2001

Proviso

Pyrus Malus—an evil fire?—burning
in the branches, perhaps, of a primitive
species of crab-apple, cultivated
in all temperate zones into so many
varieties: the apple of discord
awarded to the fairest (in beauty
not justice) who caused the burning of Troy,
the apple of Sodom that Josephus
claimed dissolved into smoke and ashes
when grasped by a traveler's hand,
Adam's apple, the *apple of love,*
the *apple of the eye,* the *Apple John*
said to be perfect only when shriveled,
any number of erroneous fruits, any
disappointing thing. "*Faith (as you say)*
there's small choice in rotten apples" or
"*Feed an enemy the skin of a peach,*
a friend the skin of an apple." But tree
of knowledge or morning snack, you can have
the gala skin, the blush of the apple,
even the white succulent flesh, if you save
me the core—that earthly constellation
usually tossed to horses or thrown away.
I'll be with the Gypsies who cut to the star
of seeds at the heart of each orb, for
it's the core I want—intensely *apple,*
medicinal with a dash of arsenic, the zing
of earth, the crisp bite of becoming.

CAROLYN KIZER

from *Cool, Calm & Collected: Poems 1960–2000*, 2002

Suppressing the Evidence

Alaska oil spill, I edit you out.
You are too terrible to think about.
I *X*, I double-*X* you out.
The repeated floods in Bangladesh:
The starving poor who stare at us,
Stare with plaintive smiles,
Smiles without hope
As they clutch a bulbous-bellied child,
I erase your dark faces.
I edit you out.

From the dark windows of their limousines
The rich long since have waved their ringed hands,
Said Abracadabra, to disappear the poor.
Their streets are swept clear
So the homeless are sucked down the dirty drains.
Only their reflections in the tinted glass
Stare back in their complacent discontent:
The blind rich, in their blind car.

On Madison a young emaciated man
In a threadbare jacket shivers in the snow.
Help me. Please. I have no place to go.
I hold out a dollar bill between his face and mine
Like the fan of an old Japanese courtesan,
Then hurry past as his face turns to smoke.

I flee the city, back to my comfortable farm
In the valley of wine. I drink the wine.
I do not turn on the news.
I and the wine will blot it out.

And we erase more and more of the world's terrible map;
How may we bear witness, as we should?

I must hold in my mind one small dead otter pup.

CESARE PAVESE

from *Disaffections: Complete Poems 1930–1950,* 2002
Translated from the Italian by Geoffrey Brock

Poetics

The boy is aware that the tree is alive.
If the tender leaves force themselves open,
bursting ruthlessly into the light, the hard bark
must suffer extremely. And it lives in silence.
The whole world is covered with plants that suffer
in light, not daring even to breathe.
A tender light, its source unknown to the boy.
It's evening already, but each trunk stands out
against a magical background. In a moment it's dark.

The boy—and some men remain boys
for too long—who once was afraid of the dark,
walks down the street, not minding the twilight
that darkens the houses. He listens, head bowed,
to a distant memory. In the emptied-out streets
that seem like piazzas, a grave silence gathers.
A person can feel he's alone in a forest
where the trees are enormous. The light
shudders through streetlamps. The houses
are dazzling, transparent in the bluish vapor,
and the boy raises his eyes. The distant silence
that can tighten a person's breath has flowered
in the sudden light. These are the boy's
ancient trees. And the light is the spell of that time.

And somebody now is walking silently past,
through the diaphanous circle. On the street, no one
ever reveals the pain that gnaws at their life.
They move quickly, as if absorbed in their stride,
their great shadows staggering. Their faces are furrowed,

their eyes full of grief, but no one complains.
And all through the night, in a bluish haze,
they move as if through a forest, among infinite houses.

RUTH STONE

from *In the Next Galaxy*, 2002

Always on the Train

Writing poems about writing poems
is like rolling bales of hay in Texas.
Nothing but the horizon to stop you.

But consider the railroad's edge of metal trash;
bird perches, miles of telephone wires.
What is so innocent as grazing cattle?
If you think about it, it turns into words.

Trash is so cheerful, flying up
like grasshoppers in front of the reaper.
The dust devil whirls it aloft: bronze candy wrappers,
squares of clear plastic—windows on a house of air.

Below the weedy edge in last year's mat,
red and silver beer cans.
In bits blown equally everywhere,
the gaiety of flying paper
and the black high flung patterns of flocking birds.

C.D. WRIGHT

from *Steal Away: Selected and New Poems,* 2002

Floating Trees

a bed is left open to a mirror
a mirror gazes long and hard at a bed

light fingers the house with its own acoustics

one of them writes this down
one has paper

bed of swollen creeks and theories and coils
bed of eyes and leaky pens

much of the night the air touches arms
arms extend themselves to air

their torsos turning toward a roll
of sound: thunder

night of coon scat and vandalized headstones
night of deep kisses and catamenia

his face by this light: saurian
hers: ash like the tissue of a hornets' nest

one scans the aisle of firs
the faint blue line of them
one looks out: sans serif

"Didn't I hear you tell them you were born
on a train"

what begins with a sough and ends with a groan
groan in which the tongue's true color is revealed

the comb's sough and the denim's undeniable rub
the chair's stripped back and muddied rung

color of stone soup and garden gloves
color of meal and treacle and sphagnum

hangers clinging to their coat
a soft-white bulb to its string

the footprints inside us
iterate the footprints outside

the scratched words return to their sleeves

the dresses of monday through friday
swallow the long hips of weekends

a face is studied like a key
for the mystery of what it once opened

"I didn't mean to wake you
angel brains"

ink of eyes and veins and phonemes
the ink completes the feeling

a mirror silently facing a door
door with no lock no lock

the room he brings into you
the room befalls you

like the fir trees he trues her
she nears him like the firs

if one vanishes one stays
if one stays the other will or will not vanish

otherwise my beautiful green fly
otherwise not a leaf stirs

C.D. WRIGHT

from *Steal Away: Selected and New Poems*, 2002

Girl Friend

When I first saw her a few summers ago I felt.
                    Her photogenic spit.
I was climbing a coruscating staircase.
In my flammable skin. To be so full of.
Everything. At her age. It is very difficult.
A singer manqué. Among a small host of poets.
                    Noisier
than the men. Quaffing schnapps. No lens
could describe her.
                    Shoulders. Hands.
Such longings: Errant. Verdant.
To have a good time. And dream. In one's own
country. The lack. Of. Everything.
The confusion. It is very difficult. One needs.
One's own set of golden books. What if.
A ladder were. Miraculous. Extended. Across
a nursery for new stars.
                    And then.

                    for Nina

JEAN FOLLAIN

from *Transparence of the World,* 2003
Translated from the French by W.S. Merwin

Voluntary Mutilation

Rather than have to serve
in the emperor's armies
one fine evening the master
took the ax to himself
cut from his hand two great fingers,
his young blonde wife
gently bandaged the place
and the yellow hearted
pansies shook in the border
the master's two dogs howled
as he was carried to bed
then the lamps smoked
surrounded by moths
but the women who gathered
on the village square
facing the red clouds said
that what they saw was the blood
of soldiers.

from *Threshold,* 2003

Daily Ritual

              its own vocabulary

settling accounts
                targets
strategic approach
                 assessing

the situation the goddamn
situation

everyone arguing at once

litter of legs
             little torn legs
of the latest

Taha Muhammad Ali begins
his poem

        what makes me love
being alive

          he sells olivewood camels
to tourists in Nazareth

                his book
walks barefoot
            on *coins with holes*
at their center
          bullet casings
old ladies' copper rings
thrown away by grandsons

it is called *Never Mind*

                    I'm not sure
what (if)
          I love today
ask me next week

.   *the world* Ali says
                    and *dreams*

ANTONIO MACHADO

from *Border of a Dream: Selected Poems of Antonio Machado,* 2003
Translated from the Spanish by Willis Barnstone

from "Proverbs and Songs"

1907–1917

29

Walker, your footsteps
are the road, and nothing more.
Walker, there is no road,
the road is made by walking.
Walking you make the road,
and turning to look behind
you see the path you never
again will step upon.
Walker, there is no road,
only foam trails on the sea.

43

You say nothing is lost.
Maybe you say the truth,
but we lose everything
and everything loses us.

47

A man has four things
that don't work on the sea:
anchor, rudder and oars,
and fear of drowning.

ANTONIO PORCHIA

from *Voices,* 2003
Translated from the Spanish by W.S. Merwin

from *Voices*

The little things are what is eternal, and the rest, all the rest, is brevity, extreme brevity.

*

Without this ridiculous vanity that takes the form of self-display, and is part of everything and everyone, we would see nothing, and nothing would exist.

*

Truth has very few friends and those few are suicides.

*

Treat me as you should treat me, not as I should be treated.

*

I know what I have given you. I do not know what you have received.

RABINDRANATH TAGORE

from *The Lover of God,* 2003
   Translated from the Bengali by Tony K. Stewart and Chase Twichell

from "The Poems of Sun Lion"

3

He never came to me.
In the whole long dark he never came
to tend my lacerated heart.
I'm a girl with nothing, a tree
with neither flowers nor fruit.

> Go home, poor tragedy. Distract yourself
> with chores, dry your eyes. Go on now,
> dear tattered garland, limp with shame.

How can I bear this staggering weight?
I'm budding and blooming at once,
and dying, too, crushed by thirst
and the leaves' incessant rustling.
I need his eyes in mine, their altar's gold fire.
Don't lie to me. I'm lost in that blaze.
My heart waits, fierce and alone.
He'll leave me. If he leaves me, I'll poison myself.

> He drinks at love's fountain, too,
> my friend. His own thirst will call him.
> Listen to Bhānu: a man's love
> whets itself on absence if it's true.

MARVIN BELL

from *Rampant,* 2004

Around Us

We need some pines to assuage the darkness
when it blankets the mind,
we need a silvery stream that banks as smoothly
as a plane's wing, and a worn bed of
needles to pad the rumble that fills the mind,
and a blur or two of a wild thing
that sees and is not seen. We need these things
between appointments, after work,
and, if we keep them, then someone someday,
lying down after a walk
and supper, with the fire hole wet down,
the whole night sky set at a particular
time, without numbers or hours, will cause
a little sound of thanks—a zipper or a snap—
to close round the moment and the thought
of whatever good we did.

TED KOOSER

from *Delights & Shadows,* 2004

A Happy Birthday

This evening, I sat by an open window
and read till the light was gone and the book
was no more than a part of the darkness.
I could easily have switched on a lamp,
but I wanted to ride this day down into night,
to sit alone and smooth the unreadable page
with the pale gray ghost of my hand.

TED KOOSER

from *Delights & Shadows*, 2004

Mother

Mid April already, and the wild plums
bloom at the roadside, a lacy white
against the exuberant, jubilant green
of new grass and the dusty, fading black
of burned-out ditches. No leaves, not yet,
only the delicate, star-petaled
blossoms, sweet with their timeless perfume.

You have been gone a month today
and have missed three rains and one nightlong
watch for tornadoes. I sat in the cellar
from six to eight while fat spring clouds
went somersaulting, rumbling east. Then it poured,
a storm that walked on legs of lightning,
dragging its shaggy belly over the fields.

The meadowlarks are back, and the finches
are turning from green to gold. Those same
two geese have come to the pond again this year,
honking in over the trees and splashing down.
They never nest, but stay a week or two
then leave. The peonies are up, the red sprouts
burning in circles like birthday candles,

for this is the month of my birth, as you know,
the best month to be born in, thanks to you,
everything ready to burst with living.
There will be no more new flannel nightshirts
sewn on your old black Singer, no birthday card
addressed in a shaky but businesslike hand.
You asked me if I would be sad when it happened

and I am sad. But the iris I moved from your house
now hold in the dusty dry fists of their roots
green knives and forks as if waiting for dinner,
as if spring were a feast. I thank you for that.
Were it not for the way you taught me to look
at the world, to see the life at play in everything,
I would have to be lonely forever.

TED KOOSER

from *Delights & Shadows,* 2004

On the Road

By the toe of my boot,
a pebble of quartz,
one drop of the earth's milk,
dirty and cold.
I held it to the light
and could almost see through it
into the grand explanation.
Put it back, something told me,
put it back and keep walking.

BEN LERNER

from *The Lichtenberg Figures,* 2004

"I did it for the children. I did it for the money"

I did it for the children. I did it for the money.
I did it for the depression of spirit and the cessation of hope.
I did it because I could, because it was there.
I'd do it again. Oops, I did it again.

What have I done? What have I done
to deserve this? What have I done with my keys,
my youth? What am I going to do
while you're at tennis camp? What are we going to do

with the body? I don't do smack. I don't do
toilets. I don't do well at school. I could do
with a bath. Unto others, I do
injurious, praiseworthy, parroted acts.

Let's just do Chinese. Just do as I say. Just do me.
That does it. Easy does it. That'll do.

JONATHAN WILLIAMS

from *Jubilant Thicket: New & Selected Poems*, 2004

The Photographer Looks at His Prints and Turns Poet

for Ralph Eugene Meatyard, 1925–1972

this picture for
instance
of Lucybelle with Wendell Berry
on his farm

he raised a small crop of peanuts
which is there
in its entirety

the shadows
are my contribution
to the construction
of the picture

*

I find
a background

and put
content

in front
of it

*

the rear
of the truck

swing-ropes coming down
branch coming across

shadows on the side
of Lucybelle

there's got
to be more in a picture

than the billboard sight
we first
get

of it

        *

in the doctor's office
the other day

people had lines running on their jawline
where the mask-line would come

if they were 70 years old
instead of 40 years old

        *

how demure some
people can look

how frightened how
pleased

all this that & the other
all become

of importance

        *

hard time
getting this little boy
to wear the mask

looks as if
he was having a hard time
doing it

      *

the hands
on this man

on the play-toy they're
sitting on

      *

how Lucybelle
raises
her eyebrows

sometimes

      *

the toes
of this little girl

the important part
of this
particular picture

      *

it could be you

or you or
you

you know there's a person
back there

you have no idea in the world
who

add a little mask

ELEANOR RAND WILNER

from *The Girl with Bees in Her Hair*, 2004

The Girl with Bees in Her Hair

came in an envelope with no return address;
she was small, wore a wrinkled dress of figured
cotton, full from neck to ankles, with a button
of bone at the throat, a collar of torn lace.
She was standing before a monumental house—
on the scale you see in certain English films:
urns, curved drives, stone lions, and an entrance far
too vast for any home. She was not of that place,
for she had a foreign look, and tangled black hair,
and an ikon, heavy and strange, dangling from
an oversize chain around her neck, that looked
as if some tall adult had taken it from his,
and hung it there as a charm to keep her safe
from a world of infinite harm that soon
would take him far from her, and leave her
standing, as she stood now—barefoot, gazing
without expression into distance, away
from the grandeur of that house, its gravel
walks and sculpted gardens. She carried a basket
full of flames, but whether fire or flowers
with crimson petals shading toward a central gold,
was hard to say—though certainly, it burned,
and the light within it had nowhere else
to go, and so fed on itself, intensified its red
and burning glow, the only color in the scene.
The rest was done in grays, light and shadow
as they played along her dress, across her face,
and through her midnight hair, lively with bees.
At first they seemed just errant bits of shade,
until the humming grew too loud to be denied
as the bees flew in and out, as if choreographed

in a country dance between the fields of sun
and the black tangle of her hair.
                              Without warning
a window on one of the upper floors flew open—
wind had caught the casement, a silken length
of curtain filled like a billowing sail—the bees
began to stream out from her hair, straight
to the single opening in the high facade. Inside,
a moment later—the sound of screams.

The girl—who had through all of this seemed
unconcerned and blank—all at once looked up.
She shook her head, her mane of hair freed
of its burden of bees, and walked away,
out of the picture frame, far beyond
the confines of the envelope that brought her
image here—here, where the days grow longer
now, the air begins to warm, dread grows to
fear among us, and the bees swarm.

GEOFF BOUVIER

from *Living Room,* 2005

Living Arrangement

Overnight, the slowly dripping faucet fills a bowl. Brings a music to our dreams
and water for the morning.

Distant Relations

In the sideyard, a rock's trying hard. The wind's kind of Zen. Between them, a
million miles (by analogy) although they're touching.

Myth Gave Birth to Philosophy

What happened when the gods learned that their word wasn't good enough?

Truth is the Person Who is There

The sky meets the mountain with no further obligation.

A Bee's Advice

Open slowly, little red flower. Out here is the Irrational.

SCOTT HIGHTOWER

from *Part of the Bargain,* 2005

At the Trough

> *. . . something unspoken, then . . .*

> J.D. McClatchy, "My Sideshow"

I'd gone from rinsing
toys with the hose
to fencing with my father

and his men. One afternoon,
preparing to wash off
the day's grime at the trough,

I began to undress
beside the sun-warmed
water. A lingering hand,

who had worked that day
alone, came in. A line
of wire had snapped:

the vicious recoil
of its teeth had sliced
his pants and gashed him.

I squatted and tried my best
to stanch and clean
his wounds. In the end,

the nearly exhausted man
brushed aside the conventional
goodbye-grip. Instead, he grazed

me with a kiss. That night, I
washed alone; for the first time
turning an undisclosed tension.

DANA LEVIN

from *Wedding Day,* 2005

Ars Poetica

Six monarch butterfly cocoons
        clinging to the back of your throat—

        you could feel their gold wings trembling.

You were alarmed. You felt infested.
In the downstairs bathroom of the family home,
        gagging to spit them out—
                        and a voice saying, *Don't, don't—*

W.S. MERWIN

from *Migration: New & Selected Poems,* 2005

Place

On the last day of the world
I would want to plant a tree

what for
not for the fruit

the tree that bears the fruit
is not the one that was planted

I want the tree that stands
in the earth for the first time

with the sun already
going down

and the water
touching its roots

in the earth full of the dead
and the clouds passing

one by one
over its leaves

W.S. MERWIN

from *Migration: New & Selected Poems*, 2005

Vixen

Comet of stillness princess of what is over
    high note held without trembling without voice without sound
aura of complete darkness keeper of the kept secrets
    of the destroyed stories the escaped dreams the sentences
never caught in words warden of where the river went
    touch of its surface sibyl of the extinguished
window onto the hidden place and the other time
    at the foot of the wall by the road patient without waiting
in the full moonlight of autumn at the hour when I was born
    you no longer go out like a flame at the sight of me
you are still warmer than the moonlight gleaming on you
    even now you are unharmed even now perfect
as you have always been now when your light paws are running
    on the breathless night on the bridge with one end I remember you
when I have heard you the soles of my feet have made answer
    when I have seen you I have waked and slipped from the calendars
from the creeds of difference and the contradictions
    that were my life and all the crumbling fabrications
as long as it lasted until something that we were
    had ended when you are no longer anything
let me catch sight of you again going over the wall
    and before the garden is extinct and the woods are figures
guttering on a screen let my words find their own
    places in the silence after the animals

JANE MILLER

from *A Palace of Pearls*, 2005

Coda

The horizon is totaled by clouds

A foot soldier seized in sight of his own squadron

No one will be responsible least of all

Please call for several hundred thousand physicians quickly

As they move about the intestines of my backyard

We have our secrets

The theme of the hero brought low

The last days of and so on

The natural light of the night

Caravaggio the bull and Goya the dark horse

More or less on a fool's journey

One should not stand in for someone else unless the choice is clear

In the south they will kill for a pomegranate

To fell the precious redwood to live in a redwood house

When the soft flesh falls off the fallen giants

Dead the features of the sick man are barely visible

Just my father is not my father anymore

Those strangers seemed far away and harmless

A patron who has paid to be amused

The full pale moon rising in lavender sky

I think it is a lovely day

Cherries blueberries white peaches and limes

To drag recruits from their families

On quivering bones it makes a ringing of bells

The whole family will enjoy singing in fellowship around a piano

One mustn't take public transport during a war

Four times until they finally blow away

Be careful of murderers in a palace

Perfumed with warm pineapple

Beyond what is humanly possible must be an astonishing figure

The grand piano crammed into our ear

The ancestors are asleep in a safe place

Streaking toward the emergency room of my eardrum

A palace of pearls

CHASE TWICHELL

from *Dog Language,* 2005

Soul in Space

How did it come to be
that a particular human loneliness
set forth into clouds of ignorance
so as to more closely examine itself?
Why one and so few others?

I stand among shoulder-high canes,
looking directly into their barbed
inner dark to the snake, or caterpillar—
actually a handful of blackberries
in the green shade, reptilian
yet warm, momentarily still.

I want my obituary to say that
I wrote in the language of dogs
and not that I sat sprinkling
black letters on a white ladder,
leading my own eye down
one rung at a time
until the dog was gone.

AMY UYEMATSU

from *Stone Bow Prayer,* 2005

The Meaning of Zero: A Love Poem

> *And is where space ends*
> *called death or infinity?*
>
> Pablo Neruda, *The Book of Questions*

A mere eyelid's distance between you and me.

It took us a long time to discover the number zero.

John's brother is afraid to go outside.
He claims he knows
the meaning of zero.

I want to kiss you.

A mathematician once told me you can add infinity
to infinity.

There is a zero vector, which starts and ends
at the same place, its force
and movement impossible
to record with
rays or maps or words.
It intersects yet runs parallel
with all others.

A young man I know
wants me to prove
the zero vector exists.
I tell him I can't,
but nothing in my world
makes sense without it.

CHRISTIAN WIMAN

from *Hard Night*, 2005

Done

Men living in the dark regard
of their own faces
in the night's black panes
pause finally as if for air,

and standing there
at desks or kitchen drains
are so ghosted by those spaces
they look into and are

that something in them goes hard.
They are their choices.
They are what remains.
And they stare and stare

until a man who had their eyes, their hair,
who answered to their names
and spoke with their voices,
falls from them like a star.

TAHA MUHAMMAD ALI

from *So What: New & Selected Poems, 1971–2005,* 2006
Translated from the Arabic by Peter Cole, Yahya Hijazi, and Gabriel Levin

Revenge

At times . . . I wish
I could meet in a duel
the man who killed my father
and razed our home,
expelling me
into
a narrow country.
And if he killed me,
I'd rest at last,
and if I were ready—
I would take my revenge!

*

But if it came to light,
when my rival appeared,
that he had a mother
waiting for him,
or a father who'd put
his right hand over
the heart's place in his chest
whenever his son was late
even by just a quarter-hour
for a meeting they'd set—
then I would not kill him,
even if I could.

*

Likewise . . . I
would not murder him

if it were soon made clear
that he had a brother or sisters
who loved him and constantly longed to see him.
Or if he had a wife to greet him
and children who
couldn't bear his absence
and whom his gifts would thrill.
Or if he had
friends or companions,
neighbors he knew
or allies from prison
or a hospital room,
or classmates from his school . . .
asking about him
and sending him regards.

      *

But if he turned
out to be on his own—
cut off like a branch from a tree—
without a mother or father,
with neither a brother nor sister,
wifeless, without a child,
and without kin or neighbors or friends,
colleagues or companions,
then I'd add not a thing to his pain
within that aloneness—
not the torment of death,
and not the sorrow of passing away.
Instead I'd be content
to ignore him when I passed him by
on the street—as I
convinced myself
that paying him no attention
in itself was a kind of revenge.

TAHA MUHAMMAD ALI

from *So What: New & Selected Poems, 1971–2005*, 2006
Translated from the Arabic by Peter Cole, Yahya Hijazi, and Gabriel Levin

Twigs

Neither music,
fame, nor wealth,
not even poetry itself,
could provide consolation
for life's brevity,
or the fact that *King Lear*
is a mere eighty pages long and comes to an end,
and for the thought that one might suffer greatly
on account of a rebellious child.

*

My love for you
is what's magnificent,
but I, you, and the others,
most likely,
are ordinary people.

*

My poem
goes beyond poetry
because you
exist
beyond the realm of women.

*

And so
it has taken me
all of sixty years
to understand

that water is the finest drink,
and bread the most delicious food,
and that art is worthless
unless it plants
a measure of splendor in people's hearts.

*

After we die,
and the weary heart
has lowered its final eyelid
on all that we've done,
and on all that we've longed for,
on all that we've dreamt of,
all we've desired
or felt,
hate will be
the first thing
to putrefy
within us.

MAHMOUD DARWISH

from *The Butterfly's Burden,* 2006
   Translated from the Arabic by Fady Joudah

We Were Missing a Present

Let's go as we are:
a free woman
and a loyal friend,
let's go together on two different paths
let's go as we are united
and separate,
with nothing hurting us
not the divorce of the doves or the coldness between the hands
nor the wind around the church . . .
what bloomed of almond trees wasn't enough.
So smile for the almonds to blossom more
between the butterflies of two dimples

And soon there will be a new present for us.
If you look back you will see only
the exile of your looking back:
your bedroom,
the courtyard willow,
the river behind the glass buildings,
and the café of our trysts . . . all of it, all
preparing to become exile, so
let's be kind!

Let's go as we are:
a free woman
and a friend loyal to her flutes.
Our time wasn't enough to grow old together
to walk wearily to the cinema
to witness the end of Athens's war with her neighbors
and see the banquet of peace between Rome and Carthage
about to happen. Because soon
the birds will relocate from one epoch to another:

Was this path only dust
in the shape of meaning, and did it march us
as if we were a passing journey between two myths
so the path is inevitable, and we are inevitable
as a stranger sees himself in the mirror of another stranger?
"No, this is not my path to my body"
"No cultural solutions for existential concerns"
"Wherever you are my sky
is real"
"Who am I to give you back the previous sun and moon"
Then let's be kind . . .

Let's go, as we are:
a free lover
and her poet.
What fell of January snow
wasn't enough, so smile
for snow to card its cotton on the Christian's prayer,
we will soon return to our tomorrow, behind us,
where we were young in love's beginning,
playing Romeo and Juliet
and learning Shakespeare's language . . .
The butterflies have flown out of sleep
as a mirage of a swift peace
that adorns us with two stars
and kills us in the struggle over the name
between two windows
so, let's go
and let's be kind

Let's go, as we are:
a free woman
and a loyal friend,
let's go as we are. We came
with the wind from Babylon
and we march to Babylon . . .
My travel wasn't enough
for the pines to become in my trace
an utterance of praise to the southern place.

We are kind here. Northerly
is our wind, and our songs are southerly.
Am I another you
and you another I?
"This isn't my path to my freedom's land"
this isn't my path to my body
and I won't be "I" twice
now that my yesterday has become my tomorrow
and I have split into two women
so I am not of the east
and I am not of the west,
nor am I an olive tree shading two verses in the Quran,
then let's go.
"No collective solutions for personal scruples"
it wasn't enough that we be together
to be together . . .
we were missing a present to see
where we were. Let's go as we are,
a free woman
and an old friend
let's go on two separate paths
let's go together,
and let's be kind . . .

LISA OLSTEIN

from Radio Crackling, Radio Gone, 2006

Jupiter Moon May Hold Hidden Sea

The roof is leaking but we don't mind,
we're glad for the sound, the plip of water

filling the pot we've laid on the floor.
On that first night we took a boat across a harbor.

It must have been an effort,
keeping track of me in the dark.

And in the morning, sunlight through
the east window, the air still cool.

How many times will one person imagine light
shining through one small east-facing window?

More than I would have imagined.
Each day something makes us walk out

to the sandbars and later say I walked out
to the sandbars, I put my foot down on a shore.

THEODORE ROETHKE

from *Straw for the Fire: From the Notebooks of Theodore Roethke, 1943–63*, 2006
Edited by David Wagoner

from "Straw for the Fire"

What dies before me is myself alone:
What lives again? Only a man of straw—
Yet straw can feed a fire to melt down stone.

*

To love objects is to love life.
The pure shaft of a single granary on the prairie,
The small pool of rain in the plank of a railway siding . . .

*

Am I too old to write in paragraphs?

*

I need to become learned in the literature of exasperation. In my worst state,
    once I think of my contemporaries, I'm immediately revived.

*

I always wonder, when I'm on the podium, why I am there: I really belong
    in some dingy poolhall under the table.

*

O Mother Mary, and what do I mean,
That poet's fallen into the latrine,—
And no amount of grace or art
Can change what happens after that.

*

I don't know a thing except what I try to do.

*

My courage kisses the ground.

*

Sure I'm crazy
But it ain't easy.

*

I seek first and last, that *essential* vulgarity I once thought charming.

*

Feeling's a hard
Thing to do well—
And slightly absurd;
I'd rather smell.

*

Some vast and shabby uncle of disorder: an old dog barking in a cellar . . .

*

They've sat on the secret of life so long, they no longer realize it's there.

*

O dealer in momentous bromides, O odious ethereal chimney . . .

*

Their poems are not so much hewn as spewn.

*

The most bitter of intellectuals: he who was once a poet.

*

It's not that many Americans can't think: they just don't want to.

*

The delusion that there is some hidden mystery in the banal that escapes us.

*

The academic tendency to rest: that profound impulse to sit down.

*

What we need is more people who specialize in the impossible.

*

The serious problems of life are never fully solved but some states can be resolved rhythmically.

MARAM AL-MASSRI

from *A Red Cherry on a White-tiled Floor: Selected Poems,* 2007
Translated from the Arabic by Khaled Mattawa

from *I Look to You*

98   I will wipe
the traces of the night
off of me
with cotton
and milk
and rose water,

I will strip his warmth
like a nightgown
and toss it
on the nearest chair,
to greet
daylight,
my luminous lover.

99   Whenever a man
leaves me
my beauty increases.

100   Increases . . .

The Human Line, 2007

Gate C22

At gate C22 in the Portland airport
a man in a broad-band leather hat kissed
a woman arriving from Orange County.
They kissed and kissed and kissed. Long after
the other passengers clicked the handles of their carry-ons
and wheeled briskly toward short-term parking,
the couple stood there, arms wrapped around each other
like he'd just staggered off the boat at Ellis Island,
like she'd been released at last from ICU, snapped
out of a coma, survived bone cancer, made it down
from Annapurna in only the clothes she was wearing.

Neither of them was young. His beard was gray.
She carried a few extra pounds you could imagine
her saying she had to lose. But they kissed lavish
kisses like the ocean in the early morning,
the way it gathers and swells, sucking
each rock under, swallowing it
again and again. We were all watching—
passengers waiting for the delayed flight
to San Jose, the stewardesses, the pilots,
the aproned woman icing Cinnabons, the man selling
sunglasses. We couldn't look away. We could
taste the kisses crushed in our mouths.

But the best part was his face. When he drew back
and looked at her, his smile soft with wonder, almost
as though he were a mother still open from giving birth,
as your mother must have looked at you, no matter
what happened after—if she beat you or left you or
you're lonely now—you once lay there, the vernix
not yet wiped off, and someone gazed at you
as if you were the first sunrise seen from the Earth.

The whole wing of the airport hushed,
all of us trying to slip into that woman's middle-aged body,
her plaid Bermuda shorts, sleeveless blouse, glasses,
little gold hoop earrings, tilting our heads up.

JUNE JORDAN

from *Directed by Desire: The Collected Poems of June Jordan,* 2007
Edited by Jan Heller Levi and Sara Miles

Poem about My Rights

Even tonight and I need to take a walk and clear
my head about this poem about why I can't
go out without changing my clothes my shoes
my body posture my gender identity my age
my status as a woman alone in the evening/
alone on the streets/alone not being the point/
the point being that I can't do what I want
to do with my own body because I am the wrong
sex the wrong age the wrong skin and
suppose it was not here in the city but down on the beach/
or far into the woods and I wanted to go
there by myself thinking about God/or thinking
about children or thinking about the world/all of it
disclosed by the stars and the silence:
I could not go and I could not think and I could not
stay there
alone
as I need to be
alone because I can't do what I want to do with my own
body and
who in the hell set things up
like this
and in France they say if the guy penetrates
but does not ejaculate then he did not rape me
and if after stabbing him if after screams if
after begging the bastard and if even after smashing
a hammer to his head if even after that if he
and his buddies fuck me after that
then I consented and there was
no rape because finally you understand finally
they fucked me over because I was wrong I was

wrong again to be me being me where I was/wrong
to be who I am
which is exactly like South Africa
penetrating into Namibia penetrating into
Angola and does that mean I mean how do you know if
Pretoria ejaculates what will the evidence look like the
proof of the monster jackboot ejaculation on Blackland
and if
after Namibia and if after Angola and if after Zimbabwe
and if after all of my kinsmen and women resist even to
self-immolation of the villages and if after that
we lose nevertheless what will the big boys say will they
claim my consent:
Do You Follow Me: We are the wrong people of
the wrong skin on the wrong continent and what
in the hell is everybody being reasonable about
and according to the *Times* this week
back in 1966 the C.I.A. decided that they had this problem
and the problem was a man named Nkrumah so they
killed him and before that it was Patrice Lumumba
and before that it was my father on the campus
of my Ivy League school and my father afraid
to walk into the cafeteria because he said he
was wrong the wrong age the wrong skin the wrong
gender identity and he was paying my tuition and
before that
it was my father saying I was wrong saying that
I should have been a boy because he wanted one/a
boy and that I should have been lighter skinned and
that I should have had straighter hair and that
I should not be so boy crazy but instead I should
just be one/a boy and before that
it was my mother pleading plastic surgery for
my nose and braces for my teeth and telling me
to let the books loose to let them loose in other
words
I am very familiar with the problems of the C.I.A.
and the problems of South Africa and the problems
of Exxon Corporation and the problems of white

America in general and the problems of the teachers
and the preachers and the F.B.I. and the social
workers and my particular Mom and Dad/I am very
familiar with the problems because the problems
turn out to be
me
I am the history of rape
I am the history of the rejection of who I am
I am the history of the terrorized incarceration of
my self
I am the history of battery assault and limitless
armies against whatever I want to do with my mind
and my body and my soul and
whether it's about walking out at night
or whether it's about the love that I feel or
whether it's about the sanctity of my vagina or
the sanctity of my national boundaries
or the sanctity of my leaders or the sanctity
of each and every desire
that I know from my personal and idiosyncratic
and indisputably single and singular heart
I have been raped
be-
cause I have been wrong the wrong sex the wrong age
the wrong skin the wrong nose the wrong hair the
wrong need the wrong dream the wrong geographic
the wrong sartorial I
I have been the meaning of rape
I have been the problem everyone seeks to
eliminate by forced
penetration with or without the evidence of slime and/
but let this be unmistakable this poem
is not consent I do not consent
to my mother to my father to the teachers to
the F.B.I. to South Africa to Bedford-Stuy
to Park Avenue to American Airlines to the hardon
idlers on the corners to the sneaky creeps in
cars
I am not wrong: Wrong is not my name

My name is my own my own my own
and I can't tell you who the hell set things up like this
but I can tell you that from now on my resistance
my simple and daily and nightly self-determination
may very well cost you your life

JUNE JORDAN

from *Directed by Desire: The Collected Poems of June Jordan,* 2007
Edited by Jan Heller Levi and Sara Miles

Poem for My Love

How do we come to be here next to each other
in the night
Where are the stars that show us to our love
inevitable
Outside the leaves flame usual in darkness
and the rain
falls cool and blessed on the holy flesh
the black men waiting on the corner for
a womanly mirage
I am amazed by peace
It is this possibility of you
asleep
and breathing in the quiet air

JUNE JORDAN

from *Directed by Desire: The Collected Poems of June Jordan,* 2007
Edited by Jan Heller Levi and Sara Miles

These Poems

These poems
they are things that I do
in the dark
reaching for you
whoever you are
and
are you ready?

These words
they are stones in the water
running away

These skeletal lines
they are desperate arms for my longing and love.

I am a stranger
learning to worship the strangers
around me

whoever you are
whoever I may become.

CHRIS MARTIN

from *American Music,* 2007

American Music

I don't plan to address the physical
Impossibility of understanding
Death, but when you close my fingers

In your own, each bone comes
Alive, the skeleton jangles
In its perfunctory sleeve and even

As the bald man at the table
Next to ours thumbs
Through a magazine about guns

I can look out the window to where
A blossom of birds issues
From an abandoned skyscraper or traffic

Enacts its unwitting algorithms
Of pulse, it is in
This pulse that such thought

Arrives, in pulse
That it recedes, just as these city
Bodies orbit relative

To the attention they are
Paid, one eye
Ogling another, space

A capacity for the patent
Enumeration of our feelings
Some of them

Essential: love, carousal, wonder
Loss, breakfast, noise, terror, I refuse
The counsel of stupidity

Regarding such matters—this equals
That, take it from us, buy
A car, make loads of money only

To further the inventions
Of self, and so the dissociations
Of velocity continue unabated

Halving and trebling
Ourselves into metropolitan collage
Involved or unloved, the chalky

Abstinence or slick slip of our
Nowadays fraught
With a stubbornness to dissolve

Into pixels, our greatest
Poets hounded by lavender, the yelp
Of an old catamount plaguing

The suburbs, in Bhutan
It's said the local yeti survives
On a diet of frogs and I tend

To these stories carefully, knowing
The ease with which
An overly pleased public scoffs

At unsanctified dreams, my beard
Hedging outward as
Rote continuance happens

Only in the face
Of encapsulated truths, my truths
Equal suddenly to any

Small observation of cheer
The weeds reaching
Dutifully toward what gravity

Deems us opposite to, the sopor
Of a steadily impinging commonplace
And for the same reason

Each monarch is doomed
To revisit the same tree with the same
Poison, we think to

Lay our androgynous howling before
Suns of uninhabitable
Chemistry or *the lonely wail*

Of that old Cannonball blazing
Through the night, it's American
Music I have come to

Bring you you redoubtable ear.

PETER PEREIRA

from *What's Written on the Body,* 2007

Anagrammer

If you believe in the magic of language,
then *Elvis* really *Lives*
and *Princess Diana* foretold *I end as car spin.*

If you believe the letters themselves
contain a power within them,
then you understand
what makes *outside tedious,*
how *desperation* becomes *a rope ends it.*

The circular logic that allows *senator* to become *treason,*
and *treason* to become *atoners.*

That *eleven plus two* is *twelve plus one,*
and an *admirer* is also *married.*

That if you could just rearrange things the right way
you'd find your true life,
the right path, the answer to your questions:
you'd understand how *the Titanic*
turns into *that ice tin,*
and *debit card* becomes *bad credit.*

How *listen* is the same as *silent,*
and not one letter separates *stained* from *sainted.*

C.D. WRIGHT

from *One Big Self: An Investigation,* 2007

In the Mansion of Happiness:

Whoever possesses CRUELTY

Must be sent back to JUSTICE

Whoever gets into IDLENESS

Must come to POVERTY

Whoever becomes a SABBATHBREAKER

Must be taken to the Pillory and there remain until he loses 2 turns

       I want to go home, Patricia whispered.

                  I won't say I like being in prison, but I have
learned a lot, and I like experiences. The terriblest part is being away
from your families. —Juanita
                I miss my screenporch.

I know every word to every song on *Purple Rain.* —Willie

       I'm never leaving here. —Grasshopper, in front of the woodshop,
posing beside a coffin he built

       This is a kicks' camp. Nothing positive come out of here except the
praying. Never been around this many women in my life. Never picked
up cursing before. —down for manslaughter, forty years

            I've got three. One's seven. One, four. One, one.
I'm twenty-three. The way I found out is, I was in an accident with my
brother. He was looking at some boys playing ball. We had a head-on.

       At the hospital, the doctor says, Miss, why didn't you tell us you
were pregnant. I'm pregnant? I wasn't afraid of my mama. I was afraid of
my daddy. I was supposed to be a virgin. He took it real good though.

The last time you was here I had a headful of bees.

See what I did was, I accidentally killed my brother.
                                        He spoke without inflection.

Asked how many brothers and sisters did he have—

On my mother's side, two brothers, well now, one brother, and
        two sisters.
On my father's side, fifteen sisters.

When I handed Franklin his prints, his face broke.
Damn, he said to no one, *I done got old.*

                        I kept a dog.

When you walk through Capricorn, keep your arms down and close to
    your body.

                        That's my *sign.*

No, she can't have no mattress. No, she can't have no spoon.
        See if she throwed her food yet.

                        No, she can't have no more.

    I am only about thirty-four minutes from home. That's hard.
—George, field line seated on a bag of peas on a flatbed

    My auntie works here, and two of my cousins. If I get in trouble,
get a write-up, my mama knows before supper. —George

    My name is Patricia, but my real name is Zabonia, she spoke softly.

Some have their baby and are brought back on the bus the next day
and act like it doesn't bother them a bit. Some cry all the way. And for
days. —guard

                                That's hard.
                                I don't go there.

My mama was fifteen when she had me. That's common
in the country.

Some can learn, and will be okay.
Some could stay in the class forever and not learn. S—— when she was a
little girl was struck in the head with a machete, and I don't think she'll
learn much more . . .

She is *so* sweet. You wouldn't believe she had did all the things they say
she did.

Don't ask.

My mug shot totally turned me against being photographed.

I miss the moon.
I miss silverware, with a knife,
and maybe even something to cut with it.

I miss a bathtub.
And a toilet. With a lid. And a handle.
And a door.

When Grasshopper came to Big Gola his wife was pregnant. He saw the
baby once. Next when he was twenty. Now he's inside. In Texas. Second
time. But he's short now. He'll get out soon.

That's hard.
I don't go there.

I miss driving.

We're both here because of love. —Zabonia of herself and her best
friend

I am highly hypnotizable.

I would wash that man's feet and drink the water.

MATTHEW DICKMAN

from *All-American Poem,* 2008

Grief

When grief comes to you as a purple gorilla
you must count yourself lucky.
You must offer her what's left
of your dinner, the book you were trying to finish
you must put aside
and make her a place to sit at the foot of your bed,
her eyes moving from the clock
to the television and back again.
I am not afraid. She has been here before
and now I can recognize her gait
as she approaches the house.
Some nights, when I know she's coming,
I unlock the door, lie down on my back,
and count her steps
from the street to the porch.
Tonight she brings a pencil and a ream of paper,
tells me to write down
everyone I have ever known
and we separate them between the living and the dead
so she can pick each name at random.
I play her favorite Willie Nelson album
because she misses Texas
but I don't ask why.
She hums a little,
the way my brother does when he gardens.
We sit for an hour
while she tells me how unreasonable I've been,
crying in the check-out line,
refusing to eat, refusing to shower,
all the smoking and all the drinking.
Eventually she puts one of her heavy
purple arms around me, leans

her head against mine,
and all of a sudden things are feeling romantic.
So I tell her,
things are feeling romantic.
She pulls another name, this time
from the dead
and turns to me in that way that parents do
so you feel embarrassed or ashamed of something.
Romantic? She says,
reading the name out loud, slowly
so I am aware of each syllable
wrapping around the bones like new muscle,
the sound of that person's body
and how reckless it is,
how careless that his name is in one pile and not the other.

OLAV H. HAUGE

from *The Dream We Carry: Selected and Last Poems of Olav H. Hauge,* 2008
Translated from the Norwegian by Robert Bly and Robert Hedin

This Is the Dream

This is the dream we carry through the world
that something fantastic will happen
that it has to happen
that time will open by itself
that doors shall open by themselves
that the heart will find itself open
that mountain springs will jump up
that the dream will open by itself
that we one early morning
will slip into a harbor
that we have never known.

RB

SARAH LINDSAY

from *Twigs & Knucklebones,* 2008

Song of a Spadefoot Toad

We stand by the patch of grass marked his.
But he is no longer subject
to the whims of this bewildering sphere,
with its sound waves, cancers, specific gravity, spring,
where we still live, where ostrich chicks
before hatching sing through the eggshell,
where filarial worms in bloodstream darkness
know when it's night, and drift to the skin
of their host, so mosquitoes
will drink them and bear them away.

Did he look without eyes
once more as if over his shoulder,
did his old home shrink
to a rolling marble?—
where elephants hollow out caves in a mountain
to eat its salt, where ants shelter aphids
and drink their sweet green milk,
where a black-tailed prairie dog bolts
through a tunnel with an infant head
and scarlet neck in its mouth.

We who still recoil from death,
how can we picture where he is now?—
when we labor to comprehend
this place, where minute crustaceans
pierce the side of a swordfish
to lodge in its heart, where spadefoot toads
wake from eleven months' sleep and sing
till their throats bleed, where humans
do everything humans do, where a fig wasp
pollinates a flower while laying her eggs,
then lies on her side as baby nematodes

crawl from her half-eaten gut, and where faithfully
every day in mangrove shallows
paired seahorses—armless, legless, without expression—
dance with each other at sunrise.

W.S. MERWIN

from *The Shadow of Sirius*, 2008

Blueberries After Dark

So this is the way the night tastes
one at a time
not early or late

my mother told me
that I was not afraid of the dark
and when I looked it was true

how did she know
so long ago

with her father dead
almost before she could remember
and her mother following him
not long after
and then her grandmother
who had brought her up
and a little later
her only brother
and then her firstborn
gone as soon
as he was born
she knew

W.S. MERWIN

from *The Shadow of Sirius,* 2008

Note

Remember how the naked soul
comes to language and at once knows
loss and distance and believing

then for a time it will not run
with its old freedom
like a light innocent of measure
but will hearken to how
one story becomes another
and will try to tell where
they have emerged from
and where they are heading
as though they were its own legend
running before the words and beyond them
naked and never looking back

through the noise of questions

W.S. MERWIN

from *The Shadow of Sirius,* 2008

Rain Light

All day the stars watch from long ago
my mother said I am going now
when you are alone you will be all right
whether or not you know you will know
look at the old house in the dawn rain
all the flowers are forms of water
the sun reminds them through a white cloud
touches the patchwork spread on the hill
the washed colors of the afterlife
that lived there long before you were born
see how they wake without a question
even though the whole world is burning

VALZHYNA MORT

from *Factory of Tears*, 2008
> Translated from the Belarusian by the author with Elizabeth Oehlkers
> Wright and Franz Wright

Factory of Tears

And once again according to the annual report
the highest productivity results were achieved
by the Factory of Tears.

While the Department of Transportation was breaking heels
while the Department of Heart Affairs
was beating hysterically
the Factory of Tears was working night shifts
setting new records
even on holidays.

While the Food Refinery Station
was trying to digest another catastrophe
the Factory of Tears adopted a new economically advantageous
technology of recycling the wastes of the past—
memories mostly.

The pictures of the employees of the year
were placed on the Wall of Tears.

I'm a recipient of workers' comp from the heroic Factory of Tears.
I have calluses on my eyes.
I have compound fractures on my cheeks.
I receive my wages with the product I manufacture.
And I'm happy with what I have.

DENNIS O'DRISCOLL

from *Reality Check,* 2008

Cassandra

after Hans Magnus Enzensberger

For years, all we showed
    her for her pains
were two deaf ears,
    as she fumed over
global warming,
    emitting dire predictions
in her smoky voice:
    catastrophic floods, etc.,
high-rise high-rent condos
    marinating in brine . . .
Though we'd buried
    our heads for ages
like spent fuel rods,
    her prophecies are
a hot topic suddenly
    on every chat show.
There's not a taxi driver
    who can't repeat
her words like racehorse
    tips, a dead cert.
Her rumours spread
    at hurricane speed.
Her hoarse phrases
    —"before long," "too late"—
sink in at last.

      *

Hang on a minute, though.
How many years does
"before long" add up to?

How late is "too late"?
How up-to-date is she on
current scientific R & D?

We carry on as bravely as we can
in these uncertain times:
4x4s at every door.

Low-fare airlines for cheap access
to nest-egg second houses.
All-year strawberries in supermarkets.

BUSINESS AS USUAL signs
displayed on hoardings everywhere,
with so much construction underway.

BRENDA SHAUGHNESSY

from *Human Dark with Sugar,* 2008

A Poem's Poem

If it takes me all day,
I will get the word *freshened* out of this poem.

I put it in the first line, then moved it to the second,
and now it won't come out.

It's stuck. I'm so frustrated,
so I went out to my little porch all covered in snow

and watched the icicles drip, as I smoked
a cigarette.

Finally I reached up and broke a big, clear spike
off the roof with my bare hand.

And used it to write a word in the snow.
I wrote the word *snow.*

I can't stand myself.

RUTH STONE

from *What Love Comes To: New & Selected Poems,* 2008

Curtains

Putting up new curtains,
other windows intrude.
As though it is that first winter in Cambridge
when you and I had just moved in.
Now cold borscht alone in a bare kitchen.

What does it mean if I say this years later?

Listen, last night
I am on a crying jag
with my landlord, Mr. Tempesta.
I sneaked in two cats.
He screams, "No pets! No pets!"
I become my Aunt Virginia,
proud but weak in the head.
I remember Anna Magnani.
I throw a few books. I shout.
He wipes his eyes and opens his hands.
OK OK keep the dirty animals
but no nails in the walls.
We cry together.
I am so nervous, he says.

I want to dig you up and say, look,
it's like the time, remember,
when I ran into our living room naked
to get rid of that fire inspector.

See what you miss by being dead?

from *What Love Comes To: New & Selected Poems*, 2008

Fragrance

Edna St. Vincent Millay—
her friends called her Vincent—
lived for a time in New York,
in the Village.
E.E. Cummings lived there, too—
and even I was living then—
but in the Midwest,
in Indianapolis.

Then, my father,
sitting at his Linotype machine,
the hot lead slugs
clicking and falling,
would sometimes print
a poem of mine—
something he found
around the house.

Poems came to me
as if from far away.
I would feel them coming.
I would rush into the house,
looking for paper and pencil.
It had to be quick,
for they passed through me
and were gone forever.
What are children's poems?
Like the sudden breeze
that pulls the petals
from the honeysuckle.

Much later,
when I lived in the Village,

E.E. Cummings was a faint legend.
Poets come and go,
like squills that bloom
in the melting snow.

RUTH STONE

from *What Love Comes To: New & Selected Poems,* 2008

Yes, Think

Mother, said a small tomato caterpillar to a wasp,
why are you kissing me so hard on my back?
You'll see, said the industrious wasp, deftly inserting
a package of her eggs under the small caterpillar's skin.
Every day the small caterpillar ate and ate the delicious
tomato leaves. I am surely getting larger, it said to itself.
This was a sad miscalculation. The ravenous hatched
wasp worms were getting larger. O world, the small
caterpillar said, you were so beautiful. I am only a small
tomato caterpillar, made to eat the good tomato leaves.
Now I am so tired. And I am getting even smaller. Nature
smiled. Never mind, dear, she said. You are a lovely link
in the great chain of being. Think how lucky it is to be born.

EMILY WARN

from *Shadow Architect*, 2008

Shin: Instruction for Lighting Fires

O My Soul

I forged you with my speech.
No longer bereft, you blaze.

The futility of deciphering you—
spark, seed, script, star.

I am yours and you are mine.
No words describe you.

I burn each one so you can see
    within the walls.

Instruction for Lighting Fires

Dry oak leaves, three crossed sticks, and a match.
You fight to kindle it with your breath.

When damp wood sputters and flares,
you doze on branches piled near shore.

Flickering wakes you at midnight.
To lean beyond the circle of light

and puzzle how galaxies and coals—
fitful, appearing and disappearing—

signal each other in the dark.
Leaves rattle and stir, waves sigh,

erasing the border between dreams and fire.
When dawn smudges in the shapes of trees,

the loons talk, the wind murmurs,
illuminating your way home.

SHERWIN BITSUI

from *Flood Song,* 2009

"I bite my eyes shut between these songs"

I bite my eyes shut between these songs.

They are the sounds of blackened insect husks
                                folded over elk teeth in a tin can,

they are gull wings fattening on cold air
                flapping in a paper sack on the chlorine-stained floor.

They curl in corners, spiked and black-thatched,
stomp across the living-room ceiling,
pull our hair one strand at a time from electric sockets
and paint our stems with sand in the kitchen sink.

They speak a double helix,
zigzag a tree trunk,
bark the tips of its leaves with cracked amber—

        they plant whispers where shouts incinerate into hisses.

"Stepping through the drum's vibration"

Stepping through the drum's vibration,
I hear gasoline
      trickle alongside the fenced-in panorama
of the reed we climb in from
and slide my hands into shoes of ocean water.

I step onto the gravel path of swans paved across lake scent,
wrap this blank page around the exclamation point slammed between us.

The storm lying outside its fetal shell
folds back its antelope ears
and hears its heart pounding through powdery earth
underneath dancers flecking dust from their ankles to thunder into rain.

MICHAEL DICKMAN

from *The End of the West,* 2009

Seeing Whales

You can go blind, waiting

Unbelievable quiet
except for their
soundings

Moving the sea around

Unbelievable quiet inside you, as they change
the face of water

The only other time I felt this still was watching Leif shoot up when we
      were twelve

Sunlight all over his face

breaking
the surface of something
I couldn't see

You can wait your
whole life

    *

The Himalayas are on the move, appearing and disappearing in the snow
      in the Himalayas

Mahler
begins to fill
the half-dead auditorium
giant step by
giant step

The Colorado
The Snake
The Salmon

My grandfather walks across the front porch
spotted with cancer, smoking
a black cigar

The whales fold themselves back and back inside the long hallways of salt

You have to stare back at the salt
the sliding mirrors
all day

just to see something
maybe

for the last time

       *

By now they are asleep
some are asleep
on the bottom of the world
sucking the world in
and blowing it out
in wave-
lengths

Radiant ghosts

Leif laid his head back on a pillow and waited for all the blood inside him
    to flush down
     a hole

After seeing whales what do you see?

The hills behind the freeway

power lines

green, green
grass

the green sea

DAVID HUERTA

from *Before Saying Any of the Great Words: Selected Poems,* 2009
Translated from the Spanish by Mark Schafer

Silence

for Coral Bracho

It lies obliquely in the tender or harsh words
of every day. It is an inevitable presence
in which every human voice recognizes itself
before or after speaking.

In the lightning bolt it is the pure light of imminence and in the reliable thunder
it is like the blackness of the blast, its negative face, its flip side
of potentialities, its deep mirror.

I recognize in this long, smooth hand
reaching for my face in the morning
its wealth of unspeakable meaning.

I am grateful to silence like him who is enamored of invisibility
and the power of a divine gift.
It inhabits certain texts whose printed or handwritten muteness
barely hints at its defiant plenitude. For it is not the same
as the muteness of those signs, which it sustains, nourishes, completes,
fertilizes—and makes possible its display of form and meaning.

Without it music would possess neither substance nor structure
and many poems would be drained of their tangible magic,
turning at last into tepid shells,
useless or unplugged machinery.

Years ago I gathered silence from the eyes of a woman
who was slowly dying and could see the abyss.
She gave me a shining, deaf scrap of the world
that surrounded her at that very moment,
along with the bitter gifts of suffering, in the final test.

Juan de Yepes and John of Patmos felt its depth
in the loving or turbulent acts of God.

Its existence bears all the qualities of nothingness
but is replete and overwhelms. At times it possesses the delicacy
of a superhuman spirit that could annihilate us
like the Angel in Rilke's Elegies.

Made of negation and transparency,
it is neither one thing nor the other—and it resembles thought,
which seeks it frequently, late at night
and during the loud and indifferent days.

It carries a flame and places it in the heart, like
death and fully resembling the life we live
and that lives us impersonally and abstractly.

I have entrusted to that fire the wealth or poverty
of thousands of perhaps unnecessary words.

LAO-TZU

from *Lao-tzu's Taoteching: With Selected Commentaries from the Past 2,000 Years,* 2009
   Translated from the Chinese by Red Pine

11

Thirty spokes converge on a hub
but it's the emptiness
that makes a wheel work
pots are fashioned from clay
but it's the hollow
that makes a pot work
windows and doors are carved for a house
but it's the spaces
that make a house work
existence makes a thing useful
but nonexistence makes it work

HEATHER MCHUGH

from *Upgraded to Serious,* 2009

Not to Be Dwelled On

Self-interest cropped up even there,
the day I hoisted three, instead
of the ceremonially called-for two,
spadefuls of loam on top
of the coffin of my friend.

Why shovel more than anybody else?
What did I think I'd prove? More love
(mud in her eye)? More will to work?
(Her father what, a shirker?) Christ,
what wouldn't anybody give
to get that gesture back?

She cannot die again; and I
do nothing but re-live.

GREGORY ORR

from *How Beautiful the Beloved,* 2009

"All those years"

All those years
I had only to say
Yes.
      But I couldn't.

Finally, I said Maybe,
But even then
I was filled with dread.

I wanted to step carefully.
I didn't want to leap.

What if the beloved
Didn't catch me?
What if the world
Disappeared beneath my feet?

GREGORY ORR

from *How Beautiful the Beloved*, 2009

"Words, of course, but"

Words, of course, but
Also the silence
Between them.

Like the silence
Between
The beloved and you.
Silence full
Of the unspoken
As a seed is full
Of all
It will become.

No poem made only
Of silence.
No poem
Made only of words.

LUCIA PERILLO

from *Inseminating the Elephant,* 2009

Inseminating the Elephant

The zoologists who came from Germany
wore bicycle helmets and protective rubber suits.
So as not to be soiled by substances
that alchemize to produce laughter in the human species;
how does that work biochemically is a question
whose answer I have not found yet. But these are men
whose language requires difficult conjugations under any circumstance:
first, there's the matter of the enema, which ought to come
as no surprise. Because what the news brings us
is often wheelbarrows of dung—suffering,
with photographs. And so long as there is suffering,
there should be also baby elephants—especially this messy,
headlamp-lit calling-forth. The problem lies
in deciding which side to side with: it is natural
to choose the giant rectal thermometer
over the twisted human form,
but is there something cowardly in that comic swerve?
Hurry an elephant
to carry the bundle of my pains,
another with shiny clamps and calipers
and the anodyne of laughter. So there, now I've alluded
to my body that grows ever more inert—better not overdo
lest you get scared; the sorrowing world
is way too big. How the zoologists start
is by facing the mirror of her flanks,
that foreboding luscious place where the gray hide
gives way to a zeroing-in of skin as vulnerable as an orchid.
Which is the place to enter, provided you are brave,
brave enough to insert your laser-guided camera
to avoid the two false openings of her "vestibule,"
much like the way of entering death, of giving birth to death,
calling it forth as described in the Tibetan Book.

And are you brave enough to side with laughter
if I face my purplish, raw reflection
and attempt the difficult entry of that chamber where
the seed-pearl of my farce and equally opalescent sorrow
lie waiting?

WEI YING-WU

from *In Such Hard Times: The Poetry of Wei Ying-wu*, 2009
Translated from the Chinese by Red Pine

On a Moonlit Night Meeting at Hsu Eleven's Thatched Hut

In an empty study with nothing to do
you loosened your hat strings and waited for a friend
it wasn't a night for reading
but for writing poems about the moon
after listening to the bell and sleeping in comfort
we rolled up dew-covered blinds
and sensed another fall was near
while the fading river tried to hold off dawn

2010—2019

CHRIS ABANI

from *Sanctificum,* 2010

Om

I

The hills of my childhood are purple with dusk and wings—
guinea fowl launched like a prayer to the still forming moon.
I hold Bean's shell to my ear. There is no sea. But only sea.
By my bed, in an empty chair, my shirt unwinds.
I remember my aunt counting the dead in the newspaper.
I never told anyone that every sliver of orange I ate
was preceded by words from high mass.
Per omnia saecula saeculorum.
Spit out pit. Amen.
Juice. Amen. Flesh.

2

A full moon leaning on a skyscraper. The taste:
qat and sweets on a tropical afternoon.
The dog's black tongue was more terrifying than its teeth.
The gravestone rising out of the puddle was more sinister
than the body we discovered as children swinging
in the summer-hot orchard.

3

The old woman singing a dirge has a voice of dust.
Sorrow lodged like a splintered bullet next to the heart.
A man once asked me in the street:
Do you own your own bones?
She likes the home I come in, I say to Cristina
as we drive toward the Golden Gate.
Bean, I repeat.
She loves the home I come in

and I am alive with fire and scars.
Here is my body, I say, eat it, do this,
remember me—

    4

Even now melancholy is a skin flayed
and worn in dance through the city.
Yes, the city becomes skin too and wears me
as skin and I want to say, *This is my body*, as I stroke
the curve of the fountain in the park.
This is my blood. Drink it. Remember.
The safety of doorways is an illusion.
They lead nowhere.
This is why we build houses.
Sand, when there is no water, can ablute,
washing grain by grain even the hardest stone of sin.
But you, but you, you are a sin that I live for.
Ne Me Quitte Pas. Ne Me Quitte Pas. Ne Me Quitte Pas.
Nina's voice walks in dragging bodies,
dead black men that bled unseen in the dark
of southern nights, shaded by leaves
and the veiled eyes of hate.
And in a poem, Lucille stands in the shadow of a tree
and pours libations for our souls,
for our salt, for our gospel.

    5

Somewhere a man speaks
in the dark, voice lost to rain.
I know this hunger, this need
to make patterns, to build meaning
from detritus; also the light
and the wood floor bare but for the lone slipper
tossed carelessly to one side. I admit the lies I've told.
Look, nothing has been true
since that picture of hell on the living-room wall lost its terror.
I say I want a strong woman, but unlike Neto

I cannot have the woman and the fish.
The war followed.
Children are losing their souls to the heat.
That is to say, poor American soldiers.
The rich have found a way to charge theirs to Amex.
Ask this: what is the relationship of desire to memory?
Here is a boy in the airport café, hair cropped from service.
And he closes his eyes to take a sip of coffee.
And smiles as the dark washes the desert away.

6

Los Angeles:
A red sky and angels thick like palm trees,
and garbage blown in the wind like cars
and the gluttony of SUVs
in an endless river of traffic.
Through the dark, we say, through the dark:
but do we ever really know?
There is a man in a field and he is searching for God.
Father, he says, Father.
In the distance, birds, traffic, and children.
There is a blue sky. There is a sky blue with night.
The call of the earth is a primitive song,
stomping feet and broken men.
There is a blue sky. And night.
The city is a flock of lights.
The darkness of tunnels like caves is knowledge,
also mortal. Maps are like God.
They are the city yet not the city.
They contain the city but yet do not.
We trace the lines in loss.
Sometimes we find treasure.
Sometimes something fills the mind,
something at which we pause, stopped.
The way a photograph cannot remember the living.

7

To die is to return.
To fly is to be a bird's heart.
Neither is freedom.
If it were we would have no name for it.
No language. Not even the temptation of wind
blowing a dark woman's hair away from a cliff's edge.
Instead, feathers are brought to my door every day by mystery.
Kindling for a fire, a beacon, an epiphany I cannot light.
This is the body of Christ.
Sanctificum.

JON DAVIS

from *Preliminary Report,* 2010

The Immortals

for John Langdon

That they have sidestepped death makes them powerful.
That each day is thick with opportunity.
That one takes guitar lessons, that one paints landscapes.
Another is sculpting her abs in the gym.

Most days, they avoid reminiscing.
Most days they spend perfecting a minor art.
They lunch on a salad of gratitude and bliss.
Dine early. Sleep soundly.

But sometimes, before dawn, an image from the past flares—
betrayal, death of a child, twisted metal, sirens.
Something somebody said that was hurtful.
Something they thought was theirs taken away.

And sadness flames up from somewhere in the chest.
And burns there, fading and flaring, almost unbearable.
Until the earth tilts.
Until sunlight brings color to roses, and birds begin to stir.

And they are called once again to their activities and appointments.
Their duties, distractions.
And the sadness fades, leaving them efficient and eager and prompt.

STEPHEN DOBYNS

from *Winter's Journey*, 2010

Poem

Who has the time? he asked.
But none in the room wore a watch.

On the hearth lay a dog, its two
front paws making parallel lines.

It's eleven o'clock, said another,
the day has scarcely begun.

But the dog was a black dog,
black with one blind eye.

It's nearing midnight, said a third,
and which of us is ready?

BENJAMIN ALIRE SÁENZ

from *The Book of What Remains*, 2010

Meditation on Living in the Desert

No. 3

There is a gray bird smaller than a pigeon but bigger than a sparrow nesting in a tree in my backyard. I don't know what kind of bird it is. Denise Levertov would chastise me for my laziness and remind me that a poet's job was to know the names of all things.

Even though I don't know what kind of bird is sitting on the nest, I *do* know the name of the tree: sweet acacia. Its formal name is *Vachellia farnesiana.* (There, Denise, are you happy now?)

A sweet acacia is a desert tree that has thousands of thorns.

The nest the bird has made is made of the thorny twigs of the tree she has chosen for laying her eggs. The bird is unbothered by the thorns. She is content to sit on the eggs she has laid.

Every day I go out to see if she is still there.

I pretend not to see her as she sits perfectly still.

She pretends not to see me, either.

I am playing a game. The bird is not.

JOHN TAGGART

from *Is Music: Selected Poems*, 2010

Magdalene Poem

Love enters the body

enters

almost

almost completely breaks and enters into the body

already beaten and broken

peaceful if breaking if breaking

and entering the already broken is peaceful

untouchable fortunately

untouchable.

JOHN TAGGART

from *Is Music: Selected Poems,* 2010

Slow Song for Mark Rothko

I

To breathe and stretch one's arms again

to breathe through the mouth to breathe to

breathe through the mouth to utter in

the most quiet way not to whisper not to whisper

to breathe through the mouth in the most quiet way to

breathe to sing to breathe to sing to breathe

to sing the most quiet way.

To sing to light the most quiet light in darkness

radiantia radiantia

singing light in darkness.

To sing as the host sings in his house.

To breathe through the mouth to breathe through the

mouth to breathe to sing to

sing in the most quiet way to

sing *the seeds in the earth breathe forth*

not to whisper *the seeds* not to whisper *in the earth*

to sing *the seeds in the earth* the most quiet way to

sing *the seeds in the earth breathe forth.*

To sing to light the most quiet light in darkness

radiant light of *seeds in the earth*

singing light in the darkness.

To sing as the host sings in his house.

To breathe through the mouth to breathe to sing

in the most quiet way not to

whisper *the seeds in the earth breathe forth*

to sing totality of *the seeds* not to eat to

sing *the seeds in the earth* to

be at ease to sing totality totality

to sing to be at ease.

To sing to light the most quiet light in darkness

be at ease with radiant *seeds*

with singing light in darkness.

To sing as the host sings in his house.

2

To breathe and stretch one's arms again

to stretch to stretch to straighten to stretch to

rise to stretch to straighten to rise

to full height not to torture not to torture to

rise to full height to give to hold out to

to give the hand to hold out the hand

to give to hold out to.

To give self-lighted flowers in the darkness

fiery saxifrage

to hold out self-lighted flowers in darkness.

To give as the host gives in his house.

To stretch to stretch to straighten to stretch to

rise to full height not to torture not to

to rise to give to hold out to

give the hand to hold out the hand to give

hope hope of hope of perfect hope of perfect rest

to give hope of perfect rest

to give to hold out to.

To give self-lighted flowers in the darkness

perfect and fiery hope

to hold out lighted flowers in darkness.

To give as the host gives in his house.

To stretch to stretch to straighten to stretch to

rise to full height not to torture to

give the hand to hold out the hand to

give hope to give hope of perfect rest to

rest not to lay flat not to lay out

to rest as *seeds* as *seeds in the earth*

to give rest to hold out to.

To give self-lighted flowers in the darkness

fiery hope of perfect rest

to hold out light flowers in darkness.

To give as the host gives in his house.

3

To breathe and stretch one's arms again

to join arm in arm to join arm in arm to

join to take to take into

to join to take into a state of intimacy

not in anger not in anger

to join arm in arm to join arms

to take into intimacy.

To take into the light in the darkness

into the excited phosphor

to be in light in the darkness.

To take as the host takes into his house.

To join arm in arm to join arm in arm to

join to take to take into

to join to take into a state of intimacy

not anger not anger

to take as *the earth* takes *seeds* as

the poor the poor must be taken into

to take into intimacy.

To take into the light in the darkness

into the phosphor star-flowers

to be in the light in the darkness.

To take as the host takes into his house.

To join arm in arm to join arm in arm to

join arms to take to take into a state of intimacy

not anger

to take as *the earth* takes *seeds* as

the poor must be taken into

to end the silence and the solitude

to take into intimacy.

To take into the light in the darkness

into star-flowers before sunrise

to be in light in the darkness.

To take as the host takes into his house.

CHASE TWICHELL

from *Horses Where the Answers Should Have Been:
New and Selected Poems*, 2010

Mask of a Maiden

My lips are clay, for centuries unkissed.
I thought middle age would not pass so quickly.
Time is cruel. I look in the mirror.
Now the word *cruel* scares me.

My ambition was once
to write the starlit poems of our age,
our final words, which in any case
are just graffiti from here on out,
yesteryear straight through to the afterlife
(though wasn't the middle part
supposed to be longer?).

I wanted words to contain consciousness,
so I was a child until I was old.

CONNIE WANEK

from *On Speaking Terms,* 2010

Monopoly

We used to play, long before we bought real houses.
A roll of the dice could send a girl to jail.
The money was pink, blue, gold as well as green,
and we could own a whole railroad
or speculate in hotels where others dreaded staying:
the cost was extortionary.

At last one person would own everything,
every teaspoon in the dining car, every spike
driven into the planks by immigrants,
every crooked mayor.
But then, with only the clothes on our backs,
we ran outside, laughing.

MATTHEW ZAPRUDER

from *Come On All You Ghosts,* 2010

Little Voice

I woke this morning to the sound of a little voice
saying this life, it was good while it lasted, but I just
can't take it any longer. I'm going to stop shaving
my teeth and chew my face. I'm going to finish inventing
that way to turn my blood into thread and knit
a sweater the shape of a giant machete and chop
my head right off. The leaves had a green
aspect, all their faces turned down towards the earth.
This is exactly how I wanted to act, but I didn't
know where the little voice had hidden, and anyway
who talks like that? What a loss, another tiny
brilliant mind switched off by that same big boring finger.
Clearly life is a drag, by which I mean a net that keeps
pulling the most unsavory and useful boots we
either put on lamenting, or eat with the hooks of some
big idea gripping the sides of our mouths and yanking them
upward in a conceptual grimace. Said the little voice,
that is. I was just half listening, one quarter wondering
what the little park the window looked onto was named,
and one quarter thanking the war I knew was somewhere
busy returning all those limbs to their phantoms.

MARIANNE BORUCH

from *The Book of Hours,* 2011

"The mosquito brings you blood, it"

The mosquito brings you blood, it
doesn't bleed you. The voice was sure.
What? he said. Like the bullet's all solace
to the wound? That thing *takes* my blood.

She does, with those eggs inside to consider.
Not true, the voice said. I swear on her
needle of light. Think what she gives you
for nothing, a pinpoint, her single thread

splayed on your arm or aloft at your ear.
Poems, he said, they've wacko-ed you right out!
Knock knock! She siphons my blood to hoard it.
Her dark monotony—*now now now now*—

the whole summer's in it, intrusion and blinding
endlessness, each day without time.
What fun to tell you things, the voice said. As if
I'm wrong—look, how she kneels with it.

MARIANNE BORUCH

from *The Book of Hours,* 2011

"To make a life inside, you"

To make a life inside a life, you
do that—how? My grandmother willed
her chair into a city-state, the porch
a fiefdom, the house itself

a realm. There is music like this,
relentlessly inward. Water meets water
and divides and grows dark all
afternoon at the pond. Down there,

bottom-heavy boxes,
jars, a letter torn in half
and first floated until rain
took it, until even the weave

in the paper unraveled. That life
you wanted secret. Do you
make that? Or does it come and you
remember, it was here once.

ROBERT BRINGHURST

from *Selected Poems,* 2011

Larix Lyallii

> *. . . es sind*
> *noch Lieder zu singen jenseits*
> *der Menschen*
>
> Paul Celan

In the threadbare
air, through the tattered
weave of leaves,
the blue light cools
into ash-black shadow.

Tree: the high
thought roots itself
in the luminous clay
of the caught light's closeness
to audibility.

So we know that again
today, there are songs
still to be sung. They
exist. Just on the other
side of mankind.

W.S. DI PIERO

from *Nitro Nights,* 2011

April

It isn't good to have too much.
Good lies, I tell myself, in having less.
The rain that cuts the sun's dense rays,
a look that feels too much like touch
in too many places, the heart's fine distress
that perfume brings, or sight, or taste.

I wake and have to check my haste
to suck her juices, his love, their faith,
taking what I know they won't offer,
the leafy trees and wisteria like wraiths . . .
Love and touch shouldn't take such effort
this season, when nothing goes to waste.

JIM HARRISON

from *Songs of Unreason*, 2011

Death Again

Let's not get romantic or dismal about death.
Indeed it's our most unique act along with birth.
We must think of it as cooking breakfast,
it's that ordinary. Break two eggs into a bowl
or break a bowl into two eggs. Slip into a coffin
after the fluids have been drained, or better yet,
slide into the fire. Of course it's a little hard
to accept your last kiss, your last drink,
your last meal about which the condemned
can be quite particular as if there could be
a cheeseburger sent by God. A few lovers
sweep by the inner eye, but it's mostly a placid
lake at dawn, mist rising, a solitary loon
call, and staring into the still, opaque water.
We'll know as children again all that we are
destined to know, that the water is cold
and deep, and the sun penetrates only so far.

LAURA KASISCHKE

from *Space, in Chains,* 2011

Pharmacy

A knife plunged into the center
of summer. Air

and terror, which become teeth together.

The pearl around which the sea
formed itself into softly undulating song—

This tender moment when my father
gives a package of cookies to my son.

They have been saved
from the lunch tray
for days.

Hook
in a sponge. The expressions on both of their faces. A memory I will carry with me
always, and which will sustain me, despite all the years I will try to prescribe this
memory away.

LAURA KASISCHKE

from *Space, in Chains*, 2011

Space, in chains

Things that are beautiful, and die. Things that fall asleep in the afternoon, in sun.
Things that laugh, then cover their mouths, ashamed of their teeth. A strong man
pouring coffee into a cup. His hands shake, it spills. His wife falls to her knees when
the telephone rings. *Hello? Goddammit, hello?*

Where is their child?

Hamster, tulips, love, gigantic squid. *To live.* I'm not endorsing it.

Any single, transcriptional event. The chromosomes of the roses. Flagella, cilia, all
the filaments of touching, of feeling, of running your little hand hopelessly along
the bricks.

Sky, stamped into flesh, bending over the sink to drink the *tour de force* of water.

It's all space, in chains—the chaos of birdsong after a rainstorm, the steam rising off
the asphalt, a small boy in boots opening the back door, stepping out, and someone
calling to him from the kitchen,

Sweetie, don't be gone too long.

SUNG PO-JEN

from *Guide to Capturing a Plum Blossom*, 2011
Translated from the Chinese by Red Pine

90. Windblown

where does that hidden scent come from
wafted here by a winter gale
may the Lord of the East protect it
keep it from gracing palace faces

JAMES ARTHUR

from *Charms Against Lightning,* 2012

Distracted by an Ergonomic Bicycle

On a rainy morning in the worst year
of my life, as icy eyelets shelled the street,
I shared a tremor with a Doberman
leashed to a post. We two were all the world
until a bicyclist shot by, riding

like a backward birth, feetfirst,
in level, gentle ease, with the season's hard breath
between his teeth. The rain was almost ice, the sky
mild and pale. I saw a milk carton bobbing by
on a stream of melting sleet.

   A bicyclist. A bicyclist. He rode away—
to his home, I guess. I went home,
where I undressed, left my jacket
where it fell, went straight to bed, and slept
for two days straight. But those clicking wheels

kept clicking in my head, and though
I can't say why, I felt not only *not myself*
but that I'd never been . . . that I

was that man I hardly saw, hurling myself
into the blast, and that everything
I passed—dog, rain, cold, the other guy—
I left in my wake, like afterbirth.

NATALIE DIAZ

from *When My Brother Was an Aztec*, 2012

No More Cake Here

When my brother died
I worried there wasn't enough time
to deliver the one hundred invitations
I'd scribbled while on the phone with the mortuary:
Because of the short notice no need to RSVP.
Unfortunately the firemen couldn't come.
(I had hoped they'd give free rides on the truck.)
They did agree to drive by the house once
with the lights on— It was a party after all.

I put Mom and Dad in charge of balloons,
let them blow as many years of my brother's name,
jails, twenty-dollar bills, midnight phone calls,
fistfights, and ER visits as they could let go of.
The scarlet balloons zigzagged along the ceiling
like they'd been filled with helium. Mom blew up
so many that she fell asleep. She slept for ten years—
she missed the whole party.

My brothers and sisters were giddy, shredding
his stained T-shirts and raggedy pants, throwing them up
into the air like confetti.

When the clowns came in a few balloons slipped out
the front door. They seemed to know where
they were going and shrank to a fistful of red grins
at the end of our cul-de-sac. The clowns played toy bugles
until the air was scented with rotten raspberries.
They pulled scarves from Mom's ear—she slept through it.
I baked my brother's favorite cake (chocolate, white frosting).
When I counted there were ninety-nine of us in the kitchen.
We all stuck our fingers in the mixing bowl.

A few stray dogs came to the window.
I heard their stomachs and mouths growling
over the mariachi band playing in the bathroom.
(There was no room in the hallway because of the magician.)
The mariachis complained about the bathtub acoustics.
I told the dogs, *No more cake here,* and shut the window.
The fire truck came by with the sirens on. The dogs ran away.
I sliced the cake into ninety-nine pieces.

I wrapped all the electronic equipment in the house,
taped pink bows and glittery ribbons to them—
remote controls, the Polaroid, stereo, Shop-Vac,
even the motor to Dad's work truck—everything
my brother had taken apart and put back together
doing his crystal meth tricks—he'd always been
a magician of sorts.

Two mutants came to the door.
One looked almost human. They wanted
to know if my brother had willed them the pots
and pans and spoons stacked in his basement bedroom.
They said they missed my brother's cooking and did we
have any cake. *No more cake here,* I told them.
Well, what's in the piñata? they asked. I told them
God was and they ran into the desert, barefoot.
I gave Dad his slice and put Mom's in the freezer.
I brought up the pots and pans and spoons
(really, my brother was a horrible cook), banged them
together like a New Year's Day celebration.

My brother finally showed up asking why
he hadn't been invited and who baked the cake.
He told me I shouldn't smile, that this whole party was shit
because I'd imagined it all. The worst part he said was
he was still alive. The worst part he said was
he wasn't even dead. I think he's right, but maybe
the worst part is that I'm still imagining the party, maybe
the worst part is that I can still taste the cake.

LIDIJA DIMKOVSKA

from *pH Neutral History,* 2012
> Translated from the Macedonian by Ljubica Arsovska and Peggy Reid

Memory

My memory is a soldier's tin of bully beef
with no best-before date. I return to places
I have trodden with only one tongue in my mouth
and beat egg yolks for the natives to give them a good voice.
In the snow of the whites Jesus lies crucified as if in jest.
It takes two tongues for a French kiss,
now that I have several I'm no longer a woman but a dragon.
Like Saint George, I never learned
to give mouth-to-mouth resuscitation; my nose being blocked for years
I myself only breathe through others' nostrils, the world's paying.
"Aha! There's something fishy about you, something's fishy here,"
the little fallen angels
collecting old paper and plastic cry after me.
I love them best when they take their cots
out into the corridor to air the DNA away,
then A. and I sprawl out on them, a side each,
and in a carefully worked-out act of love
all our porcelain teeth chip off,
our gums turn into wide-open eyes, before which
our tongues in the darkness trip each other up,
growling, whimpering and moaning, and we
feel neither fear nor sorrow.
My memory is the black box from a crashed warplane
with no sell-by date. I return to places I have trodden
with only one blood under my skin,
I cross off fertile days for the natives on the calendars
with their name days and family feasts,
tame animals long for the wild, the wild for the tame.
Like a Jewish couple during fasts and monthly periods,
so God and I have been sleeping in separate beds for years.

DAN GERBER

from *Sailing through Cassiopeia,* 2012

Postscript

I think I may have startled you,
signing this letter
with *love* at the end,
that you may think
I'm being too familiar,
sending the wrong signal,
that we don't know each other
that well,
that there's so much about you
I'd find unlovable
if I *really*
knew the real you,
that I've overstepped,
invaded your space,
that I may want you
to love me, that this
could complicate our lives
impossibly,
that . . .

among people,
I think of my father
telling me an hour
before he died,
how he thought of all the
men and women he'd loved
and how
he wished he'd told them
when he could've.

LUCIA PERILLO

from *On the Spectrum of Possible Deaths,* 2012

Autothalamium

On my wedding night I drove the white boat,
its steering wheel a full yard wide. The dress
bellied out behind me like a sail
as I gripped the lacquered wood
and circuited the bay. The poem
by Akhmatova having already
been read, the calamari and cake
already eaten, I stood alone
in the wheelhouse while my friends
danced to the balalaikas outside
on the deck. I could not speak
for the groom, who left me
to the old motor's growl
and the old boards' groan; I also
couldn't speak for the moon
because I feared diverging
from my task to look. Instead I stuck
my eyes to the water, whose toxins shined
with a phosphor that I plowed and plundered.
And no matter what has happened since,
the years and the dead,
the sadness of the bound-to-happen,
the ecstasy of the fragile moment,
I know one night I narrowed my gaze
and attended to my captaining, while the sea
gave me more serious work than either love or speech.

BRENDA SHAUGHNESSY

from *Our Andromeda,* 2012

Hide-and-Seek with God

There are no hiding places left, Cal.
Every dark space isn't really dark
but pinkish black, flesh and oblivion,
filled with me, with us, deathly
and breathless and holding on, skin
about to split and give us away.

Is it better to run? Run down
the street—the floating red hand
that means *don't walk* looks
like a heart. But I'm too afraid.
If we just close our eyes truly enough,
believing hard, no peeking, we can
be invisible. Don't let him find
us, Cal. Don't let him find us again.

GEORG TRAKL

from *Song of the Departed: Selected Poems of Georg Trakl,* 2012
Translated from the German by Robert Firmage

Gródek

At evening autumn forests drone
With deadly weapons, the golden plains
And the blue lakes, above which somberly
The sun rolls down. The night
Embraces dying warriors, the wild laments
Of their shattered mouths.
But in the willow valley silently
The outspilled blood collects, red clouds
In which an angry god dwells, lunar coolness;
All roads disgorge to black decay.
Beneath the golden boughs of night and stars
The sister's shadow flutters through the silent grove
To greet the spirits of the heroes, bleeding heads.
And softly in the reeds drone the dark flutes of autumn.
O prouder grief! you brazen altars;
Tonight a mighty anguish feeds the hot flame of spirit:
Unborn grandchildren.

DAVID WAGONER

from *After the Point of No Return,* 2012

After the Point of No Return

After that moment when you've lost all reason
for going back where you started, when going ahead
is no longer a yes or no but a matter of fact,
you'll need to weigh, on the one hand, what will seem
on the other, almost nothing against something
slightly more than nothing and must choose
again and again, at points of fewer and fewer
chances to guess, when and which way to turn.

That's when you might stop thinking about stars
and storm clouds, the direction of wind,
the difference between rain and snow, the time
of day or the lay of the land, about which trees
mean water, which birds know what you need
to know before it's too late, or what's right here
under your feet, no longer able to tell you
where it was you thought you had to go.

JOHN YAU

from *Further Adventures in Monochrome,* 2012

Ill-Advised Love Poem

Come live with me
And we will sit

Upon the rocks
By shallow rivers

Come live with me
And we will plant acorns

In each other's mouth
It would be our way

Of greeting the earth
Before it shoves us

Back into the snow
Our interior cavities

Brimming with
Disagreeable substances

Come live with me
Before winter stops

To use the only pillow
The sky ever sleeps on

Our interior cavities
Brimming with snow

Come live with me
Before spring

Swallows the air
And birds sing

DEAN YOUNG

from *Bender: New & Selected Poems*, 2012

Frottage

How goofy and horrible is life. Just
look into the faces of the lovers
as they near their drastic destinations,
the horses lathered and fagged. Just
look at them handling the vase
priced beyond the rational beneath
the sign stating the store's breakage
policy, and what is the rational but
a thing we must always break? I am not
the only one composed of fractious murmurs.
From the point of view of the clouds,
it is all inevitable and dispersed—
they vanish over the lands to reconstitute
over the seas, themselves again
but no longer themselves, what they wanted
they no longer want, daylight fidgets
across the frothy waves. Most days
you can't even rub a piece of charcoal
across paper laid on some rough wood
without a lion appearing, a fish's umbrella
skeleton. Once we believed it told us
something of ourselves. Once we even believed
in the diagnostic powers of ants. Upon
the eyelids of the touched and suffering,
they'd exchange their secretive packets
like notes folded smaller than chemicals
the dancers pass while dancing with another.
A quadrille. They told us nearly nothing
which may have been enough now that we know
so much more. From the point of view
of the ant, the entire planet is a dream
quivering beneath an eyelid and who's to say

the planet isn't? From the point of view
of the sufferer, it seems everything will
be taken from us except the sensation
of being crawled over. I believe everything
will be taken from us. Then given back
when it's no longer what we want. We
are clouds, and terrible things happen
in clouds. The wolf's mouth is full
of strawberries, the morning's a phantom
hum of glories.

ALFONSO D'AQUINO

from *fungus skull eye wing: Selected Poems of Alfonso D'Aquino*, 2013
Translated from the Spanish by Forrest Gander

Written in a Grain of Salt

In the mindful light of the stars
Halite / salt / fate
Reading the salt
Water and stone / the first earth
Saliva's salt
Fathomless dawn alive in my skull / lips backlit with incandescence
Air and salt / nothing else
Salt Eros

White mountains / at hand
A fly licking the salt
Each face / reflects / another sky / reflected
Adarce of light in the leaves
Geometric constructions / of the mind's water
Fractures in salt flowers / reversed in fissures / fissures / in fossilizing salt
Cryptic minerals / colorless and pure
Elemental mind salt

Ah the marvelous distances of the umbratile
Minimum emerge / as lucid invisible / untranslucent salt / silica

Encrypted in its white script / as the star in each grain
Reflective / reflectant / reflected . . . water
And on my lips . . . its traces

KWAME DAWES

from *Duppy Conqueror: New and Selected Poems,* 2013

Dirt

> *I got one part of it. Sell them watermelons and get me another part.*
> *Get Bernice to sell that piano and I'll have the third part.*

August Wilson

We who gave, owned nothing,
learned the value of dirt, how
a man or a woman can stand
among the unruly growth,
look far into its limits,
a place of stone and entanglements,
and suddenly understand
the meaning of a name, a deed,
a currency of personhood.
Here, where we have labored
for another man's gain, if it is fine
to own dirt and stone, it is
fine to have a plot where
a body may be planted to rot.
We who have built only
that which others have owned
learn the ritual of trees,
the rites of fruit picked
and eaten, the pleasures
of ownership. We who
have fled with sword
at our backs know the things
they have stolen from us, and we
will walk naked and filthy
into the open field knowing
only that this piece of dirt,
this expanse of nothing,

is the earnest of our faith
in the idea of tomorrow.
We will sell our bones
for a piece of dirt,
we will build new tribes
and plant new seeds
and bury our bones in our dirt.

KERRY JAMES EVANS

from *Bangalore,* 2013

Packed in Ice

My wife   pulls a peach   from   the freezer,
then   stares   at the knives   stuck

in their wooden   block.   I want   the right   line
for our   marriage,   but the exact   emotion

is a peach   packed in ice.   I cannot accept   this,
though   clearly,   here   it is,   cold

and ripe, and now,   in hand,   passed
between us like a desperate   artifact.

JENNIFER MICHAEL HECHT

from *Who Said*, 2013

Drummond's "Don't Kill Yourself"

Carlos Drummond de Andrade
will never be a major poet
because his name is too long and
difficult to remember.

Carlos, me, stop flipping out.
You've been kissed.
Maybe you'll get another kiss tomorrow,
maybe not, ad infinitum. Nothing
can be done about this
exciting series of possibilities.
The only way to stop it would be to kill
yourself, so don't. Just stay
and hope for more kisses, even sex.

You, tellurian, earth-beast, are flipping out
because you have spent the night
enraptured by love, a common thing
in the world.

Your insides are going nuts with panic
and emotion, also pretty normal.
The feelings and hormones and thoughts
going on in my head right now are a cacophony,
like a symphony of prayers, old record players,
Catholic signs and wonders, commercials
for soap and better living. There's no way
to make any sense of this racket inside.

Meanwhile you are walking around town,
looking normal but with such a slammed heart
that you are identifying with every passing tree.
When someone lets out one of those moans

that might be anything, might just be the sigh
of sitting down, it's such a relief. *Oh!* someone
cries out and you agree. *Oh,* me too.
And the lights go out in the theater. Me too.

Carlos is alone and says to himself that love,
especially in the light of day, is always sad,
and it is true, but it's not all that's true,
and he knows it, calling himself a boy to hint
that someone too young to know is trying to know,
while nearby, also inside the poet, is the sublime
and graceful knowing. See what he says,
in the last lines? *Tell it to nobody, / nobody knows*
nor shall know. He's closing the poem there,
tucking his scarf into his overcoat.
But also he's counseling himself
to keep the crazy hidden, keep the despair hidden;
he says *Hide it,* but he's telling us.

It's safer to keep it to himself,
but he gets it on paper
and hands it out across the century to me,
and I take it and I say, *Thank you*
Carlos Drummond de A . . . I wish I could
remember your name.
I get stuck on the Andrade part.

Now reader, what I wanted the poem to say
was less, *Self, don't flee from feeling,*
even though it is so frightening that you almost feel
like running off a ledge, and more, *Friends,*
selves, countrymen of the realms of gold, fellows
and sisters of outrageous despair, don't kill yourselves.

I wanted to say: We have to talk to each other.
We broken. We need to keep drinking tea
or wine and tell each other the one thing
we don't have to trance out to hear: I was there.
It sucked. It was insane, the things I said to myself
to stay sane. You too? Got a hot brain

from coping too long all up in your head alone?
Don't kill yourself.
Come over and drink coffee
or beer with us and tell us.

People who do not ever feel this way pity us.

Maybe you don't want to be pitied, but I'm ready
to know that being someone who has hard times
is often awful, as awful as other awful things,
and that's how it is for me. So pity away,
ye normals, and freaks come sit by me.

TOM HENNEN

from *Darkness Sticks to Everything: Collected and New Poems,* 2013

Found on the Earth

The simple words no longer work.
Neither do the grand ones.
Something about
The hanging bits of dark
Mixed with your hair.
The everlasting quietness
Attached to the deserted barn
Made me think I'd discovered you
But you already knew all about yourself
As we stood on the edge of a forest
With your dress as languid as the air,
The day made of spring wind and daffodils.
Then the sky appeared in blue patches
Among slow clouds,
Oak leaves came out on the trees,
Grass suddenly became green,
Filled with small animals that sing.
All the parts of spring were gathering.
The earth was being created all over again
One piece at a time
Just for you.

BOB HICOK

from *Elegy Owed,* 2013

Ode to magic

Do the one where you bring the woman
back from the dead, his host, the king, commanded,
but the magician would not.

He did the one in which he was one half
of the folk-indie duo Heartwind.

He did the one that required a volunteer tornado
from the audience.

He did the one in which the lungs of a warlord
are filled with lava.

But he would not bring the woman back from the dead.

The king wanted to cut his head off
but the queen said, *Perhaps this is just a poem.*

This is just a poem.

Everyone is alive as long as the poem is alive.

The king wears a crown of a thousand crows.

The queen keeps three lovers inside the castle
of her dress, the third a spare for the second,
the second a technical advisor to the first.

The magician's tongue is nothing but the word
abracadabra and the dead woman has just written
cotton candy on her shopping list, just written
antelopes and reminded the poet
he is running out of things to say.

The queen asks him, *Do the one in which your heart*
is folded over and pounded with moonlight,
in which you claim to miss everything—
I like how big your arms are in that one,
your throat the size of the universe
before silence gets the last word.

Oh, that one, the poet says, *is this one,*
is the only one.

Listen to it sound like shucked corn,
like a single blade of grass eating sun,
like any train or noisemaker or hallelujah
that will keep this line from being
the last line, and this line
but not the coming line, the hush,
the crush it is.

TUNG-HUI HU

from *Greenhouses, Lighthouses,* 2013

Ars Poetica

The new words will be spring and summer.
Poems will continue to pose questions of existence
Though not as probingly as before
Owing to the change in vocabulary
Which stresses the social over the existential
And having over not having. In the new poems,
Endings will be soft, quiet, understated, and
Images will contain recycled content.
Some poems may be made entirely of
Used rubber tires; others, of canvas.
Canvas and *luminous* will be featured;
"Bougainvillea," however, will be replaced
By creeping myrtle and a sense of grace.
Unlike the winter writing, the new writing
Will be light and thrifty. Those lines once
Celebrated for their texture of brocade
Will not be mourned. Instead, they will be
Freed of unnecessary language, as when
Eliminating your job made unnecessary
The word *fired.* That anger, the least complex
Of emotions, thus the hardest to write about,
Succeeds the topic of malaise. Not disdain,
Vengeance, or regret. Just impotent anger
That the new city bears no resemblance
To the old city but keeps the same name.
It is like the Sicilian town of Noto: after an
Earthquake, citizens voted to build a town
Ten kilometers over, also called Noto.
Having lived here all your life,
You can't find your way around.
Water-blue skyscrapers are everywhere,
And there is a luminous river where
Old streets once meandered.

FADY JOUDAH

from *Alight*, 2013

Into Life

Mouths that breathe like fishes out of water
Faster then slower pursed lips then gaping mouths billowing chests and all

The fixed stare that gives its sense up and over to other sense and reflex

I can't bear it
Am frightened
Of the dorsal fins fanning out to puncture the hand that wants the hook

Out of the mouth to throw the fish back in

I don't blame the fish its indiscriminate violence it cannot know
It was my daughter's hand that threaded the bait and cast the line

She too wants them back in the water
But can't let go of the desire
To catch what she can't see but knows is teeming

An idea of absence a little blue
Heron partakes in and dives after
Each fish I unhook and toss into life

And not once did the bird come up beak-filled or gulping

I eat fish
Same as I eat rabbit

Without nearing the look on its face
When my mother would grab it
By its long ears the blade approaching

Then skinning it by hand like peeling a banana

The fish's pulled out and is plopped on the deck
Fluttering like a startled bird or an epileptic

I pin it down by the gills with my index
Retrieve the hook with my other hand

Then under and across its belly where the spikes are short
I dart it

That's before I thought of a towel

That stare that white light
Of the day's operating theater burning

The retina like a flash without an image
To behold a clean slate a blank page

A summation of color in the final cortex
(Which fishes don't have)

Then the electric shock the pain of coming
Back into life

DENNIS O'DRISCOLL

from Dear Life, 2013

Memoir

It has been
absolutely

fascinating
being me.

A unique
privilege.

Now my
whole life

lies ahead
of you.

No thanks
at all are

called for,
I assure you.

The pleasure
is all mine.

ROGER REEVES

from *King Me,* 2013

In a Brief, Animated World: The Marriage of Anne of Denmark to James of Scotland, 1589

Nature always begins with resistance—
The small congregation of ants refusing
To allow the femur bone of the fox
To rest, meatless, the heavy head of flies
In January straying from the graves
Which are the corners of this house—
The four Negroes at Queen Anne's wedding
Dancing in the snow, naked, before her
Carriage, the creak of carriage wheels
Counting out steps—*1-2-3-Turn-Jump-*
Turn—their arms wide as goose wings,
Bow, then a breaking at the waist,
Mucus spills from their mouths onto—
And before a guest from Oslo can point
To the blood-tinged saliva, the wagon wheels
Gather every stitch of spit, grind,
Then smear—the body, if allowed,
Will dance even as it is ruined—a mule
Collapsing in a furrow it's just hewed—
The sway and undulation of the famished—
There are no straight lines but unto death—
Four men turning circles in the snow—
The arch of their toes calling Anne to lean
Forward, admire the work of the unshod
Sinking below all this white. She thinks:
In a brief, animated world, this would not be
Agony. The leg of her fox stole slips
From her shoulders and points to the men
Shivering in their last plié. *Yes,* she thinks,
But agony is sometimes necessary.

YOSA BUSON

from *Collected Haiku of Yosa Buson,* 2013
Translated from the Japanese by W.S. Merwin and Takako Lento

318

This is happiness
crossing the stream in summer
carrying my straw sandals

527

Under the harvest moon
a servant is on his way
to abandon a puppy

814

Oh you who call loudly upon Buddha
beating your gourds go now
have a drink and get some sleep

MALACHI BLACK

from *Storm Toward Morning,* 2014

Coming & Going

All day long I plunge into the ether
like a tongue into a fragile glass

of water. Thirsty for an urgency
to squint in the crouched sun, to turn

the doorknob of a corner, to open
up into an avenue and run,

I clop unevenly along the sidewalks,
crooked and vaguely caving in,

like some demented, avid mailman.
Though I know no one is expecting me,

worrying a wristwatch, pacing
and awaiting and awaiting

my delivery, I stroll just the same:
there must be something in the air to blame.

JERICHO BROWN

from *The New Testament,* 2014

Heart Condition

I don't want to hurt a man, but I like to hear one beg.
Two people touch twice a month in ten hotels, and
We call it long distance. He holds down one coast.
I wander the other like any African American, Africa
With its condition and America with its condition
And black folk born in this nation content to carry
Half of each. I shoulder my share. My man flies
To touch me. Sky on our side. Sky above his world
I wish to write. Which is where I go wrong. Words
Are a sense of sound. I get smart. My mother shakes
Her head. My grandmother sighs: He ain't got no
Sense. My grandmother is dead. She lives with me.
I hear my mother shake her head over the phone.
Somebody cut the cord. We have a long-distance
Relationship. I lost half of her to a stroke. God gives
To each a body. God gives every body its pains.
When pain mounts in my body, I try thinking
Of my white forefathers who hurt their black bastards
Quite legally. I hate to say it, but one pain can ease
Another. Doctors rather I take pills. My man wants me
To see a doctor. What are you when you leave your man
Wanting? What am I now that I think so fondly
Of airplanes? What's my name, whose is it, while we
Make love. My lover leaves me with words I wish
To write. Flies from one side of a nation to the outside
Of our world. I don't want the world. I only want
African sense of American sound. Him. Touching.
This body. Aware of its pains. Greetings, Earthlings.
My name is Slow And Stumbling. I come from planet
Trouble. I am here to love you uncomfortable.

OLENA KALYTIAK DAVIS

from *The Poem She Didn't Write and Other Poems,* 2014

The Poem She Didn't Write

began
when she stopped

began in winter and, like everything else, at first, just waited for spring
in spring noticed there were lilac branches, but no desire,
no need to talk to any angel, to say: sky, dooryard, _____,
when summer arrived there was more, but not much
nothing really worth noting
and then it was winter again—nothing had changed: sky, dooryard,
_____, white, frozen was the lake and the lagoon, some froze the ocean
(*now you erase that*) (*you cross that out*)
and so on and so forth
didn't want
didn't want to point, to catalogue, to inquire,
to acknowledge, to uncover, not even to transcend
wasn't ambitious, wasn't ambiguous, wasn't
____-reflexive, ____-referential,
the "poet-narrator" did not "want to be liked"
got even stronger: no longer wanted
"to be"
until "wasn't"
was what was missing
was enough

the paper need not (was) not
function(ing) as air (*please stop*) (*please shut the fuck up*)

THE POEM SHE DIDN'T WRITE

had no synecdoches, no metonymy, no pattern, if it rhymed—it was
purely accidental,
no non sequitur, no primogenitor, wasn't
influenced by homer or blake or yeats   auden   contained

no anxiety, hadn't even heard of
louise glück franz wright billy (budd?) collins

(in the margin: "*then why are you so sad?*")

spring summer fall
and so on and so forth
it was and it was and it was

done

she did not read it to anyone
she did not send it out "for publication"   when asked
she said she "was not writing" because
"she wasn't"

          But somehow   (like a rumor)

                    THE POEM

SHE DIDN'T WRITE got out   maybe
she talked about it in her sleep   maybe
she was betrayed by a lover

(and in the margin: "*and why are you so sad?*")

In   THE POEM SHE DIDN'T WRITE
there was nothing poetic.
In   THE POEM
there were no hidden references to _____.
In   THE POEMSHEDIDN'TWRITE
arthur rimbaud was not a hero.
In   THEPOEMSHEDIDN'TWRITE
people did not turn to each other in mania or desperation   preservation
In   THEPOEM
away in boredom   disappointment   despair

                    THE POEM

was equally hailed and dismissed by the critics.
harold bloom said: "otherness to such a degree that loneliness was

created and alleviated at once".

helen vendler wrote: "a posthumous consciousness imputed to the poet's corpse; a hoped-for future represented as though it has already happened".

_____: "the marriage of marivaux and poussin, i.e., poussinesque maurivaudage"
: "an anti-master floribund disaster"
: "fawn meets wolf"
: "exudes sexuality like a dark french perfume"

poets turned in their tombs
hopkins's skull shifted   nothing could be counted   was this finally
S=P=R=U=N=G rhythm?
there was hysteria and histrionic personality   disorder   low affect
aphonia   apophasis   andyet
                    THE POEM
(people need(ed) shorthand and so the rest of the title began to be
elided) was   some how   able to act
some said   THE POEM

    "could not exist, because it, um, didn't"
some said "it existed only in that space between 'out there' and 'in
here'   catullus's   mistress's   sandaled foot stepping/suspended
over the threshold
some exegesised that "rilke had already not written it"
some opined that like all the other poems—it only didn't exist in
academia, if it didn't exist at all
    i.e., somewhere in a park near athens "duh", said
some, "ever heard of derrida? as the poet need not be present then
why present the poem?"
some said its presence   as with all poetry   written or not was
"contingent

    on a reader (or non-
    reader, as the case may be) and only if that reader bent over it late
    at night
    called it 'beloved'"
others agreed because now they could quote some stevens: "yes, yes,
they said,

293

late and leaning"
others maintained that it SO didn't matter, they would go on the way
they had been doing and their parents before them and their parents'
parents
        (a cat's flux)

: "tries, but fails, to cross over into different worlds"
: "not worthy of my love"
: "an assassination at an assignation"
: "(nothing is(n't) real, everything is(n't) possible)"

but the lilacs, the lilacs
blooming, blooming   (on) (in) winter

i.e., nothing had changed   and yet   and   none
the   less: a new world order
the point had been made: things that didn't exist   existed more
existed ever   existed over . . . (*watchit!*)
("*because complexity never made anyone feel better")
she had given them permission (not) to   proceed
soon   hopefully   other writers would stop

(writing(;))
       THEPOEM

was some body's thesis and some body's else's dumbest joke
it made literary terms like _____ and _____ obsolete
it made literary theories like _____ and _____ sound
stupider than ever

in the 22nd century they would talk about   "she" being hit with a
"fish"
they would confuse "she" with all the great poets who really weren't so
good, were they?
        (all small and flawed men)
five hundred years later a fragment would be found   a fragment
                that also couldn't   didn't

exist

and so forth and so on   on in

lilacs   on in
winters

       THEPOEM

      was repeatedly misattributed   it crossed and re-crossed
genres
some said it had once been   a charlie kaufman movie or
           a novel by davidfosterwallace
was it rauschenberg or   was it dekooning?
who erased whom?

      what?

it was the ascension and the ceiling and the sonnets except
better   'cause   refused   to be
refused to participate in a world made up of and by   ants and
dogs and   armadillos   peacocks   skunks
(ref. swarthmore chart)

my name is verdant greene.

i am the HUNTER GRACCHUS.

call me . . . .

      BUT by now (then)   every   one   was   dead

      but for now,

in the year of
     THEPOEM
20__
finally:

a poetry the masses could rally around—
"so simple" they intoned "and yet so brilliant"
people began crossing poetry off the list of what they, too, disliked
someone began carrying a sign, as if it was a demonstration: "CLEAR

YOUR MIND OF CANT" someone else copied it but added an apostrophe
splinter groups became political (INSERT SOMETHING HERE ON
KANT) (*the starry skies above me and the moral law inside me?*)
"why didn't the poets invent it sooner?" they bemusedly wondered
(smelling their faux lilac boutonnieres)
slightly giddy with relief they became a little careless and self-
aggrandizing
"why didn't WE think of it?"
"my six-year-old could have done it!"
"how did we live (not) not thinking about poetry, when, after all, that was
all there ever wasn't".

TED KOOSER

from *Splitting an Order,* 2014

Splitting an Order

I like to watch an old man cutting a sandwich in half,
maybe an ordinary cold roast beef on whole wheat bread,
no pickles or onion, keeping his shaky hands steady
by placing his forearms firm on the edge of the table
and using both hands, the left to hold the sandwich in place,
and the right to cut it surely, corner to corner,
observing his progress through glasses that moments before
he wiped with his napkin, and then to see him lift half
onto the extra plate that he asked the server to bring,
and then to wait, offering the plate to his wife
while she slowly unrolls her napkin and places her spoon,
her knife, and her fork in their proper places,
then smooths the starched white napkin over her knees
and meets his eyes and holds out both old hands to him.

TED KOOSER

from *Splitting an Order,* 2014

Swinging from Parents

The child walks between her father and mother,
holding their hands. She makes the shape of the *y*
at the end of *infancy,* and lifts her feet
the way the *y* pulls up its feet, and swings
like the *v* in *love,* between an *o* and an *e*
who are strong and steady and as far as she knows
will be there to swing from forever. Sometimes
her father, using his free hand, points to something
and says its name, the way the arm of the *r*
points into the future at the end of *father.*
Or the *r* at the end of *forever.* It's that *forever*
the child puts her trust in, lifting her knees,
swinging her feet out over the world.

W.S. MERWIN

from *The Moon before Morning*, 2014

How It Happens

The sky said I am watching
to see what you
can make out of nothing
I was looking up and I said
I thought you
were supposed to be doing that
the sky said Many
are clinging to that
I am giving you a chance
I was looking up and I said
I am the only chance I have
then the sky did not answer
and here we are
with our names for the days
the vast days that do not listen to us

RAINER MARIA RILKE

from *Rilke: New Poems,* 2014
> Translated from the German by Joseph Cadora

Archaic Torso of Apollo

We could not ever know his wondrous head,
with eyes like apples that are ripening.
But the lamp of his torso is still glowing,
although it is turned down low, to spread

his glance, which abides and glimmers within.
Else the curve of the breast could not dazzle you,
nor, in turning, could a smile play through
those loins to the center of procreation.

Else this stone would seem stunted and defiled
and could not shimmer so, like a wild
beast's fur beneath the shoulder's sheer surface,

and it would not burst from its bounds, so rife
with light and star-like, for there is no place
that does not see you. You must change your life.

ARTHUR SZE

from *Compass Rose,* 2014

Confetti

Strike, rub, crumple—rip paper into shreds:
you can make confetti form a quick orange
blossom before it collapses to the ground.
At night, a driver misses a curve and plows
through the wall into a neighbor's dining room;
twice a day, another neighbor breaks apart
ice with a pick, and her horses dip their heads
into the tub. At dawn, branches scrape,
like rough flint, against the window;
where I stare, a woman once threw a shuttle
back and forth through the alternating sheds
at her loom, and that sound was a needle
sparking through emptiness. Last night,
as sleet hit the skylight, we moved from
trough to crest to radiating wave: even as
shrapnel litters the ground, as a car flips
and scatters bright shards of CDs into the grass.

JEFFREY BROWN

from *The News,* 2015

West Point

Backpacks on benches
caps on their hooks

all stand to attention
for the professor of poetry

who mapped today's lesson plan:
death and honor at Thermopylae

the Somme, Hamburger Hill
and the names we now announce:

Baghdad, Fallujah, Najaf
Kabul, Khost, Korengal.

Will reciting a sonnet
make me a better lieutenant?

This is what they ask
of Shelley, of Owen

the clearest words, a step away
from "a bleeding world"

measuring war by meter
command by rhyme, killing

by form, victory by the time
it takes to read one's way

from Troy to Kandahar where
today the bomb explodes.

"We're here," the cadet says,
"to learn to take lives"

and art serves, we all serve
an arc of humanity in death

the ancient brutality of battle
muck and muse, books and blood.

"The most powerful tool
a soldier has," the general writes

"is not his weapon but his mind"
and art—cadets on the march—

calls forth what is best
even as men do their worst.

DEBORAH LANDAU

from *The Uses of the Body*, 2015

from "Minutes, Years"

Before you have kids,
you get a dog.

Then when you get a baby,
you wait for the dog to die.

When the dog dies,
it's a relief.

When your babies aren't babies,
you want a dog again.

DENNIS O'DRISCOLL

from *Update: Poems 2011–2012*, 2015

Update

God, I still miss you some days,
fondly recall our happier times.
You used to take me into
your confidence, while I
fessed up to my transgressions,
owned up to grievous flaws.
And, granted absolution, I would
ascend to cloud nine,
mind on higher things,
ears only for your voice that conversed,
not in our inarticulate vernacular
but through lapidary Latin,
plainchant, exultant motet.
I recall the wet cathedral evenings
when your fair-weather friends
had absented themselves,
and we settled down by the fire
of the votive candle shrine
for a heart-to-heart confab,
our conversation never flagging.

What a good listener you always were
to me, God. I so wish we had not quarrelled,
gone our separate ways, making
too big an issue of the Jesuitical
distinctions that divided us, failing
to see eye-to-eye on articles of faith.

I still watch out for news of you,
gossip column tattle, and—an obsessive
divorcee—track your movements, eager
to learn which lovers take my place,
what types you hang about with these days,

what you're up to elsewhere
as you expand your horizons,
establishing new branches of your empire,
propagating universes by the second.

And you must feel a loneliness
close to empty nest syndrome
now that so many of your
erstwhile acolytes have flown the coop,
escaped your cage, questioned
your discretion, no longer prepared
to submit to your rough justice,
remain prisoners of your conscience.

God, how much I miss the comfort food
of your home-baked communion host.
And hush. The megaphones roped
to the telegraph poles relay around
the town your May procession:
The blue-gowned Child of Mary
women join with the choir.
The petal-strewing schoolgirls,
the banner-carrying sodality men,
and the canopy-bearing deacons
—custodians of the fragile Marian shrine
buoyant on its wildflower-brimming float—
break into song, give 'full-throated' voice
to the humming fecundity of early summer.

The year, refurbished, kitted out afresh,
is soaking up warm pastel colours,
reaching perfect pitch, oozing
through rejuvenated fields
a slow sempiternal note.

ALBERTO RÍOS

from *A Small Story about the Sky*, 2015

Sudden Smells, Sudden Songs

Where does it all come from,
The sap of strangeness inside us,

The sudden flow of feeling—*I love that song!*—
That lighter blood, that second breath,

That *something* where in the darkness
A knob is turned.

Who are we then? In that moment
We are not who we were a second ago:

A quick smell of rosemary changes us, that fast.
We stand up, familiar to ourselves,

Then sit down strangers. We are
Two people. Maybe more.

RICHARD SIKEN

from *War of the Foxes*, 2015

Birds Hover the Trampled Field

I saw them hiding in the yellow field, crouching low
in the varnished dark. I followed them pretending
they were me because they were. I wanted to explain
myself to myself in an understandable way. I gave
shape to my fears and made excuses. I varied my
velocities, watched myselves sleep. Something's not
right about what I'm doing but I'm still doing it—
living in the worst parts, ruining myself. My inner life
is a sheet of black glass. If I fell through the floor
I would keep falling. The enormity of my desire
disgusts me. I kissed my mouth, it was no longer
a mouth. I threw a spear at my head, I didn't have
a head. Fox. At the throat of. The territory is more
complex than I supposed. What does a body of
knowledge look like? A body, any body. Look away
but I'm still there. Birds flying but I'm still there,
lurk there. Not just one of me but multitudes in
the hayfield. Want something to chase you? Run.
Take a body, dump it, drive. Take a body, maybe
your own, and dump it gently. All your dead,
unfinished selves and dump them gently. Take only
what you need. The machine of the world—if you
don't grab on, you begin to tremble. And if you do
grab on, then everything trembles. I spent my lamp
and cleft my head. Deep-wounded mind, I wasn't
doing anything with it anyway. And the birds looking
for a place to land. I would like to say something
about grace, and the brown corduroy thrift store coat
I bought for eight-fifty when you told me my
paintings were empty. Never finish a war without
starting another. I've seen your true face: the back
of your head. If you were walking away, keep walking.

FRANK STANFORD

from *What About This: Collected Poems of Frank Stanford,* 2015
Edited by Michael Wiegers

from *The Battlefield Where the Moon Says I Love You*

I seemed to hear the hog beater
even before I saw him coming
I followed him
I stepped on the back of his cut down
cowboy boots I followed him so close
he reach around and grab me
and tells me how he stole the hog back
how no one would know
cause the evidence was not
there the marked ears were buried
in a stump and the hog was shot
through the nose with a pistol
so no one could tell
it just dropped dead on his place
by the water and he skinned him
and in court they couldn't put it on him
and lord jesus christ I seen it all
and I'm seeing it all somebody get me off this river there's going to be
a WAR I see it the high temperature bullets is going through me clean
up into the sky like the stars the little nailheads in the coffins it's a place
called VIETNAM goodbye mammy wind blowing through dead american hair
o these cosmologies sadder than the sea
and the long presidential horseshit
and the moon say get up you want some more so I open my eyes think see tell

FRANK STANFORD

from *What About This: Collected Poems of Frank Stanford*, 2015
Edited by Michael Wiegers

What About This

A guy comes walking out of the garden
Playing Dark Eyes on the accordion.
We're sitting on the porch,
Drinking and spitting, lying.
We shut our eyes, snap our fingers.
Dewhurst goes out to his truck
Like he doesn't believe what he's seeing
And brings back three half-pints.
A little whirlwind occurs in the road,
Carrying dust away like a pail of water.
We're drinking serious now, and O.Z.
Wants to break in the store for some head cheese,
But the others won't let him.
Everybody laughs, dances.
The crossroads are all quiet
Except for the little man on the accordion.
Things are dying down, the moon spills its water.
Dewhurst says he smells rain.
O.Z. says if it rains he'll still make a crop.
We wait there all night, looking for rain.
We haven't been to sleep, so the blue lizards
On the side of the white porch
Lose their tails when we try to dream.
The man playing the music looks at us,
Noticing what we're up to. He backs off,
Holding up his hands in front, smiling,
Shaking his head, but before he gets halfway
Down the road that O.Z. shoots him in the belly.
All summer his accordion rotted in the ditch,
Like an armadillo turning into a house payment.

JEAN VALENTINE

from *Shirt in Heaven,* 2015

God of rooms

God of rooms, of this room made of taken-away
papers and books, of removal, this single
room made of taken-away
empty now, god of empty rooms, god of
one unable to speak, god of turned-over boats
in the wind (god of boat and mouth and ear)
listen to someone, be of-you
needful to someone

for Paul Celan

JEAN VALENTINE

from *Shirt in Heaven*, 2015

[The ship] is slowly giving up her sentient life. I cannot write about it.

Shackleton, diary

Next to where their ship went down
they pitched their linen tents.

You, mountain-climbing,
mountain-climbing,
wearing your dead father's flight jacket—

My scalp is alive,
love touched it. My eyes are open water. Yours too.

Sitting in the dark Baltimore bar
drinking Coke
with you with your inoperable cancer
with your meds

no tent
no care what we look like
what we say

Later that night, in my room
looking into the mirror, to tell the truth I was loved.
I looked right through into nothing.

DEAN YOUNG

from *Shock by Shock*, 2015

Gizzard Song

Dean, it's Harry. No birds are nesting
in my birdhouses. What could it mean?
I don't know why I answered the phone,
there's already too much going on in
Nacogdoches and not even hello. Harry,
you haven't even asked about my operation.
You sick? No, I had a heart transplant.
They do those with lasers now, right? Lapra-
dazically? No, mine was more complicated, I say,
with knives. Ouch, he deducts, but you must
be okay now. Antlers are growing out of my floors,
a snowman, an evil snowman delivers my mail
and I'm taking so many pills my tongue's purple
and hair's growing out of my forehead so no.
Well, sorry, but you're the only person I
can call. No one knows the habits and inklings
of our winged friends like you. A query about
a foundling fledgling, a moody rooster, an owl
with self-esteem issues, you're the go-to guy.
Even if you feel like a wobbly oblong peg
driven into a wedge of cheddar, you're the guy
who holds it all together not only in avian
affairs but all atmospheric matters: comets
and Martians your métier, angels and even clouds
for crying out loud. What would we do without
you? One day: no birds then stars all falled down
then what? Nothing! The void! The dark maw
of zilch! He was working himself into a fine
fettle and I had to admit, even if he was feeding
you regurgitated worm, he could make you feel
special and all my pains, my multitudinous pains
would shrink to a single whinge like what a word

makes when it's misspelled. Pilgrim, I say,
you need to clear out the old nests, your houses
probably jammed with others' twigs and mud and stuff.
Birds, like the rest of us, like clean starts
and as I spoke I felt my new heart roost deeper
in my chest, fluffing out its blue breast, looking
for something to peck and this is how mercy
and poetry move through the world.

JOSH BELL

from *Alamo Theory,* 2016

Notes Toward an Imperial Poetry

No more masturbating in the gift shop
No more days dropping like child actors
Days like something Antigone might have buried
Days in which my friend and I hold hands in the street and eat up what the
      palmerworm hath not yet eaten
And watch young people exercise
And remind me what the old evil was, again?
Scrap of flag poking out of the dirt
We must deliver the claw hammer
Annihilator, step into the calendry
Rip off the head and gnaw on the neck peg, as if we are dolls
Where the wages of capitalism are wages
Where puncture to the small beasts who are deserving of it
Snood of the living body with the spirit bursting from its fold as lamprey,
      microscopics from another plane wriggling in its teeth
Where we're bringing King George back
No more darkrooms, no more dressing rooms
Not a doll that pees itself but a doll that pees on other dolls
I did not feel the spirit's anger was anarchic
Your body in the back of every ambulance in New York City
Call of Duty: the Battle of Tel Megiddo
Annihilator, if one wants a mother, one puts a mother
If one wants a father, then one goes ahead and puts one
Third-person-limited omniscient shooter
In the dark of the VIP room Death's going to let us put our little stickies on it
Elegy for it (how you tried to fit it: how you couldn't keep it fit)
And of the even smaller beasts who are deserving of it
And was it Monday's child who was full of hair?
Is lubricant the only apology we'll ever need?
No sundress, for any sex or species, in or around the Annihilator

Antigone's holding hands with her friends in the street and she's sending out the
	Polaroids
Summer's still the heavy favorite
Parts of the day left scattered behind in motel refrigerators all across the Northeast
Gnostic reviser, time clicking in the horse, voice the departure point of spirit from
	the flesh, and God's assent as my thumb slips to its fit in the jugular notch
Antigone keeping lookout in the whale watch
And all these seaside cottages with photographs of seaside cottages on their
	bedroom walls
Annihilator, your voice is holy and it goes wherever you go
Do not take it with you into the gift shop
Do not hand its body to the adult acoustics
Death's going to let us put our little stickies on it, one last time
Elegy for it (and how I put it out of my misery: lit it: how it won't stay lit)

JIM HARRISON

from *Dead Man's Float,* 2016

Bridge

Most of my life was spent
building a bridge out over the sea
though the sea was too wide.
I'm proud of the bridge
hanging in the pure sea air. Machado
came for a visit and we sat on the
end of the bridge, which was his idea.

Now that I'm old the work goes slowly.
Ever nearer death, I like it out here
high above the sea bundled
up for the arctic storms of late fall,
the resounding crash and moan of the sea,
the hundred-foot depth of the green troughs.
Sometimes the sea roars and howls like
the animal it is, a continent wide and alive.
What beauty in this the darkest music
over which you can hear the lightest music of human
behavior, the tender connection between men and galaxies.

So I sit on the edge, wagging my feet above
the abyss. Tonight the moon will be in my lap.
This is my job, to study the universe
from my bridge. I have the sky, the sea, the faint
green streak of Canadian forest on the far shore.

from *Garden Time,* 2016

The Present

As they were leaving the garden
one of the angels bent down to them and whispered

I am to give you this
as you are leaving the garden

I do not know what it is
or what it is for
what you will do with it

you will not be able to keep it
but you will not be able

to keep anything
yet they both reached at once

for the present
and when their hands met

they laughed

LUCIA PERILLO

from *Time Will Clean the Carcass Bones: Selected and New Poems,* 2016

In the Confessional Mode, with a Borrowed Movie Trope

. . . and then there is the idea of another life
of which this outward life is only an expression,
the way the bag floating round in the alley
traces out the shape of wind
but is not wind. In a fleabag hotel
in Worcester, Mass., a man is dying,
muscles stiff, their ropes pulled taut,
his voice somewhere between a honk and whisper.
But float down through the years, many years,
and it's us, meaning me and the man
as a boy upstairs in the house
where I've finagled my deflowering.
Maybe finagled. Hard to say if it's working.
It reminds me of trying to cram a washrag
down a bottle neck—you twist and twist
to make it reach, but it does not,
and in the end the inside of me
was not wiped clean. Oh I was once
in such a hurry. The job had to be done
before the pot roast was, his stepmother
thumping the ceiling under us: *Whatever*
you're doing, you better get out
of your sister's room. But her voice
carried more of the wasp's irritation
than the hornet's true rage, so we forged on—
while our jury of trusty busty Barbies
perched on their toes, their gowns iridescent,
a sword of gray light coming through the curtain crack
and knighting me where I contorted
on the rug. And it's clear to me still,
what I wanted back then; namely, my old life
cut up into shreds so I could get on

with my next. But the boy was only
halfway hard, no knife-edge there,
though the rest of him looked as if it were bronze,
with muscles rumpling his dark-gold skin.
Meaning this is a story about beauty after all.
And when the roast was ready, I slipped outside,
where November dusk was already sifting down
into the ballrooms underneath the trees.
It was time to go home to my own dinner,
the ziti, the meatballs, *Star Trek* on TV,
but how could I sit there, familiar among them,
now that I was this completely different thing?
Sweat was my coat as I flew from his house
while the brakes of my ten-speed sang like geese.
But now it's his voice that resembles a honk
in a room where the empty amber vials
rattle underneath his narrow bed. Meaning
he's trying hard to take himself out.
And while I have as yet no theory
to unlock the secret forces of the earth, still
I think there's a reason why the boy and I,
when we grew up, both got stuck
with the same disease. Meaning the stiffness,
the spasms, the concrete legs—
oh I was once in such a hurry. Now
my thighs are purple from all the drugs
I'm shooting in, & I don't even want to know
how the boy looks racked and wrecked.
Sometimes in the midst of making love
that kind of body will come floating in,
but quickly I'll nudge it away in favor of
the airbrushed visions. But not him,
the young him, the brass plate of whose belly
would be more lovely than I could bear,
though in chaster moments I will visit
that alcove of me where his torso is struck
by all the dark-gold light that still slants in.
Oh we are blown, we are bags,
we are moved by such elegant chaos.

Call it god. Only because it is an expletive that fits.
His body, his beauty, all fucked up now.
God. Then the air cuts out, and then we drop.

CAMILLE RANKINE

from *Incorrect Merciful Impulses,* 2016

Contact

Out of respect for the departed, I still my hands, I hold
the volume of my wailing low. I gather
my spit and sweat and sorrow beneath my raincoat.
I make a blanket of all the letters
no one writes anymore. I didn't tell you
that the wind so urgent, the sound
like a wave, the dresses fluttering bright
from the storefront, my high
society, my commerce, my undimmed
night, my neon hum. Today, a near collision
with a stranger. How I tried to touch, be
known. To think a body moves me, moves
for me. To think it doesn't. To think we are alone.
Today, I feel an alien. If I could disappear.
Not a danger, not in danger. Belonging here. If I could
be the shape of your breath in the cold. What camouflage
have we. How we bury our living
within us. This precious ache I cradle, my treasure,
my dread. What barren, what beauty it makes of me.

PAISLEY REKDAL

from *Imaginary Vessels,* 2016

Self-Portrait as Mae West One-Liner

I'm no moaning bluet, mountable
linnet, mumbling nun. I'm
tangible, I'm gin. Able to molt
in toto, to limn. I'm blame and angle, I'm
lumbago, an oblate mug gone notable,
not glum. I'm a tabu tuba mogul, I'm motile,
I'm nimble. No gab ennui, no bagel bun boat: I'm one
big megaton bolt able to bail
men out. Gluten iamb. Male bong unit.
I'm a genial bum, mental obi, genital
montage. I'm Agent Limbo, my blunt bio
an amulet, an enigma. Omit élan. Omit bingo.
Alien mangle, I'm glib lingo. Untangle me,
tangelo. But I'm no angel.

JAMES RICHARDSON

from *During,* 2016

Indispensable

The world
is very small.
Inhale,
and the birds fall.

JAMES RICHARDSON

from *During,* 2016

One of the Evenings

After so many years, we know them.
This is one of the older Evenings: its patience,
settling in, its warmth that needs nothing in return.
So many Augusts sitting out through sunset,
first a dimness in the undergrowth like smoke,
and then like someone you hadn't noticed
has been watching a long time . . .

It has seen everything that can be done in the dark.
It has seen two rifles swing around
to train on each other, it has seen lovers meet and revolve,
it has seen the wounds grayscale in low light.
It has come equally for those who prayed for it
and those who switched on lamp after lamp
until they could not see. It deals evenhandedly
with the one skimming the stairs as rapidly as typing,
the one washing plates a little too loudly,
the one who thinks there is something more important,
since it does not believe in protagonists,
since it knows anyone could be anyone else.

It has heard what they said aloud to the moon, to the stars
and what they could not say,
walking alone and together. It has gotten over
I cannot live through this, it has gotten over *This did not have to happen*
and *This is experience one day I will be glad for.*
It has gotten over *How even for a moment*
could I have forgotten? though it never forgets,
leaves nothing behind, does not believe in stories,
since nothing is over, only beginning somewhere else.

It could be anywhere but it is here
with the kids who play softball endlessly not keeping score,

though it's getting late, way too late,
holding their drives in the air like invisible moons a little longer,
giving way before them so they feel like they're running faster.
It likes trees, I think. It likes summer. It seems comfortable with us,
though it is here to help us be less ourselves.
It thinks of its darkening as listening harder and harder.

BRENDA SHAUGHNESSY

from So Much Synth, 2016

I Have a Time Machine

But unfortunately it can only travel into the future
at a rate of one second per second,

which seems slow to the physicists and to the grant
committees and even to me.

But I manage to get there, time after time, to the next
moment and to the next.

Thing is, I can't turn it off. I keep zipping ahead—
well not *zipping*— And if I try

to get out of this time machine, open the latch,
I'll fall into space, unconscious,

then desiccated! And I'm pretty sure I'm afraid of that.
So I stay inside.

There's a window, though. It shows the past.
It's like a television or fish tank.

But it's never live; it's always over. The fish swim
in backward circles.

Sometimes it's like a rearview mirror, another chance
to see what I'm leaving behind,

and sometimes like blackout, all that time
wasted sleeping.

Myself age eight, whole head burnt with embarrassment
at having lost a library book.

Myself lurking in a candled corner expecting
to be found charming.

Me holding a rose though I want to put it down
so I can smoke.

Me exploding at my mother who explodes at me
because the explosion

of some dark star all the way back struck hard
at mother's mother's mother.

I turn away from the window, anticipating a blow.
I thought I'd find myself

an old woman by now, traveling so light in time.
But I haven't gotten far at all.

Strange not to be able to pick up the pace as I'd like;
the past is so horribly fast.

ED SKOOG

from *Run the Red Lights,* 2016

Run the Red Lights

When my mother sent me for cigarettes
I'd buy a candy bar too, sign her name
to the book, and walk out with the green-
and-white carton, Virginia Slims 100s,
under my arm, the chocolate already gone.
Sugar, my god! like newspaper cartoon
panels spread out on the kitchen table
where I'd pretend to smoke, imitating her.
After the corner store closed we made our groceries
at Dillon's, joined the impersonal. A villain
snatched her purse there when I was away at college
and on the phone she told me, excitedly,
how Topeka police chased the culprit, and she named
each street, each intersection and landmark,
the whole adventure, just for her.
I'm grateful now to the sedentary house
though I've grown as large on candy as John Candy.
My older brothers left home and our meals stayed
the same, a skillet high with beef Stroganoff,
pot roast in broth, chili con carne,
cheese sandwiches with mayo, flocks of fried chicken.
Then the whole house went on a diet of cold
tofu cubes, a broken disk of lemon in a water glass,
cottage cheese measured onto lettuce,
and then back to London broil the next night,
no questions asked—lovely. We were emotions
without form, and I carry it with me,
not just in frame, arm and jowl and belly,
but here in the intergalactic space of written
thought, the infinite stage where we come
talk to each other. Sugar makes me curious.
After Katrina, I took the diet where you eat meat,

and lost almost a hundred pounds from a surfeit
of bacon, sautéed pork medallions, beef & lamb.
The weight fell away like a knight's armor
after a joust. I bought shirts at a regular store.
I played softball and ran bases, bounded them,
as if on a new, more forgiving planet. And
I went crazy, evened out, broke down again,
inconsolable at the finale of *Six Feet Under*,
tears for my mother, postponed, and more
torrented for delay. Opening the book of grief
requires you read all the way to the end,
every time. Driving to work, I stopped
bewildered at a gas station, paid cash for two
Snickers providing more salvation
than I have ever known from religion's acres.
I write about the West and the South and home,
their tenderness and trouble and the weird spirits
breaking the best days. Still I find myself down
by the river at twilight. On the bridge deliberate-
seeming people walk by like victorious aliens,
past the consequential palaces lit as before,
the faces turning in their rotisseries.
In profile, my mother looked like Alex Chilton,
lead singer of the Box Tops, and then Big Star.
I used to see Chilton around New Orleans,
in line at the grocery store, walking down Esplanade.
My mother also had a solo career, playing
solitaire and watching her own TV in the kitchen
and dying before everyone else. Dying, Chilton
urged his wife to run the red lights, his last words,
and when I had to leave my mother in the hospital
that was hard, and then again at the funeral
I set a marble under her folded hands,
don't know why. It's been ten years.
Ten fingers, the closed eye of each knuckle,
each nail its years' fullest day moon.
Which shed the other? My scar from opening
a window, such force to move the wood frame,

so little to shatter glass it held. To be held so
again. Ten years, so forty seasons, eighty endings
and beginnings, well, always a gust in them
which is the sigh of how she would note leaf and bird.
One hand to hold the coffee cup, one the cigarette.
The red ember she became at midnight. Red light. Eye.

OCEAN VUONG

from *Night Sky with Exit Wounds,* 2016

Telemachus

Like any good son, I pull my father out
of the water, drag him by his hair

through white sand, his knuckles carving a trail
the waves rush in to erase. Because the city

beyond the shore is no longer
where we left it. Because the bombed

cathedral is now a cathedral
of trees. I kneel beside him to see how far

I might sink. *Do you know who I am,*
Ba? But the answer never comes. The answer

is the bullet hole in his back, brimming
with seawater. He is so still I think

he could be anyone's father, found
the way a green bottle might appear

at a boy's feet containing a year
he has never touched. I touch

his ears. No use. I turn him
over. To face it. The cathedral

in his sea-black eyes. The face
not mine—but one I will wear

to kiss all my lovers good-night:
the way I seal my father's lips

with my own & begin
the faithful work of drowning.

C.D. WRIGHT

from The Poet, the Lion, Talking Pictures, El Farolito, a Wedding in St. Roch, the Big Box Store, the Warp in the Mirror, Spring, Midnights, Fire & All, 2016

In a Word, a World

I love them all.

I love that a handful, a mouthful, gets you by, a satchelful can land you a job, a well-chosen clutch of them could get you laid, and that a solitary word can initiate a stampede, and therefore can be formally outlawed—even by a liberal court bent on defending a constitution guaranteeing unimpeded utterance. I love that the Argentine gaucho has over two hundred words for the coloration of horses and the Sami language of Scandinavia has over a thousand words for reindeer based on age, sex, appearance—e.g., a *busat* has big balls or only one big ball. More than the pristine, I love the filthy ones for their descriptive talent as well as transgressive nature. I love the dirty ones more than the minced, in that I respect extravagant expression more than reserved. I admire reserve, especially when taken to an ascetic *n*th. I love the particular lexicons of particular occupations. The substrate of those activities. The nomenclatures within nomenclatures. I am of the unaccredited school that believes animals did not exist until Adam assigned them names. My relationship to the word is anything but scientific; it is a matter of faith on my part, that the word endows material substance, by setting the thing named apart from all else. *Horse,* then, unhorses what is not horse.

C.D. WRIGHT

from *The Poet, the Lion, Talking Pictures, El Farolito, a Wedding in St. Roch, the Big Box Store, the Warp in the Mirror, Spring, Midnights, Fire & All,* 2016

from "Concerning Why Poetry Offers a Better Deal Than the World's Biggest Retailer"

Poetry digs through. Its castings make some growth possible even on contaminated ground. Though forced to make do with shrinking day-length, though forced to go the worm's way, poetry ensures new shoots. It could be that an international vault will have to be established for poetry, to ensure the renewal of the greatest variety of voices, of lines capable of challenging the uniformity of thought. The vault that must by definition of its mission reject the Walmart cheer. Spring clings to poetry. It brings forth possibility, "the greatest good."

That the poems we snatch from the language must bear the habit of our thinking.

That their arrangement strengthens the authority on which each separate line is laid.

That they extend the line into perpetuity.

That they enlarge the circle.

That they awaken the dreamer. That they awaken the schemer.

That they rectify the names.

That they draw not conclusions but further qualify doubt.

That they avail themselves of the shrapnel of everything: the disappearance of cork trees and coral, the destroyed center of Ramadi, the shape of buildings to come, the pearness of pears.

That they clear the air.

That they keep a big-box sense of humor at the ready (like an ax in a glass case).

That they bring the ship nearer to its longing.

That they resensitize the surface of things.

That they resonate in the bowels.

That they will not stand alone.

This is our mind. Our language. Our light. Our word. Our bond.

In the world.

VICTORIA CHANG

from *Barbie Chang,* 2017

Barbie Chang's Tears

Barbie Chang's tears are the lights of
    the city that go off on

off on Mr. Darcy walks around the city
    but Barbie Chang can't

follow him she can't promote herself
    if she had legs she would

stop begging if she had hands she would
    stop her own wedding

the city has no extra bedding it is not
    ready yet the maids are

still making beds Barbie Chang is still
    looking for small openings

there are always storms long arms drinks
    with pink umbrellas

because they know she is confused like a
    sea horse light avoids her

town on the map B2 C4 she wants to
    be used she doesn't

want to be with you or you it is morning
    again and she is already

mourning the men the night men who
    never fight who never

write back she prefers to sleep on her
    back so she can see the

eyes of her attackers in the morning
    a bed with questions

with her depression on each side two
    small holes from knees

TYREE DAYE

from *River Hymns,* 2017

Neuse River

Tell them not to go
to the banks alone.

Tell them where
they can drink

without watching
over their shoulders.

Tell them drowning
is third on your list

of concerns.
First is *lie down,*

second, *come here.*
Even the water

I was baptized in
isn't safe.

I knew God
was a man

because he put
a baby in Mary

without her
permission.

ALEX DIMITROV

from *Together and By Ourselves,* 2017

You Were Blond Once

I have a photograph . . .
when I describe it, you'll know.
On a long train ride they sat and said nothing.
In a pocket, a ticket stub of two hours on a night five years ago.
If you left your life, what life would you leave for? Tell me.
A lot of terrible things used to make me happy.
For years, my friend looked for the perfect chair,
that space he wanted to be in.
Found it two summers ago—never sits in it.
They sat in the back of the restaurant
so he could be upset privately and in public.
You know those streets that have two names,
one before and one after they intersect with another?
How sometimes we can't find them on maps.
Well, I got lost every day that summer in London.
It's the kind of film you want to see by yourself,
but take a car home, don't get lost on me.
None of this is important—and still—
I have a photograph of you . . .
when we ate an orange in bed.
What month was that in? What did you want from me?
Every book is a book, is a thing you feel by yourself.
You are here. I am alone in this poem.
The window open all day: rain on the white desk, wood floor,
that strange curve on the back of your head (only I knew).
Sometimes I go outside just to feel movement.
Is that why you live here?
Did you imagine your life would turn out this way?
It takes the way someone asks a question to know
if you really want to know them.
You were blond once. So handsome.

And the streets kept their names, and that restaurant closed
and I found the right film when I needed nothing.
Where is he going with this? *Where were you?*
How you approached the water and never went in it.
I'm telling you it's not cold. It's not cold anymore.
Today it's perfect out there. The tea's tea,
there's work, pills, unsent messages, empty glasses.
A lot of things to say with one body (unlikely).
It wasn't that long ago.
I have a photograph of you from that day . . .

JOHN FREEMAN

from *Maps*, 2017

The Boy under the Car

That night in Damascus
her job was to put
tea and cake,
a sprig of mint,
on a silver tray
and walk down
the crushed-pebble drive
to the boy paid
to sleep under the car.
She never said
his name, or what
he looked like,
or whether, when she came
upon him,
curled up,
eyes black and glossy,
she caught him
singing to himself,
before the clattering metal
made him silent.

ROBERT HEDIN

from At the Great Door of Morning: Selected Poems and Translations, 2017

The Snow Country

for Carolyn

Up on Verstovia the snow country is silent tonight.
I can see it from our window,
A white sea whose tide flattens over the darkness.
This is where the animals must go—
The old foxes, the bears too slow to catch
The fall run of salmon, even the salmon themselves—
All brought together in the snow country of Verstovia.
This must be where the ravens turn to geese,
The weasels to wolves, where the rabbits turn to owls.
I wonder if birds even nest on that floating sea,
What hunters have forgotten their trails and sunk out of sight.
I wonder if the snow country is green underneath,
If there are forests and paths
And cabins with wood-burning stoves.
Or does it move down silently gyrating forever,
Glistening with the bones of animals and trappers,
Eggs that are cold and turning to stones.
I wonder if I should turn, tap, and even wake you.

ROBERT HEDIN

from *At the Great Door of Morning: Selected Poems and Translations*, 2017

The Wreck of the Great Northern

Where the Great Northern plunged in
The river boiled with light, and we all stood
In the tall grass staring at a tangle
Of track, and four orange coaches
And one Pullman lying under the current,
Turning the current clear. We stood staring
As though it had been there all along
And was suddenly thrust up out of the weeds
That night as a blessing, as a long, sleek hallway
Dropping off into fields we'd never seen,
Into the pastures of some great god
Who sent back our steers too heavy to move,
All bloated and with green seaweed strung down
Their horns. And we all looked down
Into the lit cars at businessmen
And wives, already back to breathing water,
And saw in the cold, clear tanks of the Pullman
A small child the size of my son, a porter's
White jacket, a nylon floating gracefully
As an eel.
                    What the train and the river
Were saying, no one could understand.
We just stood there, breathing what was left
Of the night. How still the cars were,
How sleek, shimmering through the undertow.
And I saw the trees around us blossomed out,
The wind had come back and was blowing
Through the tall empty grass, through the high
Grain fields, the wind was rattling
The dry husks of corn.

LAURA KASISCHKE

from *Where Now: New and Selected Poems,* 2017

Green

Like the worm on its way to the center of the cabbage:
A crisis at the core of certain things.
Loves that couldn't last. The boy in Spain. The death-

row pen pal. The old
woman walking straight into the mirror, and then
rubbing her eyes, backing up, trying it again.

We all cried, *Stop!* but she kept walking.

And you were warned that it would be
a happy song followed by a brutal fact.
Eagle-headed god forged out of gold. A rag stuffed into a human hole.
My young son at the planetarium, and how
he asked me when they turned the lights back on,
"Are we on Earth again
now, Mom?" To end it all
on the universe's terms.

Or not:
Needleful
of pentobarbital.
And the cat, the cat, our last
green and peaceful gaze after
a lifetime of that. How, after that, in my arms, the

planet's bonds slackened.

To have reached the source of all that sweetness.
That satisfaction.
No turning back.

Who would turn back?

MAURICE MANNING

from *One Man's Dark,* 2017

Culture

Some of us in cahoots with the birds
are smiling silly smiles, because
the sun in the barn lot is warmer
today and that means nothing in
particular, but it is a change.
Someone, my neighbor's neighbor over
the hill, shears sheep and helps
with lambing. Beech Fork, the river,
is named for a tree and in a way
that's a symbol and also an idea;
we have a grove, we have a stand.
We like to be quiet and have our thoughts;
we remember the old piano teacher,
her spinet, an instrument that came
to town on a railroad car
and went by mule and wagon a ways
to the old brick house. We talk,
we graft the apple branch and wait
another season for the fruit;
we have a church house here, it's one
big room, we have a hummingbird
with a silver shiny greenish throat.

MICHAEL MCGRIFF

from *Early Hour,* 2017

I Am an Ox in the Year of the Horse

Your hands have made a yoke
a bright chain of grinding stars
around my neck
and you are pulling me into you
and you have turned me into an ox
of mineral fires and sweat
and you are working me
and I can't tell whether I'm falling inside you
or climbing the mantled dark of you
but I can feel myself moving
through the origin of numbers and carbon
and I can feel your ankles lock around my back
and they too are giving their orders
but they are also two thrushes
volleying their cries against
the invisible canyon of basalt
and you are working me
and I have reached some place in you
where I gnaw down the doors in you
and my teeth grow numb as drunk fishermen
and all the roots in you
suck the water from me
and I enter a depth in you
that pulls your name from my throat
and you are working me
and I'm telling you I am your pilgrim
your animal your thief your pyre
your anvil and echo
and I want to be bound and burned here
and collapse here and beg here and pound here
and unspool one long sound from my body

into this kingdom
where we are two wet shades of black
swimming into the first evening of the universe.

RACHEL MCKIBBENS

from *blud,* 2017

* * *

To my daughters I need to say:

Go with the one who loves you biblically.
The one whose love lifts its head to you

despite its broken neck. Whose body
bursts sixteen arms electric

to carry you, gentle
the way old grief is gentle.

Love the love that is messy
in all its too much. The body

that rides best your body, whose mouth
saddles the naked salt of your far-gone hips,

whose tongue translates the rock language
of all your elegant scars.

Go with the one who cries out for her
tragic sisters as she chops the winter's wood,

the one whose skin triggers your heart
into a heaven of blood waltzes.

Go with the one who resembles most your father.
Not the father you can point out on a map,

but the father who is here, is home,
the key to your front door.

Know that your first love will only be the first,
& the second & third & even fourth

will unprepare you for the most important:
The Blessed. The Beast. The Last Love

which is of course the most terrifying kind.
Because which of us wants to go with what

can murder us? Can reveal to us our true heart's
end & its thirty years spent in poverty?
Can mimic the sound of our bird-throated
mothers, replicate the warmth of our brothers'

tempers, can pull us out of ourselves until we are
no longer sisters or daughters or sword swallowers

but instead women who give & lead & take & want
& want
& want
& want

because there is no shame in wanting. & you will
hear yourself say: Last Love, I wish to die

so I may come back to you new & never tasted
by any other mouth but yours & I want to be the hands

that pull your children out of you & tuck them
deep inside myself until they are ready to be

the children of such a royal & staggering love.
Or you will say: Last Love, I am old & I have

spent myself on the courageless, have wasted
too many clocks on the less-deserving, so I hurl

myself at the throne of you & lie humbly
at your feet. Last Love, let me never

roll out of this heavy dream of you, let the day
I was born mean my life will end where you end

let the man behind the church do what he did
if it brings me to you. Let the girls in the

locker room corner me again if it brings me
to you. Let this wild depression throw me beneath

its hooves if it brings me to you. Let me pronounce
my hoarded joy if it brings me to you.

Let my father break me again & again if it
brings me to you.

Last Love, I have let other men borrow your children.
Forgive me.

Last Love, I once vowed my heart to another.
Forgive me.

Last Love, I have let my blind & anxious hands
wander into a room & come out empty.

Forgive me. Last Love, I have cursed the women
you loved before me. Forgive me.

Last Love, I envy your mother's body
where you resided first. Forgive me.

Last Love, I am all that is left. Forgive me.
I did not see you coming. Forgive me.

Last Love, every day without you was a life
I crawled out of. Amen.

Last Love, you are my Last Love. Amen.
Last Love, I am all that is left. Amen.

I am all that is left.
Amen.

TOMÁS Q. MORÍN

from *Patient Zero,* 2017

Gold Record

Dark was the night the *Voyager* slipped
into space carrying the music of one whale
greeting another, as well as the thud
of the stubborn heart and three,
maybe four, people laughing, the sum
of whose voices isn't that much different
from the few seconds of herded sheep,
at least to my poor, imperfect ear
that still has trouble distinguishing
a caterwaul from a stabbing victim,
two sounds our wise Sagan
did not include on his gilded handshake
to the stars, which is regrettable
because what better way to capture
our tempers and apathy than record
some pitiful soul, hand at his punctured
side, trying to groan louder than the TVs
the neighborhood keeps turning up
because they think he's a pair of cats
fucking under the luminous stars,
the very stars the *Voyager* will photograph
on the sly until it stumbles upon a ship
piloted by a race of beings so starved
for connection they cancel their plans
for the evening and sit on shag rugs—
their favorite souvenir from the seventies
—and cue our golden record
on the turntable they inherited
from their in-laws and never expected to use
for anything other than drinks and magazines
to entertain the occasional visitor, much less to hear
Blind Willie Johnson, that priest of the night

Sagan placed alongside Stravinsky
and company because in the three minutes
and twenty-one seconds Johnson sang for Columbia
in 1927 he moaned to the heavens
about homelessness or immortality or some
other mumbo jumbo any race smart enough to escape
gravity and cross the peacock-black
of galaxies would never believe because they
would know the blues are always about love
gone cold, and its light, the clammy light we might spend
years saying we can't live without and then do.

LISA OLSTEIN

from *Late Empire,* 2017

What We're Trying to Do Is Create a Community of Dreamers

Horses, airplanes, red cars,
running. The Japanese sleep
less but do they dream less?
What do women in Stockholm
dream about in wintertime?
Show me every car dream.
Show me every car dream
in Moscow. Show me every
red-car dream that involved
men living in Las Vegas.
Compare that to Tokyo or Paris.
Do famous people dream
differently? If you have
more money in the bank?
Can we run an algorithm,
can we quantify, can we teach
that? The distance widens
and narrows, sometimes
a grapefruit, sometimes
a beach ball. Invisible data.
They say Einstein came up
with relativity in a dream.
What if you could go back
and find it?

DEAN RADER

from *Self-Portrait as Wikipedia Entry,* 2017

America, I Do Not Call Your Name without Hope

after Neruda

America, I do not call your name without hope
not even when you lay your knife
against my throat or lace my hands
behind my back, the cuffs connecting
us like two outlaws trying to escape
history's white horse, its heavy whip
a pistolshot in the ear. Lost land,
this is a song for the scars on your back,
for your blistered feet and beautiful
watch, it is for your windmills, your
magic machines, for your fists. It
is for your wagon of blood, for your dogs
and their teeth of fire, for your sons
and the smoke in their hearts. This is for
your verbs, your long lurk, your whir.
This is for you and your fear, your tar,
for the white heat in your skin, and
for your blue bones that one day may sing.
This is for your singing. This is for the past,
but not for what's passed. This is for daybreak
and backbreak, for dreams, and for darkness.
This song is not for your fight but it is a song
for fighting. It is a song of flame but not for burning.
It is a song out of breath but a plea for breathing.
It is the song I will sing when you knock
on my door, my son's name in your mouth.

NATALIE SHAPERO

from *Hard Child*, 2017

God Only

The wisdom is this:
when bitten by a cobra,
pray to the skies

the cobra is full-grown.
Adults will ration
their stores of poison,

spit just enough
to stun, while the young
ones, uncontrolled,

give all they've got.
It's supposed to be
the child who

rages and wavers.
It's supposed to be
the child who clumsily

kills. I remember
my old love holding me
once over the side

of some canyon.
DROP ME, I ordered, and
he goddamn tried.

That's right—it is not
God only I have asked
to take my life.

NATALIE SHAPERO

from *Hard Child,* 2017

Mostly I Don't Want to Have a Son—

too many fears. What if he knows the ancients
believed more boys than girls were born in wartime,
to account for casualties in battle, leave
the world in balance? What if he cannot tell
whether or not it is wartime, whether or not
his purpose is mere replacement? What if he flees
to a field of ice, lucks into a research job
itemizing the stomach contents of terns,
inducing them to spit up their prey for science?
What if he makes a mistake and a bird falls ill,
and to spare pain, he must bludgeon her with a rock?
What if he forges his home on a rockless coast?
What if he has to kill her with his fist?
What if he then finds solace in superstition?
What if he won't breathe when passing a graveyard?
What if he doesn't realize so many are murdered
that graveyards run for miles? What if he goes blue,
endeavoring to avoid the breath of the dead?
What if he does not die but instead is damaged?
What if he must rely on the aid of a dog?
What if he does not care for the dog, and strikes it,
and leaves it out to swelter, and someone yells
I'D HATE TO SEE WHAT YOU WOULD DO TO A CHILD,
and runs off? I don't want to have a son.
A daughter is simpler. All she needs to learn
is neither to speed nor be caught, and if she is caught,
make him follow her to a parking lot,
somewhere bright and unclosing, before she cuts
the engine. Always ask to see a badge.

NATALIE SHAPERO

from *Hard Child,* 2017

The Sky

Whatever I care for, someone else loves it
more, deserves it more: the doe with her
whole mouth crushing the phlox or the seer
who adores my future, whereas I could

take it or leave it. I know I'll disappear.
It won't be glamorous. It won't be like when
the *Mona Lisa* was stolen and the tourists all
lined up to pay their respects at the empty
spot on the wall of the Louvre.

I've never actually even seen the sky.
I've only ever seen effluents, seen wattage.

The only night I remember is the dinner
of neighbors at which a man I never
had met before said *I don't fear dying—*

look at the past, people have been dying forever, and—

then he stopped and shook his head—
I drank too much. I was almost saying
that people have died forever and all
of them survived, but of course—he made
a hard laugh—*God, of course they didn't survive.*

JAVIER ZAMORA

from *Unaccompanied*, 2017

Let Me Try Again

I could bore you with the sunset, the way water tasted
    after so many days without it,
                the trees,
the breed of dogs, but I can't say
                there were forty people
when we found the ranch with the thin white man,
    his dogs,
        and his shotgun.

Until this 5 a.m. I couldn't remember
        there were only five,
or seven people—

We'd separated by the paloverdes.
    We, meaning:
        four people. Not forty.
The rest . . .
    I don't know.
        They weren't there
when the thin white man
        let us drink from a hose
while pointing his shotgun.
        In pocho Spanish he told us
si correr perros atacar.
        If run dogs trained attack.

When La Migra arrived, an officer
    who probably called himself Hispanic at best,

not Mejicano like we called him, said
        buenas noches
    and gave us pan dulce y chocolate.

Procedure says he should've taken us
    back to the station,

checked our fingerprints,
                  etcétera.

He must've remembered his family
    over the border,

or the border coming over them,
    because he drove us to the border

and told us
    next time, rest at least five days,

don't trust anyone calling themselves coyotes,
    bring more tortillas, sardines, Alhambra.

He knew we would try again
    and again,
            like everyone does.

GHASSAN ZAQTAN

from *The Silence That Remains: Selected Poems,* 2017
Translated from the Arabic by Fady Joudah

A Song

The glory that has been evenly split
among everyone
into medals for the leaders
praise for rank and file
and pictures for the dead
has finished its cycle
and is leaning now
on sandbags so you can roll
and smoke your whole
tobacco pack
before the next war comes

Their Absence

And what remains
but little little
and their shirts
fabric that spreads on trees
and their shirts

banners that tug
only at trees

and are not retrieved
a triumph

DANTE ALIGHIERI

from *Purgatorio: A New Verse Translation,* 2018
Translated from the Italian by W.S. Merwin

from Canto XVII

Remember, reader, if ever, high in
the mountains, the fog caught you, so you could see
only as moles do, looking through their skin,

how when the humid, dense vapors begin
to grow thinner the sphere of the sun
finds its way feebly in among them,

and your imagination will easily
picture how, at first, I came to see
the sun again, already going down.

So, keeping pace with my master's trusted
footsteps, out of a fog like that I came
when already the beams on the shore below were dead.

Oh imagination, who sometimes steal us
so from things outside us that we do not notice
if a thousand trumpets sound around us,

who moves you if the senses give you nothing?
A light moves you, in the heavens forming
by itself, or by some will that guides it downward.

Of her impious act who changed her own
shape to that bird's who most delights in singing
the form appeared in my imagination,

and at this my mind became so turned
upon itself that it took in nothing,
at the time, that came to it from outside it.

Then there rained down, in the high fantasy,
one who was crucified; scornful and fierce
he looked out, and so he was about to die.

JENNY GEORGE

from *The Dream of Reason*, 2018

Death of a Child

    I

This is how a child dies:
His breath
curdles. His hands
soften, apricots
heavy on their branches.

I can't explain it.
I can't explain it.

On the walk back to the car
even the stones in the yards
are burning. Far overhead
in the dead orchard of space
a star explodes
and then collapses
into a black door.

This is the afterlife, but
I'm not dead. I'm just
here in this field.

    2

It made a boy-shaped hole
and filled—

the way a crushed hand fills
suddenly up
with new pain,

or a well put down
taps the liquid silt.

The center pours
toward the surface.

Now the hand is given
to the earth.
The mouth draws up
clay
and drinks.

    3

There's something uneasy in the field.
A wake. A ripple in the cloth.
We see the green corn moving
but not the thing that moves it.
The atoms of our bodies turn
bright gold and silky. Aimed
at death, we live. We keep on
doing this. Night unfolds helplessly
into day. Beyond the field are more
fields and through them, too—
this current. What is it? Where
is it going? Did you see it? Can you
catch it? Can you kill it? Can you hold
it still? Can you hold it still forever?

    4

The conductor's baton hovers
for a moment in the alert
silence (a silence that leans forward
saying *Now . . . ! Now . . . !*) and then it drops
into the chasm.

Sound enters the bodies
of all the people simultaneously,
calling them to feel together

an unconcealed fear, a cup over-
flowing, a sense of absolute love
vibrating in the dark passages—
the long-ago cry of pain
and the crack of light
coming in through the bars.

BOB HICOK

from *Hold,* 2018

Pacific

This kid had never seen the ocean,
I'd never seen a kid seeing the ocean
for the first time, and the ocean
had never been this close to Main Street,
according to the woman behind the desk
at the hotel, where the night before,
a moth landed on my shoulder, along with the moon.
He told us he was from up north,
then pointed at a man and woman fighting
so far away, we couldn't hear what they were saying
while their arms were furious with the air.
It's so big, he said.
The biggest thing in the world
that isn't the world, I thought
would be a way to put it, but just nodded.
By standing still next to his standing still
and my wife's, I was hoping
we'd build a little shelter for him,
a moment he could hold in the car
during the long drive with his untamed parents
and think, It was nice,
listening to the radio of the ocean
with those people.
But that's the kind of thought
I'd have in a poem, not what a kid would think
at all. And it was rude
to tell the moth it was a symbol of death.
It reminded me of snowflakes on my shoulder,
another kind of softness
that doesn't last, except as the desire
to carry someone barefoot over broken glass.

HA JIN

from *A Distant Center*, 2018

You Must Not Run in Place

Don't say since life is short and precarious,
you want to live effortlessly.
Don't brag you will try to outsmart time—
every day you'll watch movies and eat dim sum
while chatting idly with friends.

Better keep busy like the others
who work for a sack of rice or a set of clothes.
See how steady those footsteps are on the wharf,
look at the ships leaving the port—
heavy, they are still going far.

TED KOOSER

from *Kindest Regards: New and Selected Poems,* 2018

Daddy Longlegs

Here, on fine long legs springy as steel,
a life rides, sealed in a small brown pill
that skims along over the basement floor
wrapped up in a simple obsession.
Eight legs reach out like the master ribs
of a web in which some thought is caught
dead center in its own small world,
a thought so far from the touch of things
that we can only guess at it. If mine,
it would be the secret dream
of walking alone across the floor of my life
with an easy grace, and with love enough
to live on at the center of myself.

URSULA K. LE GUIN

from *So Far So Good: Final Poems: 2014–2018,* 2018

Travelers

I

We came from the far side of the river
of starlight and will cross back over
in a little boat
no bigger than two cupped hands.

II

Thinking about compassion.
A firefly in a great dark garden.
An earthworm naked
on a concrete path.

III

I think of the journey
we will take together
in the oarless boat
across the shoreless river.

URSULA K. LE GUIN

from *So Far So Good: Final Poems: 2014–2018*, 2018

Wakeful: Islanded

Snow and silence in the streets.
Winter in the bone.
In silent houses people sleep
each one alone.
Self-islanded by thought and dream
the solitary soul
forgets the deepest depth, the earth
that joins us all.

AIMEE NEZHUKUMATATHIL

from *Oceanic,* 2018

Sea Church

Give me a church
made entirely of salt.
Let the walls hiss
and smoke when
I return to shore.

I ask for the grace
of a new freckle
on my cheek, the lift
of blue and my mother's
soapy skin to greet me.

Hide me in a room
with no windows.
Never let me see
the dolphins leaping
into commas

for this waterprayer
rising like a host
of paper lanterns
in the inky evening.
Let them hang

in the sky until
they vanish at the edge
of the constellations—
the heroes and animals
too busy and bright to notice.

DAVID ORR

from *Dangerous Household Items*, 2018

Sandbox

My child puts her hands
Into the sand with the hands
Of other children, whose hands
Are warm from the hands
Of other parents, and the sand
Is no longer merely sand
But a small history of sand
As translated by the sand
In this particular playground,
As now the background
Of hands, sand, and ground
Rises into the foreground,
And my child's small form
Blurs with the larger form
Of children drawing form
From the sand's formless form
And I want it to stop.
I want the blurring to stop,
For my child's image to stop
Eroding in sand that won't stop
Covering itself in itself
As if it had forgotten itself
And had to repeat itself
In order to maintain itself.

MELISSA STEIN

from *Terrible blooms,* 2018

Racetrack

Velvet and shit: I summoned it
and come it did. The horses' flanks
are rank with sweat and flies and I
remember you between my legs
achieving for an hour or so.
We parted on the best of terms:
the sweet unsayable loss that's gain
in drag. The day hurt a little
brighter for all that sharpening.
I have a turnstile heart; it opens
madly and shuts just so.
In morning cold, the horses'
breath takes on the shape of terrible
blooms. The hoof-stamps sound less
urgently. I'm not talking about my heart.

TANEUM BAMBRICK

from *Vantage,* 2019

New Hire

Real fine heifer / low class beauty / what do you call those blonde / feathering / got yourself a new work buddy / not the only / Victoria's Secret / pulling plastic from the reeds / she walks like she / begging / I'd give my / see her bend again / please / how many colors of lace / shoe string / her strapped black / can you imagine / bleached / I've got a family / you might be the same / like a different breed / poor thing you / couldn't compete / could learn a / thank God thank affirmative action / I'm reeling it in / calling my children / I'm a good / never cheated but / if you wonder why she's not out / spearing / in the weeds she / flashed the crew lead / he said he / right in truck 43 / ten out of / after she lifted / ballooning / can you picture / all the effort / of her / how does she walk with / gathering all that weight / into her / can you imagine her / like I already know her / out of her / clothing

LINDA BIERDS

from *The Hardy Tree*, 2019

Cento for Sydney

Between the woods and frozen lake,
Above the narrow road through pine barrens,
On the other side of the bridge,

I heard no voice in the heart, just the hum of the wires.
A shadow imperceptibly darkening
Swayed like the slow movement of a hunting bird

Then all the birds of the air
Glittered a bit above the landscape, the hills
Suffused still with a faint retroactive light.

I don't believe that we will be lifted up
                              and transfixed by radiance
But I could not resist the lovely shape
Against the sunlight and the future's glare:

A shadow imperceptibly darkening
Then all the birds of the air,
Their sudden white underwings. I follow

The cold, never letting go of you,
That day and this,
Our leaves and lakes, our woods.

I think from this distance
About things given that are taken away
And given again in another form.

I don't believe in the inextinguishable light
                              of the other world,
But I could not resist the lovely shape,
This lightest of curtains the curve of it shines.

JERICHO BROWN

from *The Tradition*, 2019

Bullet Points

I will not shoot myself
In the head, and I will not shoot myself
In the back, and I will not hang myself
With a trashbag, and if I do,
I promise you, I will not do it
In a police car while handcuffed
Or in the jail cell of a town
I only know the name of
Because I have to drive through it
To get home. Yes, I may be at risk,
But I promise you, I trust the maggots
Who live beneath the floorboards
Of my house to do what they must
To any carcass more than I trust
An officer of the law of the land
To shut my eyes like a man
Of God might, or to cover me with a sheet
So clean my mother could have used it
To tuck me in. When I kill me, I will
Do it the same way most Americans do,
I promise you: cigarette smoke
Or a piece of meat on which I choke
Or so broke I freeze
In one of these winters we keep
Calling worst. I promise if you hear
Of me dead anywhere near
A cop, then that cop killed me. He took
Me from us and left my body, which is,
No matter what we've been taught,
Greater than the settlement
A city can pay a mother to stop crying,
And more beautiful than the new bullet
Fished from the folds of my brain.

JERICHO BROWN

from *The Tradition*, 2019

Duplex

The opposite of rape is understanding
A field of flowers called paintbrushes—

      A field of flowers called paintbrushes,
      Though the spring be less than actual.

Though the spring be less than actual,
Men roam shirtless as if none ever hurt me.

      Men roam that myth. In truth, one hurt me.
      I want to obliterate the flowered field,

To obliterate my need for the field
And raise a building above the grasses,

      A building of prayer against the grasses,
      My body a temple in disrepair.

My body is a temple in disrepair.
The opposite of rape is understanding.

JERICHO BROWN

from *The Tradition,* 2019

Duplex: Cento

My last love drove a burgundy car,
Color of a rash, a symptom of sickness.

> We were the symptoms, the road our sickness:
> None of our fights ended where they began.

None of the beaten end where they begin.
Any man in love can cause a messy corpse,

> But I didn't want to leave a messy corpse
> Obliterated in some lilied field,

Stench obliterating lilies of the field,
The murderer, young and unreasonable.

> He was so young, so unreasonable,
> Steadfast and awful, tall as my father.

Steadfast and awful, my tall father
Was my first love. He drove a burgundy car.

JERICHO BROWN

from *The Tradition*, 2019

Foreday in the Morning

My mother grew morning glories that spilled onto the walkway toward her porch
Because she was a woman with land who showed as much by giving it color.
She told me I could have whatever I worked for. That means she was an American.
But she'd say it was because she believed
In God. I am ashamed of America
And confounded by God. I thank God for my citizenship in spite
Of the timer set on my life to write
These words: I love my mother. I love black women
Who plant flowers as sheepish as their sons. By the time the blooms
Unfurl themselves for a few hours of light, the women who tend them
Are already at work. Blue. I'll never know who started the lie that we are lazy,
But I'd love to wake that bastard up
At foreday in the morning, toss him in a truck, and drive him under God
Past every bus stop in America to see all those black folk
Waiting to go work for whatever they want. A house? A boy
To keep the lawn cut? Some color in the yard? My God, we leave things green.

DEBORAH LANDAU

from *Soft Targets,* 2019

the silence will be sudden then last

     *

We rocked it for a while in New York

it seemed like quite the era

and had the martinis to prove it

many magnificents

but the footlights were shining too brightly now

was our time past?

We're not in our coffinclothes, not yet

Don't mope, Mother would say

(but I'm so very good at it!)

On the other hand

I'm feeling kinda good today in my ginny way

and bought myself some cocktails

and thought of the planet wheel

and how one might

hop off

*

I'll antioxidize as best I can
bat away death with berries and flax
but there's no surviving
this slick merciless world
a bucket of guts we'll be
full-blown dead
though why wax gloomy
we're not real
just a pudding of flesh
trying gamely to preserve ourselves
my ducky grandee, glowing friend
let's sing a bit   this may end
in love may end in blood
but it will   (badly) end

*

Sybaritic afterlife I don't crave you.
I like daylight, I like crowds,
I don't think it will be charming underground.
The silence will be sudden then last—

what's chic will shrink,
there won't be any pretty, pity,
will never peaches there, or air,
we'll be so squashed and sour there.

I don't want a cold place,
don't want a threadbare
clamp and consequence all old.
Our loneliness will be prolonged then go too far.

Oh fuck it's true,
then nothing left of you.

*

Has it turned out we've wasted our time?
We've wasted our time.

Our magnificent bodies on the dissecting table,
our day after tomorrow,
our what to do now.

The stink of us so undignified—
the endgame of bloom.

We will lose the sun,
struck and disassembled
lightly down and crawling like a worm.

This earth it is a banquet and laid on its table we—
a puncture in the wound room, crude and obvious.

The raving lunatics they are upon us,
but we are raving too.

LIU TSUNG-YUAN

from *Written in Exile: The Poetry of Liu Tsung-yuan,* 2019
Translated from the Chinese by Red Pine

9. Meeting a Farmer at the Start of Spring

Spring arrives early in southern Ch'u
things start to grow while it's cold
the power of the earth is loose in the land
hibernating creatures are stirring
there's no color yet in the countryside
but farmers are already plowing
I can hear birds singing in the orchards
I can see springs flowing in the marshes
farming of course is honest work
but an exile is cut off from normal life
my old pond I imagine is overgrown
the family farm all thorns and vines
I would be a hermit but I'm not free
nothing I try succeeds
I related all this to a farmer
explaining my situation in detail
he kept rubbing the handle of his plow
and turning to look at the looming clouds

LIU TSUNG-YUAN

from *Written in Exile: The Poetry of Liu Tsung-yuan,* 2019
Translated from the Chinese by Red Pine

44. Reading Books

Living in obscurity I've given up current affairs
I bow my head in silence and reflect on the sage kings
the highs and lows of the ancient past
the ups and downs of countless paths
I laugh to myself when I'm pleased
when I'm sad I simply sigh
I take my books from their cases
I go through from front to back
despite the affliction of tropical diseases
I feel different than in the past
while reading I suddenly understand
when I'm done my mind is a blank
who can I talk with at night
if not these texts on bamboo and silk
I lie down when I get tired
after a good sleep I feel refreshed
I yawn and stretch my limbs
I read out loud to my heart's content
I enjoy doing what suits me
not to please learned men
I shut up when I've said what I want
free of restraints I relax
the clever consider me stupid
the wise think I'm a fool
but reading has managed to make me happy
what good is working till you drop
cherish this body of yours
don't use it to chase after fame

PAISLEY REKDAL

from *Nightingale,* 2019

The Cry

A man can cry, all night, your back
shaking against me as your mother
sleeps, hooked to the drip
to clear her kidneys from their muck
of sleeping pills. Each one white
as the snapper's belly I once watched a man
gut by the ice bins in his truck, its last
bubbling grunt cleaved in two
with a knife. The way my uncle's rabbit
growled in its cage, screamed
so like a child that when I woke the night
a fox chewed through the wires
to reach it, I thought it was my own voice
frozen in the yard. And then the fox,
trapped later by a neighbor, which thrashed
and barked as did the crows
that came for its eyes: the sound
of one animal's pain setting off a chain
in so many others, until each cry dissolves
into the next grown louder.
Even if I were blind
I would know night by the noise it made:
our groaning bed, the mewling
staircase, drapes that scrape
against glass panes behind which
stars rise, blue and silent.
But not even the stars
are silent: their pale waves
keen through space, echoing the dark
the way my father's disappointment
sags at my cheek, and his brother's angers

whiten his temple. And these
are your mother's shoulders shaking
in my arms tonight, her thin breath
that drags at our window where
coyotes cry: one calling to the next
calling to the next, their tender throats
tipped back to the sky.

ALISON C. ROLLINS

from *Library of Small Catastrophes,* 2019

Elephants Born without Tusks

The *Washington Post* says that green burials are on
the rise as baby boomers plan for their futures,

their graves marked with sprouting mushrooms,
little kneecaps crawling up from the dirt's skin

like Michael Brown decomposing into the concrete
ending as a natural product of the environment.

Elephants are now being born without tusks,
their genetics having studied the black market,

DNA a spiral ladder carefully carved
from wooden teeth of Founding Fathers.

Never let a chromosome speak for you, it will
only tell a myth—an ode to the survival of the fittest.

Peppered moths are used to teach natural selection,
their changes in color an instance of evolution.

Birds unable to see dark moths on soot-covered trees.
The number of blacks always rising with industry.

Life is the process of erosion, an inevitable wearing down
of the enamel. The gums posing the threat of disease.

Most websites suggest biodegradation,
a coffin made from pine or wicker.

The man in the paper said, *I want to be part of a tree,*
be part of a flower—go back to being part of the Earth.

I imagined my mother then, her short-cropped hair
like freshly cut grass, immune to the pains of mowing.

*The Natural Burial Guide for Turning Yourself into a
Forest* sits waiting in my Amazon shopping cart.

Pink salmon have now evolved to migrate earlier.
I am familiar with this type of Middle Passage,

a loved one watching you move on without a trace,
the living inheriting an ocean of time,

the sun rewiring the water-damaged insides,
cells desiring to go back where they came from,

certain strands of
your kind now extinct.

from *Lima :: Limón*, 2019

My Macho Takes Care of Me Good

because he's a citizen de los united estates.
I got a stove this big, a refri this full, a mirror
just to see my pretty face. He says:

My name's on this license. I drive la troca,
so you don't have to, mi'ja. I am a citizen
de los united estates. Because he's a citizen,

we are muy lejos de dios, but we love
los united estates. I don't wash laundry with cakes
of Jabón Zote, because my macho

takes care of me good. I bring my macho
Nescafé, American made, because he's a citizen
de los united estates. I ask for feria to go to a doctor,

& he says: *Ingrata, you're not sick.*
I clean chiles, then rub my eyes—
¡Siempre llora-lloras, chillona!

& he's right, I lloro-lloro sin saber
por qué. I bring my macho smoke in a glass
& smooth every shirt with my new electric iron.

He says: *No hay nadie en casa. ¿Why wear*
clothes at all? So I don't. I fry chicharrones.
Hiss-hiss, across my bare skin. *Bang-bang,*

my macho's fists on the table. He wants más, más,
y más in his united estates. I give him all of me
served on a platter from back home:

plump, cracked & ready-made. *Crunch-crunch,*
eats my macho. *You married him,* says my mother,
& he takes care of you good in his united estates.

JOSEPH STROUD

from *Everything That Rises,* 2019

Hovering

for Tom Marshall

Tom and I are walking Last Chance Road
down from the mountain where we had been
hunting mushrooms under a stand of coast oaks,
walking down and looking out to the Pacific
shimmering in the late fall sun, the light
on the surface like glittering flakes of mica,
when we see a white-tailed kite hovering
in the air, hovering over a green pasture,
hovering over the day, over the two of us,
our very lives hovering as well, there
on the California coast, in the fall, in the sun,
on our way home, with a sack of chanterelles,
with our love for this world, with so much time,
and so little time—all of it—hovering—
and hovering still.

from *Sight Lines,* 2019

First Snow

A rabbit has stopped on the gravel driveway:

> imbibing the silence,
> you stare at spruce needles:

>> there's no sound of a leaf blower,
>> no sign of a black bear;

a few weeks ago, a buck scraped his rack
> against an aspen trunk;
> a carpenter scribed a plank along a curved stone wall.

> You only spot the rabbit's ears and tail:

when it moves, you locate it against speckled gravel,
but when it stops, it blends in again;

> the world of being is like this gravel:

>> you think you own a car, a house,
>> this blue-zigzagged shirt, but you just borrow these things.

Yesterday, you constructed an aqueduct of dreams
> and stood at Gibraltar,
>> but you possess nothing.

Snow melts into a pool of clear water;
> and, in this stillness,

>> starlight behind daylight wherever you gaze.

KEITH S. WILSON

from *Fieldnotes on Ordinary Love,* 2019

Fieldnotes

1

in physics dark matter isn't made
of anything. it's a free citizen

that passes
unburdened through the field, through itself,

through you—

2

it helps to observe from a distance:
the field, for instance,

as a statement

the south has chosen to make,
the way whiteness too
is often rhetorical, as when an older student remarks

in those beginning days that only he observed mlk's holiday
while his black friends, working, did not

3

sometimes love is a black dot
in a field

sometimes, suddenly
it is not

4

or how can black be

the absence
of all color? take this cruiser. see the light strike blue off the car like copper
            through a fountain

5

there is a difference between what is fair and what is just,
for instance,

it is fair
that i try
to love your skin even when it is not touching my own

6

whiteness is an alibi, the way the officer was like a steam-
engine
        only i could see

7

inside where nothing shows i am of course not black
but that does not matter

to the field

8

some colors are indistinguishable
at night. *put your hands behind your back*

a different cop once asked me.
it was so sincere. he was so

polite

9

as a boy you learn to know the inside
without being required to feel it

as when, now, i understand a bucket
        or a hood

        10

he asks my girlfriend not if she is white
since even in this light

what we are is obvious

but instead he speaks philosophically:

ma'am he asks
are you here of your own free will

        11

sometimes whiteness is a form itself
of hyperbole. try this:

sit in a field. then try reading

andrew jackson's quotes on liberty
only
pretend they are being written by his slaves

        12

look at the word black
on the paper
& you will see a definite black,   a kind,

a certainty,

or if you see nothing at all that of course
is a kind of black too

13

by the road
my father showed me cotton
once

look at that
he said

DEAN YOUNG

from *Solar Perplexus,* 2019

To Poetry

The first you I tried to write
had a penguin and made me happy
to be with you even if, actually
because I couldn't understand you,
not what your atomic number was or why
O why you're so flocked with the creepy
and the dull when you can blow up the world
then origami it into a cosmic rose.
Half the time you're tilling through
my solar plexus, half I can't find you
anywhere and half you're Shari
letting me hold her canary
for cleansing. No, you don't add up
although you make some crazy square
roots and repeating decimals. Composed
of conspiracies of vowels, voices, voices,
a huge rectangle full of sticky notes,
glory in a leaf, the aster in disaster,
and—why not?—a new bill of rights.
Something reaches out of you
with a red trophy to whoever
approacheth you nude but
the Texas legislature hates you,
wants you out of college curricula
like Thomas Jefferson and evolution
out of textbooks. You, of course,
are above it all like a let-go kite
as well as below vascularizing crypts.
Maybe there ain't no such thing as death,
just shucked worm casts. Moondust
tastes like gunpowder and the universe,
we're told, is beige, a color known

to absorb pain. Poetry, I love
you certainly without any irritable
reaching after fact. Resistance
makes you shine.

MATTHEW ZAPRUDER

from *Father's Day,* 2019

Poem for Doom

Birds don't lie
they are never lost
above the earth
they never think
I stole this form
or *blue is the best*
I listen to it
singing my old man
is far away
singing American
songs stolen
from those who lived
in what now is
but was not
the park which makes
me love him
I am eating an orange
someone grabbed
from nature
over me I hear
controlled mechanical
obsidian dragonflies
search for anarchists
for a long time
I went to school
in the palm of my life
carrying a stone
obeying the law
of semblance
now each night
I bring it back
down to the land

asphodels cover
then I wake
and take my son
out on the porch
to say hello
everything hello
green hills that slept
hello tree
drawn on the side
of a white truck
exorably rumbling
toward some hole
hello magnolia
whose pink
and white blossoms
have left it
for where
oh sweet doom
we are all going
then behind us
we close
the black door
with the golden knob
and sit
in the great
chair morning light
through the shades
always makes
look like a dream
forest throne
all around
our subjects
the shadow trees
rise up
their private thoughts
filling the room
I take them
like an animal
with gentle

ungrateful ceremony
from a leaf
takes dew

2020—2023

ELLEN BASS

from *Indigo,* 2020

Indigo

As I'm walking on West Cliff Drive, a man runs
toward me pushing one of those jogging strollers
with shock absorbers so the baby can keep sleeping,
which this baby is. I can just get a glimpse
of its almost translucent eyelids. The father is young,
a jungle of indigo and carnelian tattooed
from knuckle to jaw, leafy vines and blossoms,
saints and symbols. Thick wooden plugs pierce
his lobes and his sunglasses testify
to the radiance haloed around him. I'm so jealous.
As I often am. It's a kind of obsession.
I want him to have been my child's father.
I want to have married a man who wanted
to be in a body, who wanted to live in it so much
that he marked it up like a book, underlining,
highlighting, writing in the margins, I was *here.*
Not like my dead ex-husband, who was always
fighting against the flesh, who sat for hours
on his zafu chanting *om* and then went out
and broke his hand punching the car.
I imagine when this galloping man gets home
he's going to want to have sex with his wife,
who slept in late, and then he'll eat
barbecued ribs and let the baby teethe on a bone
while he drinks a dark beer. I can't stop
wishing my daughter had had a father like that.
I can't stop wishing I'd had that life. Oh, I know
it's a miracle to have a life. Any life at all.
It took eight years for my parents to conceive me.
First there was the war and then just waiting.
And my mother's bones so narrow, she had to be slit
and I airlifted. That anyone is born,

403

each precarious success from sperm and egg
to zygote, embryo, infant, is a wonder.
And here I am, alive.
Almost seventy years and nothing has killed me.
Not the car I totaled running a stop sign
or the spirochete that screwed into my blood.
Not the tree that fell in the forest exactly
where I was standing—my best friend shoving me
backward so I fell on my ass as it crashed.
I'm alive.
And I gave birth to a child.
So she didn't get a father who'd sling her
onto his shoulder. And so much else she didn't get.
I've cried most of my life over that.
And now there's everything that we can't talk about.
We love—but cannot take
too much of each other.
Yet she is the one who, when I asked her to kill me
if I no longer had my mind—
we were on our way into Ross,
shopping for dresses. That's something
she likes and they all look adorable on her—
she's the only one
who didn't hesitate or refuse
or waver or flinch.
As we strode across the parking lot
she said, OK, but when's the cutoff?
That's what I need to know.

MARK BIBBINS

from *13th Balloon,* 2020

"A person I knew for a short time"

A person I knew for a short time

a short time after you died

guessed incorrectly that I would sleep

with him and furthermore that I slept with

a copy of *Bartlett's Familiar Quotations*

next to my bed   Though wrong

on both counts he was right

when he said I blushed absurdly

                         and too easily

but when I told him about you

he was taken a little aback

perhaps surprised that I had lived

through anything

I should remember now

what Velvet Underground song

after I turned him down

for the last time he left

on my answering machine in order

to convey that I was no

longer worthy even of his disdain

      I never told him the book

that was next to my bed was the copy

of *The Selected Poems of Frank O'Hara*

you had given me before you died

Yesterday someone told me that Frank's friend

the painter Mike Goldberg had died

and from here I can see myself

in my tenement room

on a night more than two decades gone

opening to Frank's birthday ode to Mike

when I reached down

to the floor next to my bed

to pick up the book that had been yours

    / / /

TRACI BRIMHALL

from *Come the Slumberless to the Land of Nod*, 2020

Love Poem without a Drop of Hyperbole

I love you like ladybugs love windowsills, love you
like sperm whales love squid. There's no depth

I wouldn't follow you through. I love you like
the pawns in chess love aristocratic horses.

I'll throw myself in front of a bishop or a queen
for you. Even a sentient castle. My love is crazy

like that. I like that sweet little hothouse mouth
you have. I like to kiss you with tongue, with gusto,

with socks still on. I love you like a vulture loves
the careless deer at the roadside. I want to get

all up in you. I love you like Isis loved Osiris,
but her devotion came up a few inches short.

I'll train my breath and learn to read sonar until
I retrieve every lost blood vessel of you. I swear

this love is ungodly, not an ounce of suffering in it.
Like salmon with its upstream itch, I'll dodge grizzlies

for you. Like hawks to skyscraper rooftops,
I'll keep coming back. Maddened. A little hopeless.

Embarrassingly in love. And that's why I'm on
the couch kissing pictures on my phone instead of

calling you in from the kitchen where you are
undoubtedly making dinner too spicy, but when

you hold the spoon to my lips and ask if it's ready
I'll say it is, always, but never, there is never enough.

VICTORIA CHANG

from *Obit,* 2020

America

America—died on February 14, 2018,
and my dead mother doesn't know.
Since her death, America has died a
series of small deaths, each one less
precise than the next. My tears are
now shaped like hooks but my heart
is damp still. If it is lucky, it is in the
middle of its beats. The unlucky dead
children hold telegrams they must hand
to a woman at a desk. The woman will
collect their belongings and shadows.
My dead mother asks each of these
children if they know me, have seen
me, how tall my children are now.
They will tell her that they once lived
in Florida, not California. She will see
the child with the hole in his head. She
will blow the dreams out of the hole
like dust. I used to think death was a
kind of anesthesia. Now I imagine
long lines, my mother taking in all the
children. I imagine her touching their
hair. How she might tickle their knees
to make them laugh. The dead hold the
other half of our ticket. The dead are an
image of wind. And when they comb
their hair, our trees rustle.

LEILA CHATTI

from *Deluge,* 2020

Confession

Oh, I wish I had died before this and was in oblivion, forgotten.

Mary giving birth, the Holy Qur'an

Truth be told, I like Mary a little better
when I imagine her like this, crouched
and cursing, a boy-God pushing on
her cervix (I like remembering
she had a cervix, her body ordinary
and so like mine), girl-sweat lacing
rivulets like veins in the sand,
her small hands on her knees
not doves but hands, gripping,
a palm pressed to her spine, fronds
whispering like voyeurs overhead—
(oh Mary, like a God, I too take pleasure
in knowing you were not all
holy, that ache could undo you
like a knot)—and, suffering,
I admire this girl who cared
for a moment not about God
or His plans but her own
distinct life, this fiercer Mary who'd disappear
if it saved her, who'd howl *to Hell*
with salvation if it meant this pain,
the blessed adolescent who squatted
indignant in a desert, bearing His child
like a secret she never wanted to hear.

TYREE DAYE

from *Cardinal,* 2020

On Finding a Field

I've been looking for you so long

I need you so so

soso so   much &

it snowed my woes

check my shoes   my purple hands

I've been looking for you   &

Can I plant my heart somewhere

in your mud? May I lie down awhile

under the magnolia in your middle?

Can I dig you up?

I've carried these grandmothers

and uncles for 28 years   my skin

wrapped stones   in my turning-over head

&

I need to put them down

JOHN FREEMAN

from *The Park,* 2020

The Ex–Basketball Players

The ex-basketball players
want to tell me what
it was like playing youth
tournaments during
the war how hilariously and
inappropriately they were dressed
this guy was shot they say
pointing to their point guard
now a conductor
a detail that produces roars
he has scars
for a moment I think he's
going to lift his shirt the quietest
and drollest of the group
instead he talks of an all-night drive back
to Sarajevo in 1995 and how
bandaged and bleeding
into his uniform he told the bus driver
I can't go back
got out with three friends in
Slovenia four a.m.
we took some sleep he says
in the park and phoned a friend of
a friend who asked how we were
three teenagers in a park at dawn
I had this much money in my pocket
we said fine we are okay but two days
later we weren't we had just twenty
euros our agent stalling she
didn't want us showing up smelly in
Italy so the friend of a friend took
us in for a few days it was nice showers

hot food no shelling but by day three
claps hands that's it boys so it's time
for our agent to come through and miraculously
she does we're on a train
across Europe as if our homes aren't on
fire sitting with travelers reading
newspapers as if our sisters aren't
being shot and for months the agent
she shopped us around Europe
taking us to tournaments tryouts
maybe our price was too high
the four of us it was fucking hysterical
no one wants a refugee on their team
we were like four monkeys on a rope
That's when they all double over in
laughter and form a circle and hug
and someone changes the subject

BOB HICOK

from *Red Rover Red Rover,* 2020

Having our cake and being eaten by it, too

How long can you say no
to crème brûlée and peanut butter cups, air-conditioning,
flying to San Fran, flying to New York, the big bag of Fritos,
a new iPhone, new toupee, new hair color,
remodeling the kitchen, a nose job, bigger boobs,
smaller bigger boobs when you get tired
of your bigger bigger boobs, two flat-screens
in the basement, air-conditioning, caramel corn,
sour cream on your baked potato with butter, the V-8,
the turbo V-8, the twin overhead cam turbo V-8,
masturbation, a third Coke, a thirty-second Coke, a line of coke,
a second loan on your house, building a plastic-straw factory
in Chicago, in Kuala Lampur, masturbation, the extra-large pizza
with donut-crusted crust, watering your grass,
cutting your grass, fertilizing your grass,
playing nine holes of golf, eighteen, the dream
of an air-conditioned golf course, air-conditioning:

I hate air-conditioning, resist it until July, late June,
until I sweat at night and can't sleep, until I'm tired,
until the ease of pressing a button three times
and changing the setting on the thermostat from OFF to COOL
takes all of what—a quarter-pound of pressure, two seconds,
the teamwork of a few million neurons—until convenience
kicks the ass of knowledge, until the future recedes
into the future, until I'm human, pass the Coke, the coke,
the Fritos, the next-day delivery of toilet paper, dog food,
and day-old bread: have you ever had pizza

while you masturbate, ever golfed eighteen holes on a plane
to Manitoba, ever told yourself, No, I won't eat that last piece
of chocolate cake, told yourself at six, seven, eight, nine,
ten, eleven, then got up at midnight, walked in dark

through a house your hands have memorized, flicked on a light,
snagged a plate, a fork, gently placed the cake on the plate,
walked it to the table, pulled the chair out, sat down,
and looked at love, your love of cake and your love of your life,
this air-conditioned and heated life that gives you cake,
and devoured the cake and your happiness and any chance
that you can say *No* when you need to, when we need to:

and of course now all I want is everything I want when I want it
plus chocolate cake

LEWIS HYDE

from *The Disappearing Ox: A Modern Version of a Classic Buddhist Tale,* 2020
Translated from the Chinese by Lewis Hyde and with paintings by
Max Gimblett

IX. Turning Back to First Nature

Seeking the Source, the One True Origin: why all this hard work?
Better to stay home as if ears and eyes had never opened.
Sit in the cabin. There is nothing to hunt for beyond the gate.
The streams flow and flowers open, vividly red.

X. Entering the Village with Gift-Giving Hands

Barefoot, bare-chested, he walks into town.
Dusty, spattered with mud, how broadly he grins!
He has no need of magic powers. Near him
the withered trees again come into flower.

JENNIFER L. KNOX

from *Crushing It,* 2020

Crushing It

I don't wanna brag but I'm pretty sure
I got the highest score ever on the ADHD test.
The best part was when Mike asked me to juggle
a hatchet, a balloon full of pudding, and a hamster,
and I was all, "Hold my beer, Mike!" Okay . . .
I tanked it. I could go pro at wrong. Blur—
I mean blue—ribbon wrong. You know that
feeling: you're throwing elbows like nobody's
business but when you finally get up to the window,
you can't sign your name right, and the teller gets
to keep your money? Which is not
legal in ANY state, Mike assures me.
Thank you, Mike (if that is
your real name).

PHILIP METRES

from *Shrapnel Maps*, 2020

My Heart like a Nation

for Yehuda Amichai

You threw off your exile
by clothing yourself in praise,
Yehuda, saying, *my nation
is alive,* Amichai, *in me,*

inhabiting your own body,
your mother-beloved skin.
I'm hairy like you, and afraid,
like you, I'm half animal

and half angel, uncertain
where my tenderness ends
and cruelty begins. *We
did what we had to do,*

you wrote, which in translation
reads: exile. ██████████████
Yehuda, I want your clarity—
to love you, not close the gates

of my heart like a nation
trying to make itself a home
but winding up with a state.
Psalmist, you spoke so tenderly

of peace, but the war persists.
All I have for you is this poem:
a man photographs the sudden
undulating hills. Behind him,

a woman he loves now dreams
that their bed's legs grow roots
beneath, overnight, and spread
a canopy of branches that shoot

pink blooms open and open,
now green with shushing leaves
that shelter and shadow the rucked
bedsheets, the branches burdened

with red apples, apples like eyes
ready to be praised
                              and plucked.

JAMES RICHARDSON

from *For Now,* 2020

From Up Here

From the 5th floor, by a window
no one can open, I think I can hear,
when the bus stops just at sunset,
its gasp open and sigh shut,
its struggle away from the curb.

While those it discharges, mostly alone,
a few pausing to talk, set off
north south east west from the corner,
all bending forward, as if into a wind
that blows from every way at once.

JAMES RICHARDSON

from *For Now,* 2020

from "Vectors 5.1—Otherwise: Aphorisms and Ten-Second Essays"

The secret to unhappiness is knowing exactly what you want.

*

They make a point of seeming dissatisfied, as if it were less important to love their lives than to prove they aren't fooled by them.

*

I like having choices a lot better than using them.

*

What's called creativity is an accident we learn to keep having.

*

Luck whispers *You deserved me.*

*

Self-expression? The things that sound exactly like me are exactly what I try to keep myself from saying. You have to run the water awhile before it's cool and true.

*

The road not taken also would have gotten me home.

ALBERTO RÍOS

from *Not Go Away Is My Name,* 2020

Drunk Monsoon

Drunk rain, its big spill, its heavy falling
Out of the chair of sky that held it,

Water slumping down, not able
To keep itself in the sky any longer,

Not able to stand with any attention on the horizon—
Sloppy suddenly, water everywhere,

It simply lets itself go,
A sudden collapse of the thing inside us all

That keeps us upright.
Drunk rain, it comes down not simply as water

But as so much conversation, the way drunk people talk,
A rain that can't stop or help itself,

Talking in fragments, crying but pretending not to,
But crying. Old loves. Moments remembered,

Mouths kissed. Rain, too, was young once,
But this morning it lets go.

This morning it cannot help itself,
Telling us everything.

ALBERTO RÍOS

from *Not Go Away Is My Name,* 2020

A House Called Tomorrow

You are not fifteen, or twelve, or seventeen—
You are a hundred wild centuries

And fifteen, bringing with you
In every breath and in every step

Everyone who has come before you,
All the yous that you have been,

The mothers of your mother,
The fathers of your father.

If someone in your family tree was trouble,
A hundred were not:

The bad do not win—not finally,
No matter how loud they are.

We simply would not be here
If that were so.

You are made, fundamentally, from the good.
With this knowledge, you never march alone.

You are the breaking news of the century.
You are the good who has come forward

Through it all, even if so many days
Feel otherwise. But think:

When you as a child learned to speak,
It's not that you didn't know words—

It's that, from the centuries, you knew so many,
And it's hard to choose the words that will be your own.

From those centuries we human beings bring with us
The simple solutions and songs,

The river bridges and star charts and song harmonies
All in service to a simple idea:

That we can make a house called tomorrow.
What we bring, finally, into the new day, every day,

Is ourselves. And that's all we need
To start. That's everything we require to keep going.

Look back only for as long as you must,
Then go forward into the history you will make.

Be good, then better. Write books. Cure disease.
Make us proud. Make yourself proud.

And those who came before you?
When you hear thunder, hear it as their applause.

MONICA SOK

from *A Nail the Evening Hangs On*, 2020

Recurring Dreams

0

It was a strange dinner. His empty chair.
My brother missing. Didn't ask my parents questions.

The old house. Didn't ask why.

The wooden table the kitchen cramped.
My back against the wall. I sucked in my belly.
My father rationed more food.

Ate as much as I could. My mother's soup.
Rice on my plate. She took me to the bus.
He went to work. I went to another country.

Off the last stop. In the fields. Workers gathering grain.
Black pajamas.

Someone I knew.

I ran home. In the kitchen. Found her.

What are you doing here?
Before she took me back. She said.
You must know. Your history.

I

It was a very strange dinner. I tried to ask
my parents questions. The wooden table,
the kitchen cramped. My father spooned more rice on my plate.

I went to another country, where workers
were gathering grain. *What are you doing here?*
You must know.

II

His empty chair in the old house. My back against the wall.
I ate as much as I could. She took me to the bus after dinner.
Off the last stop, they gave me black pajamas.

In the kitchen, before she took me back, she said—

III

My brother is missing. I don't need to ask why. I suck in my belly,
wanting my mother's soup. He went to work in the fields.
Someone found her, he said. *What are you doing here?*

KELLI RUSSELL AGODON

from *Dialogues with Rising Tides,* 2021

Love Waltz with Fireworks

Seventeen minutes ago, I was in love
    with the cashier and a cinnamon pull-apart,
    seven minutes before that, it was a gray-

haired man in argyle socks, a woman
    dancing outside the bakery holding
    a cigarette and a broken umbrella. The rain,

I've fallen in love with it many times,
    the fog, the frost—how it covers the clovers
    —and by clovers I mean lovers.

And now I'm thinking how much I want to rush up
    to the stranger in the plaid wool hat
    and tell him I love his eyes,

all those fireworks, every seventeen minutes, exploding
    in my head—you the baker, you the novelist,
    you the reader, you the homeless man on the corner

with the strong hands—I've thought about you. But
    in this world we've been taught to keep
    our emotions tight, a rubber-band ball where

we worry if one band loosens, the others will begin
    shooting off in so many directions. So we quiet.
    I quiet. I eat my cinnamon bread

in the bakery watching the old man still sitting
    at his table, holding his handkerchief as he drinks
    his small cup of coffee. And I never say,

I think you're beautiful, except in my head,
 except I decide I can't
 live this way. I walk over to him and

place my hand on his shoulder, lean in close
 and whisper, *I love your argyle socks,*
 and he grabs my hand,

the way a memory holds tight in the smallest
 corner. He smiles and says,
 I always hope someone will notice.

KAYLEB RAE CANDRILLI

from *Water I Won't Touch,* 2021

On having forgotten to recycle

The Arctic is a wetland

and the Dead Sea is dying, too. The chapped

lips of salt have begun to peel back, a tide in constant

surrender. Humans amaze me with their knack to kill, again

and again, so endlessly. Though I am concerned for the earth's rapid

erosion, I have done it to myself. I have cleaved whole mountains from

my chest and sent them to soak in an offshore landfill. My breasts, I imagine,

are long dead, floating alongside jellyfish and plastic straws. I feel surprised

by this new smallness—this body postanesthesia, post disposing all

the flesh I just didn't want anymore. The world is growing

warmer. And it is true; I am smaller now, with a heart

that much closer to the sun.

ALEX DIMITROV

from *Love and Other Poems,* 2021

Sunset on 14th Street

I don't want to sound unreasonable
but I need to be in love immediately.
I can't watch this sunset
on 14th Street by myself.
Everyone is walking fast
right after therapy, texting back
their lovers orange hearts
and unicorns—it's insane to me.
They're missing this free sunset
willingly! Or even worse
they're going home to cook
and read this sad poem online.
Let me tell you something,
people have quit smoking.
They don't get drinks
but they juice. There are
way too many photos
and most all of us look better
in them than we do in life.
What happened? This is
truly so embarrassing!
I want to make a case
for 1440 minutes every day
where we stop whatever else
is going on and look each other
in the eyes. Like dogs.
Like morning newspapers
in evening light. So long!
So much for this short drama.
We will die one day
and our cheap headlines

won't apply to anything.
The internet will be forgotten.
All the praise and pandering.
I'd really rather take a hike
and by the way, I'm gay.
The sunset too is homosexual.
At least today, between
the buildings which are moody
and the trees (which honestly)
they look a bit unhealthy here.
They're anxious. They're concerned.
They're wondering why
I'm broke and lonely
in Manhattan—though of course
I'll never say it—and besides
it's almost spring. It's fine.
It's goth. Hello! The truth is
no one will remember us.
We're only specks of dust
or one—one speck of dust.
Some brutes who screamed
for everything to look at us.
Well, look at us. Still terrible
and awful. Awful and pretending
we're not terrible. Such righteous
saints! Repeating easy lines,
performing our great politics.
It's just so very boring,
the real mystery in fact
is how we managed to make room
for love at all. Punk rock,
avant-garde cinema.
I love you, reader
but you should know
the sunset's over now.
I'm standing right in front of
Nowhere bar, dehydrated
and quite scared

but absolutely willing
to keep going. It makes sense
you do the same. It's far
too late for crying and quite
useless too. You can be sad
and still look so good. You can
say New York is beautiful
and it wouldn't be a headline
and it wouldn't be a lie.
Just take a cab and not the 6,
it's never once in ten years
been on time. It's orbiting
some other world
where there are sunsets
every hour and no money
and no us—that's luck!
The way to get there
clearly wasn't written down.
Don't let that stop you though.
Look at the sky. Kiss everyone
you can for sure.

TISHANI DOSHI

from *A God at the Door*, 2021

My Loneliness Is Not the Same as Your Loneliness

My loneliness is not the same
as your loneliness, although they send
each other postcards and when they meet
they relax enough to nap
on each other's sofas.

> I've never felt more alone
> than when I was being burgled,
> our bodies facing one another,
> the burglar and me. Can I help,
> I asked but really what I was saying
> was, Stay, don't leave.

You say you're sometimes jolted awake
by the horror of eating animals,
how most mornings it passes,
but once, you walked downstairs to find
a watermelon had exploded on your table,
all that rotten red froth seeping
through the tablecloth

> and even though I understood
> this explosion exploded something
> in you, that it has to do with bodies—
> animal, watermelon, burglar, your body
> and mine, the thread between us,
> I could not reach for your hand,
> could not say, Don't live among strangers.

They say it starts in childhood,
or being alive in a large country where
all the roads are empty and lead in.
They say go east, go west, go somewhere,
start something, but where can you go
if you don't know how to manage thirsty
buffaloes, if the past is a birdcage
that grows larger the farther away
from home you get?

           I left town, hit a patch of feeling blue,
           called you. Funny story, you said,
           Puppy just shredded eighteen volumes
           of the *Mahabharata.*
           What's happening
           with you?

I say, You know, I'm on the road,
it's the underground guerilla life for me,
dirt and celibacy. All I can hear
are birds and sirens, and sometimes,
birds imitating sirens.

           We're quick to tell each other
           It's okay, it's okay, we can't all
           be preceded or followed by something.
           We can't all carry around tanks of oxygen
           or storm through doors reeking
           of whiskey and Pernod.

There's no known cure.
It isn't true about daily B_{12} shots
or living in a commune. In wars
there are almost always the same number
dead from starving as from combat.
Whatever it is, it lives in the body
and will stay till the body
runs aground.

Singers say they hear the next note
before they sing it. My loneliness
is something like that. I know
not just what it is, but how
it will sound.

There's a child screaming
in the playground below, a refrain
so shrill it scrapes a layer off the air.
She's reassuring herself, she's not alone.
No one tells her, We're here together,
you've been heard.

SHANGYANG FANG

from *Burying the Mountain*, 2021

Argument of Situations

I was thinking, while making love, *this is beautiful*—this

fine craftsmanship of his skin, the texture of wintry river.

I pinched him, three inches above his coccyx, so that he knew

I was still here, still in an argument with Fan Kuan's

inkwash painting where an old man, a white-gowned literatus,

dissolves into the landscape as a plastic bag into cloud.

The man walks in the mountains. *No, he walks on rivers.*

The man moves among shapes. *He travels through colors.*

The mountains are an addendum to his silvergrass sandals.

Wrong, his embroidered sleeves are streaklines of trees.

Neither could persuade the other, as my fingers counted

along his cervical spine, seven vertebrae that held up

a minute heaven in my hand. But it isn't important.

It is not, I said. It is just a man made of brushstrokes

moving in a crowd of brushstrokes. The man walks

inside himself. The string quartet of the tap water

streamed into a vase. My arms coursed around his waist.

We didn't buy any flowers for the vase. *It's okay.*

The sunlight would soon fabricate a bouquet of gladiolus.

To walk on a mountain for so long, he must desire

nothing. Nothing must be a difficult desire. Like the smell

of lemon, cut pear, its chiseled snow. The man

must be tired. *He might.* He might be lonely.

He must be. The coastline of his spine, the alpine

of his cheekbone—here was where we stopped—this

periphery of skin, this cold, palpable remoteness

I held. The dispute persisted. Are you tired? *I'm okay.*

That means you are tired. *You're bitter.*

Whatever you say. If my hands departed from his skin,

the heavens would collapse. The limit remained

even though we had used the same soap, same shampoo;

we smelled like the singularity of one cherry's bloom.

The vase stayed empty, the sky started to rain.

My toothbrush leaned against his.

The man must be lonely, I said. *No, the mountain*

is never lonely. Burying my forehead inside his shoulder

blades, the mountain is making itself a man.

NATASHA RAO

from *Latitude,* 2021

Old Growth

Backward crossovers into years before: airy
afternoons licking the wooden spoon, pouring soft blades
of grass from a shoe, all ways of saying I miss
my mother. I wish I could remember the gentle lilt
of my brother's early voice. Instead I hear clearly
the dripping of a basalt fountain. What gets saved—

My father fed my sick goldfish a frozen pea and it lived
for another six years. Outside, pears swathed in socks
ripened, protected from birds. Those bulbous
multicolored days, I felt safe before I knew
the word for it. But how to fossilize a feeling, sustain it
in amber? I keep dreaming in reverse until I reach
a quiet expanse of forest. The dragonflies are large
and prehistoric. Mother watches from a distance
as I move wildly, without fear.

NATALIE SHAPERO

from *Popular Longing,* 2021

It Used to Be We Had to Go to War

just to make enough dead men
to give up to God. Then God stopped
caring for sacrifice, but you know
how it is with old habits. The scientist,
hauled to the Capitol to justify
his new particle lab, finally spit out
CONGRESSMAN, IT HAS NOTHING
TO DO WITH DEFENDING
OUR COUNTRY, EXCEPT TO MAKE
OUR COUNTRY WORTH DEFENDING.
Yes, it is our duty, here on the home
front, to ensure there is always
a new thing to kill and die for.
A heartier engine, a stickier resin,
a toothier starlet, a stonier statue,
a seamier alley in which you and I
might meet. A livelier, more festive
substitute for party balloons. Consider
ditching the Mylar and replacing
with paper bunting, replacing with
ivy or drumming or the smell
of something burning. Consider
replacing with high-end
angular haircuts. Consider replacing
with invitees being waited on
by serfs. Consider replacing with
colorful yet orderly mass
suicide—just make it enough
of a regular thing, and the children
won't know what they've missed.

ARTHUR SZE

from *The Glass Constellation: New and Collected Poems*, 2021

The Owl

The path was purple in the dusk.
I saw an owl, perched,
on a branch.

And when the owl stirred, a fine dust
fell from its wings. I was
silent then. And felt

the owl quaver. And at dawn, waking,
the path was green in the
May light.

FERNANDO VALVERDE

from *America,* 2021
Translated from the Spanish by Carolyn Forché

The Wound before the Tomb of Walt Whitman

You who saw the vast oceans
and the mountain peaks,
who communed with all the sailors of the world,
and you who saw Christ eat the bread of his last supper among the young
and the elders,
you who saw the executioner of Europe
with his ax soaked with blood,
you stepped on the scaffold
and the fields in which mothers cried to their dead children.

Tell me if it is still
possible to announce triumphant justice
and deliver the lessons of the New World.

I'm going to kiss your lips,
they are cold and they taste like the word *America.*

NIKKI WALLSCHLAEGER

from *Waterbaby*, 2021

Just Because We're Scared Doesn't Mean We're Wrong

When language fails me I look around.

Has language failed you, too?

I am a seaworthy underwriter,

chauffeuring the limousine malware.

You're not supposed to put new wine

in old bottles but people do it anyway.

Swelling epochs in shady hunter green,

tragic preoccupations with Hollywood.

I can still pass as a pretty young thing,

take my cue when it's time to butterfly

inside a collapsing salt mine I'm partially

shouldering, shuddering encryptions.

Blink twice if you feel betrayed as I do,

baby, it's whatever I can pull off in a day.

NIKKI WALLSCHLAEGER

from *Waterbaby,* 2021

William Carlos Williams

After I left we hung it in the sky, so everyone can see what Black
women have done for the world. Against our will or not. I discussed
it with the stars and they agreed to hold up the part of me that will
burn the longest, since the labor it took to live down here can never
be repaid. But most people recognize it as a constellation called the
Big Dipper. Anyway, once there was a poet who wrote a famous poem
about everything depending on a broken-down wheelbarrow rusting
in the rain. I think fairly highly of poets and still give them ideas,
and this man was also a doctor. Quiet and thoughtful. When he was
going about his day I whispered about the ugly wheelbarrow I spent a
lifetime with, pushing it back and forth for the fire.

"William," I said, reaching through the wind to grab his ear. He was
walking with a black umbrella and enjoying the mild rain shower.
There was a farmhouse coming up the road with a wheelbarrow in the
front yard. Someone kind had planted red geraniums in it. He slowed
and faced the direction I was pointing, noticing for the first time the
homely little wheelbarrow. Smile lines broke through the slow earth
of his face. Something good was happening, he was sure of it—and so
was I, because I told him.

NOAH WARREN

from *The Complete Stories,* 2021

The Complete Stories

Skirt leaves gone orange or torn away to reveal thorny branches, tops still flaming green
though their drowning climbed up them, the windbreak poplars glittered inverted
a moment on the flooded field until the clouds reknit. An empty road emerged
from the pools, almost touched the house. Quebec stretched to the horizon.

There were four of us but you were the one I passed the hours with.
In the long slow game, I bound you intricately to yourself with cotton ropes
and picked you up, and set you down on the carpet so I could nap.
The code is loose, therefore the sentence harsh.

Most of my life I would not believe the heart of life was making pasta
with a few people, sipping maybe two glasses of wine. In the evenings, when I was a child,
I played chess and backgammon with my father. To his credit, he never let me win.

We took a poll: most thought it was before midnight still. Talking can do that, make
a little time feel like a lot, or a lot a little, or both, in a way that makes
one feel pleasure, or loneliness, or a mix of these and many other emotions.

TANEUM BAMBRICK

from *Intimacies, Received*, 2022

New Year's Eve

At midnight, we chew twelve green grapes
in the seconds between church bells ringing.
I am with my partner's extended family
swallowing competitively around a glass table
until our little white bowls empty.
No one can speak. We are all concentrating.
His mother pulls my hand under hers
to sneak a red lace thong, which I drop
and watch unfurl on the ground
like a napkin burning. Everyone laughs but me.
The brother, the grandfather. We are all
still choking. *This is tradition,* it takes a while
for her to tell me, *wearing red for your partner*
—her son—*on New Year's Eve.*
This is how you spend the rest of the year lucky.

OLENA KALYTIAK DAVIS

from *Late Summer Ode,* 2022

Vague À L'âme

when i am alone i am happy

it is the perfect temperature
inside my house the sky is
outside and the sky is
in: [i have framed your clouds]
the wallpaper behind it cloisteresque

nothing coy nor cloying and
success is always always far away

i have strayed
and stayed

because i love my dishes
i do not wish to die

from *Content Warning: Everything,* 2022

disclosure

when i first came out i called myself bi a queer tangle of free-form dreads my mother said i was sick and in a dark place my father said i would get AIDS my father-in-law stopped speaking to me my marriage had been folded open its spine cracked my husband returned to snow in his sinuses my childhood friend screamed over the phone *what was the point of getting married* my brother said you can't live in that bubble in new york the real world is not like that but it's a lie there are no real worlds you can live in whatever bubble you like a diving bell made of tender glass clap your hands if they said you're too sensitive if they beat you because they could because you should be tougher harder gra gra ghen ghen an igbo man in my friend's home laughs and holds my food out of reach i am so tired my friend holds me in the bathroom as i cry the next day he apologizes says he likes my name but he'll never give it to his daughter because he wants her to be strong not like me i don't tell him how little he matters how i have his type at home how they already raised me with blows across the face a belt in a doorway a velvet child upholstered in incoherent rage one day a coward who will break my heart asks me how i ended up still so soft i tell him i am stubborn i wanted a better world a diving bell made of tender glass a better family i remembered how to be a god i give myself what i want no one raises their voice in my house no one lays their fleshy hands on me no one is cruel if they are fool enough to try then they die and what a death what a death to not be loved by me anymore the softest gate-opener i feast on torn herbs and fat gold the wet smear of a perfect yolk seeds burst purple beneath my hands a pulped satsuma bleeds dark juice into my mouth who knew i could love me so loudly who knew i would survive who knew their world meant nothing meant nothing meant nothing look when i last came out i called myself free.

JOHN FREEMAN

from *Wind, Trees,* 2022

Decoys

Bomber pilots knew wind could be a mercy seven thousand feet up
river like a pelican's neck   engine drone a chorus of song
clouds could be a mercy rain could be a mercy snow could be
a mercy   the wrong type of moon

did ties whistle and whip when a payload was cut began
its nearly eight-minute journey back to Earth the silence
of that descent frightening to them sitting in the sky goggled
and scarfed delivering death like a baby from above

who thought to name a thirteen-foot-long four-thousand-pound
bomb Satan   had that person ever crouched close as a plane birthed
a payload that drifted   did he wonder about the free will of objects
we set in motion how they resist us as if a silent hand

sometimes saying no   during World War I when
the Germans were using zeppelins in aerial campaigns
the French planned to build a fake Paris fifteen miles north
on the river complete with a replica street plan Arc de Triomphe

working trains snuffed-out lights that at night
might fool the bombers who'd fly right over a blacked-out Paris
engine drones a lullaby they never had to use
the war ended in 1918 all vestiges of the city outside the city

destroyed   Fernand Jacopozzi the engineer who'd designed
the stage-set Paris lit the Eiffel Tower instead
then died in his home in 1932 at age fifty-four his lasting gift
the realization that good and evil are both drawn to light

JULIAN GEWIRTZ

from *Your Face My Flag,* 2022

from *A Short History of the West*

after Canova's *Psyche Revived by Cupid's Kiss* (1793)

I

To the god. Tonight
there are no visitors.

Storm clouds rise
over the near mountains, beyond

the finch-dense forest.
For nine and ninefold nights

I have waited
in darkness, lulled

only by wind-whine—
unmoving, bedded

muddle and buzz
into body, from between

teeth seeps forth
a strange issue

and small untouchable
sores collapse open

skin-strata, shallow
basins, suppurated

sediment. I
survey the subsidence,

does blood slow
and flow around my core?

The blighting
tendons. Slough

of river, place where flow
fallows—have I fallen?

My knees draw close
and fold. My legs

lapse. I will not leave.

                *

Bright: a begonia blooms. Yolky calyx whorls
below the twisted stigmas. Petalless yellow: the sepals.

                *

A task:
                Disorder
of grain-sand and light.
The love-wind, careless,

carrying a little chaff
and seed, lifting what is
too heavy. It comes

to pass. Day
plunges into the far massif,
where I was and was,

flail's whining
unsettles the shells,
vans of air holding

the color of your hair,
husk gray. I was given

no tools. Raised my hands
to let your name rise . . .

        From height-
over-the-mountain shadows,
the winds startle cool

eddies, dry-spooled air
unweaving the grain,

hazed rain clouds
follow the crossing
currents, streaming
from the sky's raised face—

Were you there? Resting
on the low hay-bed,
looking toward me as I left

as a last breeze lazed
the wooden hold in
the granary.
What remains is only

cold and golden.

    2

The second task:
To winnow thin
sticks from the sharp-sliver
arrows. Fine fingerwork
by feel to find
the breaking down
of browns. Were I
an arrow: freed
from the bowstring
to become vector—no,
quivered into one thing.

*

As a pulley shakes
when rope runs
through it,

the bushes
new-bloomed, shivering,
opening the meadows

dowered with trees—
heavy-leaved, hovering
above, and the silent

star-pulses, alive.
Spring crawls into
eyes and scratches

its way out—
When he comes,
I almost do not

notice his light
arrival, low
breeze-blow,

the feathered air
suspending him
above me—

when he is not
here, it is as if

he is not here.

NICHOLAS GOODLY

from *Black Swim*, 2022

Evening Prayer

who bestowed upon me
this habit of wanting
music from a pen this addiction
to the gentleness of vowels
what are these notes
from people's heads
what is the point
of being the last one
to speak a beautiful language
I am a fraction
of what I could've been
what else can I contribute
I am outdone by children
with more to lose
a teenager instructing me
how to breathe
these kids are quick
they grab the hands
of their neighbors
pull each other
safely up for air
there is your enemy and son
your wife and brother
your prize and secret cross
golden fleece and weighted cast
heaven knows
I want this to be a poem
people reach for
how often have I told myself
I am not strong and time
keeps proving me wrong
when snow doesn't come

when I am not enough
let me do the right thing
and make a rope of words
let it begin with me even now
there is richness beyond belief
vulnerable warrior what risk is there
we who already die in so many places
this not even the worst of them
no one line is revolutionary
no one word ever is
I am grateful for not dying yet
I inhale what is in front of me
everything is changing
young hearts any love
I can describe for you
does not suffice but you
are worth my every effort
one day you will know love like this
and write it better than I

CATE MARVIN

from *Event Horizon,* 2022

Event Horizon

Remember when you stabbed me on my birthday?
A glass of wine itched, scratched itself off the table.

Whatever phones were then, they were dead.
Whatever phones were then, we can barely recall.

But numbers remain numbers and yours dialed
went unanswered. You were dead on the other end.

And no one knows about the flowers you sent, nor
the manner in which I sat through dullest hours

on my couch aiming a kitchen knife at my wrist.
That I do not choose the role of victim remains

unsaid. I sit across a table from you at a thesis
defense and by my silence advance the thesis

that I never sucked your dick like the broken stem
of a honeysuckle flower. For many years we continue

to act like I have never sucked your dick like the broken
stem of a honeysuckle flower. You'll ask if I'm willing

to recommend to my editor a manuscript you have
had trouble publishing. I'll oblige because it seems

I do not know what I am about. I adopt more cats.
I develop an exercise routine. I note you do not own

any pets. I don't get that and don't have much sympathy,
though I'm thankful animals are spared. The Dalai Lama

himself would have appreciated my calm that afternoon.
Walking into that room to sit across from you at that table,

months after my birthday, you smiling at me like we'd just
met: perhaps it was true. We had only just met.

There was a reason for language back then. Back then,
words meant something. I am bent down, kneeling to pick

up the bouquet you've sent that's been left by a delivery
person employed to get its message received. Across our

table, my tears are not diamonds, nor does the sun's knife
come off my smile. Remember when your floor met my knees?

You're lucky I'm as lazy as I am. Animals like me, knives like
me, strange as forgiveness. I picked those bad flowers up.

SARAH RUHL

from *Love Poems in Quarantine,* 2022

I have brought my dog with me. Why?

for Jorge

Because everything
in life is better with a
dog. Except for sex.

SARAH RUHL

from *Love Poems in Quarantine,* 2022

What are we folding when we are folding laundry in quarantine?

Standing four feet apart,
you take one edge of the sheet,
I take the other.

We walk toward one another,
creating order.

Like solemn campers folding a flag
in the early morning light.
But this is no flag.
This is where we love and sleep.

There was a time we forgot to do this—
to fold with and toward one another,
to make the edges clean together.

My grandmother might have said:

There is always more laundry to do—
and that is a blessing because it means
you did more living,
which means you get to do more cleaning.

We forgot for a while
that one large blanket
is too difficult for one chin to hold
and two hands to fold alone—

that there is more beauty
in the walking toward the fold,
and in the shared labor.

CHRISTOPHER SOTO

from *Diaries of a Terrorist*, 2022

All The Dead Boys Look Like Us

For Orlando

Last time we saw ourselves die was when police killed Jessie Hernandez

      A seventeen-year-old Brown queer // Who was sleeping in their car

Yesterday we saw ourselves die again // Fifty times we died in Orlando // &

      We remembered reading // Dr. José Esteban Muñoz before he passed

We were studying at NYU // Where he was teaching // Where he wrote shit that

      Made us feel that queer Brown survival was possible // But he didn't

Survive & now // On the dance floor // In the restroom // On the news // In our chest

      There are another // Fifty bodies that look like ours // & Are

Dead // & We've been marching for Black Lives // & Talking about police brutality

      Against Native communities too // For years // But this morning

We feel it // We really feel it again // How can we imagine ourselves // Today

      Black // Native // Brown people // How can we imagine ourselves when

All the dead boys look like us // Once we asked our nephew where he wanted

      To go to college // What career he wants // As if

The whole world was his for the choosing // Once he answered without fearing

Tombstones or cages // Or the hands from a father // The hands of our lover

Yesterday praised our whole body // Made angels from our lips // Ave Maria

Full of grace // He propped us up like the roof of a cathedral // In NYC

Before we opened the news & red // & Read about people who think two Brown queers

Can't build cathedrals // Only cemeteries // & Each time we kissed

A funeral plot opened // In the bedroom we accepted his kiss // & We lost our reflection

We're tired of writing this poem // But we wanted to say one last word about

Yesterday // Our father called // We heard him cry for only the second time in our life

He sounded like he loves us // It's something we're rarely able to hear &

We hope // If anything // His sound's what our body remembers first

MICHAEL WASSON

from *Swallowed Light*, 2022

On the Horizon

& I said
let there be dark

pouring from between
the teeth. Let there be

an aftertaste in the back
of the throat. Let each locust

leap from the slow light
being dragged over the earth.

Let every angel not named
Michael ask *do you not know*

the single click in the mouth
is a tear you are

to always live in? Let the garden
remember *fire* for it is you

who will dress the wounds
of this place. Let lesser gods

forget you were ever born.
Let light begin &

black out from remembering
flesh as a touch to tell you

the skull once kissed the blood
laced with warmth

& held a body in place years ago.
That silence is forgotten

between each soft blow of the heart
until we finally stop. A name

we never speak anymore. A head
wound by living a life

here. Tonight let me tell you
the human form is meant to be

a beauty I will continue
to ruin.

JASWINDER BOLINA

from *English as a Second Language*, 2023

A Poem, like the Soul, Which Can't Be Translated

Optimism's a funny color on a couple of Virgos,
but here we go retiling the powder room in quartz
again as if industry is rewarded by anything
other than industry in the middle of all this
whatever-this-is. First, aperitifs, then crudité.
First, boxed wine, then chitchat, over cakes,
of an almost imperceptible candor. Thus,
the seasons bustle onward rebranding themselves
so the Weber and Kingsford people keep extending
their ad buys deeper into pumpkin-picking
pigskin weather, and we feel weirdly sweaty
disemboweling a turkey on an island
in the kitchen when the older kid says,
*Momma, I'monna need a doper raincoat in this piss pot
of a winter.* It gets so you wish there were actual
barbarians at the gate, anyone to crush with a mace,
but there is no gate,
not one guy in a pelt
banging with any malice; just dad bods
and threenagers storming the bouncy castle.
And a magician at the party keeps disappearing
the rabbits and doves, but we can see plain as day
how he does it, snapping their necks,
tossing them over his shoulder—simple as that!
Don't blame me, cupcake, I voted for the other guy.
But somebody still has to pay for this shit.

NATALIE EILBERT

from *Overland,* 2023

Bacterium

In the last segment, I tried sufficiency. They moved
my femur and a single woman braiding her hair fell

from me. I tried to warn you, this desert editorializes.
A scorpion lifts its tail, *braids* more active than *braiding,*

it hisses. I, of all people, get it. In the mornings we wake
to the kind of life we want until we turn our heads east.

The night fills without us but I warned you, I was full
already. A banana inside me blasted open a door,

my mind at the threshold of such a door blank. Love
transacts, a figure in the distance crowded with window.

An enzyme eats plastic, but which kind? Synthetic polymer
or the ways you tried to keep me? This is the last segment.

My mother

draws a circle around time and this is an intercourse. My mentor
draws a circle around time and this is an intercourse. I shake

out of bed. Humans continue the first line of their suicide letter.
An enzyme invents us, we invent enzymes. The plastic we make,

we must eat it. Draw a circle around time. We designed us
in simple utterances. The political term *graft* means political

corruption. The grifter never had an *I.* In the burn unit, they
place tilapia skins over human scar tissue, the killed form on top

of afflicted form, also a graft. Also a graft of afflicted form,
the killed form on top, they place tilapia skins over human scar

tissue. In the burn unit, I never had a grifter, corruption
means political, *graft* the political term. In simple utterances

we designed us. Time draws a circle, we must eat it. We make
the plastic, enzymes invent *we, us* invents an enzyme to continue

the first line of a suicide letter. Out of bed I shake with intercourse.
Time draws a circle around my mentor. Time draws a circle around

my mother.

This is the last segment. The ways you tried to keep me? Synthetic
polymer, but which kind? An enzyme eats plastic, crowded window,

a figure in the distance transacts love. At the threshold of such
a blank door, my mind opens a door. A banana blasted inside me.

Already I was full but I warned you, the night fills without us.
We turn our heads until we want the kind of life in the mornings

we wake to. I get, of all people, it. It hisses. A scorpion, more active
than braiding, braids its tail, lifts the editorialized desert. You tried

to warn me from me. Her hair fell, braiding a single woman. My femur
was moved. They tried sufficiency in the last segment.

JORIE GRAHAM

from *To 2040, 2023*

To 2040

With whom am I speaking, are you one or many, *what* are u, are u, do I make my-
self clear, is this which we called speech what u use, are u a living form such as the
form I inhabit now letting it speak me. My window tonight casts light onto the snow,
I cast from my eye a glance, a touchless touch, tossed out to capture this shine we

cast. I pull it in, into my memory store. I have lost track. It's snowed for more
than we'd imagined at the start, it began, unexpectedly it began, it did not really
cease again, it slowed some days, melted as it fell on some, days passed thru snow
rather than snow thru days. Did it remember us at some point, when we cld hold no

more memory of day in mind. We had started with minutes. We had loved their
fullness—cells flowing thru this body of time—purging all but their passing thru us
& our letting them flow-through. But then they stopped being different. You
couldn't tell one minute from another, or an hour, day, year. Years pulled their

lengths through us like long wet strings, and we hung onto them, they strung us a
ways along, & up, they kept us from drowning in the terrible minutes. Once I sat
down & cried as I watched the sun come up & the flakes falling as if not noticing the
movmt from night into day—at least let there be difference—otherwise whatever

remains of desire will go—otherwise there will be nothing I have saved—nothing to
save—make day flower as a piece of time again—it's cold—dream is a hard thing to
catch sight of—I said *dream*—*I said dream* what is it I said—I said it because just
now, looking out, it's a reflex, I saw, as if a stain or residue of scent, a yellowing on

snow in patches, long thin stretches, like a very cold face remembering something it
wishes to forget, I saw a poverty touched by a lessening of poverty, a memory of a
chime on cold air, a strange flash as of birdshadow—so fast—though there are no
birds any longer—longer—I would have said *ever again*—but then there it is that

word I dread so—again—here where we have none of it or nothing but, we can't
tell—but it was the so-rare poking-through of the strange sun we have—& for

an instant it gave us shadows—branches that do not move moved—against snow, wall, pane, against trunk, intertwining & trembling inside other shadows, & all

was alive. You feel the *suddenly.* You feel like an itch a thing you used to call so casually yr *inwardness,* u feel yr looking at the knotting, the undoings of nothing in nothing, gorgeous—cursive golds what wld u say now, say it now, do it now yr in-wardness thinks as you feel yr greed in yr eyes yr hands yr soul—how u drink

what used to be just end-of-day, low light, any winter afternoon. Give me a day back. Give the slowing of dusk into gloaming. Give me a night. Shut something down, close your fist over it, hold us tight, then unclench unfurl slowly release us again into light. Give us a dawn. Give us the one note without warning where one call one cry breaks

& darkness releases a branch & if you wait the whole crown then the body will be unhidden and handed over into yr sight. The sight of the watching human. I turn back-in as the accident the release of light is fixed & we are back in snowlight now. How far forward r we. We used to speak of future. Speech had a different function

then. It's hard to know when to break the silence now. It has something to do with the absence of night. We never knew we shld feel the rotation. We hurled forward. Yes towards death but what joy. Didn't know it was a game. Should have loved the hurtling, the losses, the hurry dilation delay fear surprise fury. We miss

the sense of abandonment yes we miss homesickness. We miss the vector in any direction. You back there are you back there listening to me am I audible what do I do to make this audible don't forget to ask when your time comes for *presence.* Do not ask for forgiveness. Do not ask for youth. They will offer them up

pristine and innocent. Do not listen. Do not make the silly mistake do not ask for eternity. Look behind you, turn, look down as much as you can, notice all that disappears. Place as much as you can in your heart. It doesn't matter what's in your mind. When you come here all you will be left w/is a heart they spill out, a

tin cup, they count up what you put in it, they shake it into a small burlap sack, they weigh it, they tie it up, they do not give it back. It is then you are placed at your window to watch. Then the snow begins. You are told to remember the message u accidentally forgot to attend to. It is among the things they sequestered when they measured u. You must sit now and recall the message. The one put in yr hand but not opened. You were busy. There was little time. Little notice was given. Its ink is new. The fold in its paper single & crisp. The words glow in their crease. The unread shines with its particular shine. It has been weighed. It was put to yr account &

burned. What was it, u must remember, what was yr message, what were u meant to pass on?

AMANDA GUNN

from *Things I Didn't Do with This Body*, 2023

Prayer

Lord let me hand you my burden my body it's yours
what will you do with it
my bones are gone to gravel under weight
I loved her
I loved her body as it
grew broad spilled forward filled in its loosened skin filled in
with newfound weight
we stayed at the bar too late we ate with relish chorizo
syruped with figs
I put my cheek against the fat of her belly it felt
cool I felt light as if I had risen taken
a form yet to be baked
I'd stomached every pill I was asked to take some
filled my gut
with a hunger I couldn't sate so sick
from other pills I halved
or quartered meals
misplaced one hundred nine pounds of weight
women who barely knew me said you're so thin so pretty
so lucky you lost a person
it's so so so so great
she fed my body she loved me as I
grew plump again shed my wrinkled skin slowly like
heartache
my breasts so heavy I thought
they'll burst
my breasts so heavy in her hands
can a body burst I think a body can I've known its juice
pills tricked my brain into a motherhood without fruit
I made milk & I burst
I thought what new thing are you body what
are these droplets in my palm

I thought taste it
I thought maybe you'll remember your mother you must have felt
weightless in her arms she waits
for you to call you hand her your laden days she bears you
she gained baby weight to bear you
she lost weight
her muscles grew slack & weak a woman who knew her well said girl
you're wasting away
my mother said
they took you from me in the hospital you didn't know me
you wouldn't feed
it was our very first grief
don't taste no wait for the real thing the authentic thing I thought
there will be other milks to taste
there will be the sweet fat weight of a child a child
my body then refused to make
it was busy carrying weight
too late too late too late
I ask is this it
is this weightlessness
I am weak in my bones from this weight there is bone
in the milk of my knees O sweet Christ
take half my gut or half my legs or half of what's left of my life
you're holding the knife

from *The Beloved Community*, 2023

Morning Glory

Sunlight softens   helicopters hover
Skies above Brooklyn   Presidential
Visit, murder investigation, matters little
Noise in the skies, noise on the ground

You should prune the morning glories
I tell my elderly neighbor.
She refuses. She likes the way the vine has
Curled around her fence with a ferocity
That cannot be so easily cut back. I get that.

Wildness is rare on a Brooklyn city block,
Old roses return late May as if to say, ha! you
Think we do not know the season? Squirrels
Roam the bricks of buildings, while the gleaners
Fight with raccoons for the spoils of left out trash.

Huge green leaves for plants with names
Unknown to me sparkle on mornings bright
And dead tree leaves demand constant sweeping away.

The tabby is big, old, and tired—too many kittens
Not enough food—these are ungenerous cat lovers.

Neighbors greet each other and shake their heads
At the young men and women, mostly, but not
All Whitefolk running running running—or their faces
Drowning in a pool of handheld devices.

You almost wish they smoked or cursed
Had personality—but they run and run and run

Thus, the joy of this vibrant morning glory vine
Rooted in her garden's disarray—happily dominating.

Oh, morning glory—purple, green
Leaves plump as Italian cookies, blossom
Your hearty display for all to see, hold your
Vine's haven on Macon Street. Only
Winter, harsh winter will take your vines
Back to the ground—your wildness calmed.

DEBORAH LANDAU

from *Skeletons,* 2023

Skeleton

So whatever's the opposite of a Buddhist that's what I am.

Kindhearted, yes, but knee-deep in existential gloom,

except when the fog smokes the bridges like this—

like, instead of being afraid, we might juice ourselves up,

eh, like, might get kissed again? Dwelling in bones I go straight

through life, a sublime abundance—cherries, dog's breath, the sun, then

(ouch) & all of us snuffed out. Dear one, what is waiting for us tonight,

nostalgia? the homes of childhood? oblivion? How we hate to go—

Flesh

The long and short of it is a podcast can only take you so far.

There goes our summer neighbor, Wife-of-Bath'ing it at the barbecue again,

her toned shoulders, her back talk and small army of dogs. Here we still are.

Another summer, same bathing suit. Same cutoffs and blueberries.

The same sordid daydream I keep having, ashamed

here to say because someone might see.

We won't do a single new thing it turns out, just keep cycling

through the years as if they were endless, as if they'd never cease.

Will we ever run out of days? Who dares to count.

To say there are maybe thirty more Christmases, if we're lucky,

thirty more Julys.

RANDALL MANN

from *Deal: New and Selected Poems,* 2023

Double Life

Let's go
to Ocean Beach
to undermine
the line:

vultures flick
arithmetic;
pups dart,
all heart.

It's grief,
capsized,
an itch
of otherwise.

The wind
elides—
relief
a thief—

the double life
of consonants:
passing; running.
Theatrical

as the clap
of a laptop,
no one careful
does that. Careful.

Our makeup
sand,
which arranges
and repeats

itself
to protect
itself,
like CRISPR.

A stat
whisper:
Why
do snaps

numb
rather than
enhance?
Light

oversexed
yet sexless,
more edge
than gape,

or gag.
Can, oh,
anyone
be impolite

before night?
Let's do it.
Let's fall
into fear

like the veneer
grin
and weak
chin

of a
beloved
dictator.
Roll

in rash,
stud
in flesh.
You can

try
to relax.
But it's later
than syntax.

JANE MILLER

from *Paper Banners,* 2023

The Grand Piano

Our five thousand years are up
we are going to die violently
the housekeepers and gardeners burn the furniture
outside the palace in golden light
the beekeepers weep over the last red milkweeds
the artists remove the scaffolding
our job is brutal and necessary
to be with the one we love and to think
something in the heart weighs on the heart

LISA OLSTEIN

from *Dream Apartment,* 2023

Root

God made her
his vessel. No.
God made of her
a vessel. No.
The river poured
into her as if
a vessel. Yes.
God made of
her a raft. No.
Her child clung to
her as if a raft.
No. Clung to her
as a raft. Yes.
God made of her
a vassal. Yes:
landless, river
pastured, root
cut loose.

JAVIER PEÑALOSA

from *What Comes Back,* 2023
 Translated from the Spanish by Robin Myers

"It happened by the arches"

It happened by the arches on September 21, 1948.
Pablo, son of Luz and Pablo.
Eugenia, Isabel's only daughter. No record of her father's name.
  Come into the shade.
  Here.
  In the shade.
We know the scene:
Eugenia looked at the shadows cast by the trees onto the gravel
  (this is all that's left of us)
He would write her name in uppercase letters on the tree bark
  (this is all that's left of us)
She wore a white dress that flowers, years later, would bloom from.

KEVIN PRUFER

from *The Fears,* 2023

A Body of Work

One comes, eventually, to the realization
that one will leave behind only
a body of work that will grow increasingly
unintelligible to each new generation. A trace
will remain spread across the vast
internet in much the way certain particles
inhabit the emptiness of deep space—negligibly,
though perhaps measurably. I, for instance,
am childless and, therefore, most likely
will die alone, my nest feathered
with yellowing poems. One comes, eventually,
to the knowledge that one's children
are increasingly unintelligible, being yellowing
poems spread across the emptiness of deep space—
negligible, though they once seemed, in their way,
to breathe. For instance, I am alive, right here,
in the middle of my poem, having had, perhaps,
too much to drink. One comes, eventually,
to the certainty that one's body of work
is nothing like another man's progeny, being
made of language which can only veer
toward emptiness as years become empty space.
For instance, hello? I am calling out to you,
folded here between the pages
of generations. You don't know me, but once
I was particulate and alive. Now what am I?

DEAN RADER

from *Beyond the Borderless: Dialogues with the Art of Cy Twombly*, 2023

Meditation on Absolution

Cy Twombly, *Three Notes from Salalah, Note I* (2005–2007)

My heart:
green

as a lake
but not

as smooth.
White noose

after white
noose—

will I swing
or will I

sing the
words of

my note
to the

depths?
What will

I not
say? To

what will
I not kneel?

PAISLEY REKDAL

from *West: A Translation*, 2023

不灰 / **Not Ash**

> Sui Sin Far, "Leaves from the Mental Portfolio of a Eurasian"

I remember the boy who called me dirty
and the French women who hissed *pauvre*
petite as I passed on the street

and I remember the girl
like me at school who pasted her face
with white paint and blacked her brows
to pass, she said, as Mexican—

               I remember everything
for which I was made to feel

ashamed. Even the fact
my father said I would never make half
the woman my mother was because
of my heart which the doctor now calls
unusually large.

Memory is the weakness
I bear on my own. I come from a race

on my mother's side said to be the most
stolid and insensible, yet feel

so keenly alive
to suffering, it hurts to hear the words
strangers use for Chinese
shopkeepers, or watch

the Chinamen here laugh
when I say I am of their race. I,
who, but for a few phrases, remain
unacquainted with my mother tongue.

I have the name
my English father gave me. And I look
like my father; I could be loved

if I lived as if I were like him,
too. But I prefer the name
I have invented for myself.
I want the world

to see my mother in me, regardless
if the Chinese have no souls.

I do not need a soul. It is not my soul

in question here
in these hot glances,
these furious whispers—

Why care for love
when I do not know
if I should love others in return?

Love is a white loneliness that swells the heart
and shuts me out from pleasure.
What is there for one like me to do

but wander, a pioneer
traveling between West
and East, myself the link

they threaten to destroy between them.

I do not need a name
on legal papers.

Here is a match. Here is the mirror

in which my pale face burns,
its flickering allegiances.

My soul is everywhere on my person.

I lose nothing of myself
that has not already disappeared.

T'AO YUAN-MING

from *Enduring Poverty: The Complete Poems of T'ao Yuan-ming,* 2023
Translated from the Chinese by Red Pine

In Praise of Impoverished Gentlemen

I

All things have their refuge
except solitary clouds
meekly vanishing in the sky
never to see twilight again
as morning mist replaces last night's fog
birds fly off together
taking their time leaving the woods
they always return before sunset
deciding we're able to follow ancient tracks
how can we avoid cold and hunger
when no one is left who understands us
what use is lamenting that it's over

II

Freezing cold means the year is ending
I pull my robe tighter and face the south window
there's no trace of green in the garden
nothing but bare branches behind the house
I tilt my jug but not a drop comes out
I look at the stove but see no smoke
the classics are piled around my seat
but shorter days leave no time for study
my retirement isn't like it was in Chen
though I have heard some resentful words
what is it that comforts my heart
that worthies in the past did this too

III

Old Rong's belt was a rope
yet he played his zither with joy
Mister Yuan's shoes had holes
but he sang Shang tunes without restraint
since Zhonghua departed long ago
impoverished gentlemen have been known to the world
their threadbare robes and ragged sleeves
their porridge often with no rice
it's not that they disdained fine robes
they didn't approve of improper rewards
all Zigong could do was talk
he couldn't see a person's heart

IV

Content being poor and remaining humble
that was Qian Lou in the past
he didn't consider titles an honor
gifts were no reward in his eyes
the day his life came to an end
his clothes didn't cover his body
how could he not know extremes
but all that mattered was the Way
in nearly a thousand years since then
his like has not been seen
kind and just in the morning
dying that night content

V

Even with his door buried by the snow
Yuan An remained unconcerned
when Master Ruan finally earned a profit
he resigned his job that day
gathering straw for warmth
digging taro for a meal
he lived a truly hard life

but what he feared wasn't cold or hunger
it was the war between poverty and wealth
once the Way won he no longer looked distressed
his virtue was praised throughout the land
his integrity made his hometown famous

VI

Zhongwei preferred to be poor
a house surrounded by weeds
living unnoticed without social ties
still he could write a fair poem
no one in his day knew him
no one except Liu Gong
and why did Liu think him special
because he had few peers
uniquely content with his trade
happy regardless of conditions
in social affairs he was clumsy
but try to find a better guide

VII

Long ago there was Huang Zilian
he dusted off his hat and served the state
then one day he resigned and went home
in doing without he had no peer
but during a famine he was moved by his wife
facing him in tears she cried
a man must uphold his ideals
but surely he must care for his children
after just one meeting Huisun sighed
he refused to accept lavish gifts
who says enduring poverty is hard
consider these examples from long ago

TOMAS TRANSTRÖMER

from *Iron Psalm: The Collected Works of Tomas Tranströmer*, 2023
Translated from the Swedish by Patty Crane

Late May

Apple trees and cherry trees in bloom help this place to float
in the sweet dirty May night, white life vest, my thoughts widening out.
Grasses and weeds with quiet persistent wingbeats.
The mailbox shines calmly, what is written cannot be taken back.

A mild chilly wind blows through my shirt and gropes around for my heart.
Apple trees and cherry trees, they laugh quietly at Solomon,
they blossom in my tunnel. I need them
not to forget but to remember.

Sketch in October

The tugboat is freckled with rust. What's it doing here so far inland?
It's a heavy, burnt-out lamp in the cold.
But the trees have wild colors. Signals to the other shore!
As if someone needed to be picked up.

On the way home, I see inky-cap mushrooms pushing up through the lawn.
They're the help-seeking fingers of someone
who has sobbed for a long time in the darkness down there.
We are the earth's.

Indexes

Index of Authors and Translators

Index of Poem Titles

List of Copper Canyon Press Titles (1973–2023)

Abani, Chris. *Hands Washing Water,* 2006.

———. *Sanctificum,* 2010.

———. *Smoking the Bible,* 2022.

Agodon, Kelli Russell. *Dialogues with Rising Tides,* 2021.

Aleixandre, Vicente. *A Longing for the Light,* 1985, 2007. Edited by Lewis Hyde. Translated from the Spanish by Robert Bly, Lewis Hyde, Stephen Kessler, David Pritchard, David Unger, and others.

Alexander, Floyce. *Iron Country: Anthology of Washington Writers,* 1979.

Ali, Taha Muhammad. *So What: New & Selected Poems, 1971–2005,* 2006. Translated from the Arabic by Peter Cole, Yahya Hijazi, and Gabriel Levin.

Alighieri, Dante. *Purgatorio: A New Verse Translation,* 2018. Translated from the Italian by W.S. Merwin.

Allen, Heather. *Leaving a Shadow,* 1996.

al-Massri, Maram. *A Red Cherry on a White-tiled Floor: Selected Poems,* 2007. Translated from the Arabic by Khaled Mattawa.

Arthur, James. *Charms Against Lightning,* 2012.

Balaban, John. *Ca Dao Việt Nam: Vietnamese Folk Poetry,* 2003.

———. *Empires,* 2019.

———. *Locusts at the Edge of Summer: New and Selected Poems,* 1997.

———. *Path, Crooked Path,* 2006.

———. *Words for My Daughter,* 1991.

Bambrick, Taneum. *Intimacies, Received,* 2022.

———. *Vantage,* 2019.

Bass, Ellen. *The Human Line,* 2007.

———. *Indigo,* 2020.

———. *Like a Beggar,* 2014.

Bassett, Lee. *Hatsutaiken: Prose Poems,* 1980.

Beckman, Joshua. *Things Are Happening,* 1998.

Belieu, Erin. *Black Box,* 2006.

———. *Come-Hither Honeycomb,* 2021.

———. *Infanta,* 1995.

———. *One Above & One Below,* 2000.

———. *Slant Six,* 2014.

Bell, Josh. *Alamo Theory,* 2016.

Bell, Marvin. *Ardor: The Book of the Dead Man, Vol. 2,* 1997.

———. *The Book of the Dead Man,* 1994.

———. *Incarnate: The Collected Dead Man Poems,* 2019. Introduction by David St. John.

———. *Iris of Creation,* 1990.

———. *Mars Being Red,* 2007.

———. *Nightworks: Poems 1962–2000,* 2003.

———. *Rampant,* 2004.

———. *Vertigo: The Living Dead Man Poems*, 2011.

Bellen, Martine. *The Vulnerability of Order*, 2001.

Berg, Stephen. *Crow with No Mouth: Ikkyū: Fifteenth Century Zen Master*, 1989, 2000. Versions from the original Japanese.

———. *Cuckoo's Blood: Versions of Zen Poetry*, 2008.

———. *New & Selected Poems*, 1992.

———. *The Steel Cricket: Versions: 1958–1997*, 1997.

Bertolino, James. *Making Space for Our Lives*, 1975.

Bibbins, Mark. *The Dance of No Hard Feelings*, 2009.

———. *They Don't Kill You Because They're Hungry, They Kill You Because They're Full*, 2014.

———. *13th Balloon*, 2020.

Bierds, Linda. *The Hardy Tree*, 2019.

Bitsui, Sherwin. *Dissolve*, 2018.

———. *Flood Song*, 2009.

Black, Malachi. *Storm Toward Morning*, 2014.

Bode-Lang, Katherine. *The Reformation*, 2014.

Bolina, Jaswinder. *English as a Second Language*, 2023.

Boruch, Marianne. *The Anti-Grief*, 2019.

———. *Bestiary Dark*, 2021.

———. *The Book of Hours*, 2011.

———. *Cadaver, Speak*, 2014.

———. *Eventually One Dreams the Real Thing*, 2016.

Bottoms, David. *Armored Hearts: Selected & New Poems*, 1995.

———. *Otherworld, Underworld, Prayer Porch*, 2018.

———. *Vagrant Grace*, 1999.

———. *Waltzing Through the Endtime*, 2004.

———. *We Almost Disappear*, 2011.

Bouvier, Geoff. *Living Room*, 2005. Introduction by Heather McHugh.

Boyle, Kay. *Collected Poems*, 1991.

Brimhall, Traci. *Come the Slumberless to the Land of Nod*, 2020.

———. *Saudade*, 2017.

Bringhurst, Robert. *The Beauty of the Weapons: Selected Poems, 1972–82*, 1982.

———. *Pieces of Map, Pieces of Music*, 1987.

———. *Selected Poems*, 2011.

Broumas, Olga. *Perpetua*, 1989.

———. *Rave: Poems, 1975–1998*, 1999.

———. *Soie Sauvage*, 1979.

Brown, Jeffrey. *The News*, 2015.

Brown, Jericho. *The New Testament*, 2014.

———. *The Tradition*, 2019.

———. *The Tradition: Civic Dialogue Edition*, 2022.

Budbill, David. *Happy Life*, 2011.

———. *Moment to Moment: Poems of a Mountain Recluse*, 1999.

———. *Tumbling toward the End*, 2017.

———. *While We've Still Got Feet*, 2005.

Cady, Jack. *Dear friends, being a letter to the I.R.S.,* 1976.

Candrilli, Kayleb Rae. *Water I Won't Touch,* 2021.

Cardiff, Gladys. *To Frighten a Storm,* 1976.

Carruth, Hayden. *Beside the Shadblow Tree: A Memoir of James Laughlin,* 1999.

———. *Collected Longer Poems,* 1993.

———. *Collected Shorter Poems, 1946–1991,* 1992.

———. *Doctor Jazz,* 2001.

———. *Last Poems,* 2012. Introduction by Stephen Dobyns.

———. *Reluctantly: Autobiographical Essays,* 1998.

———. *Scrambled Eggs & Whiskey: Poems 1991–1995,* 1996.

———. *Selected Essays,* 1995.

———. *Toward the Distant Islands: New and Selected Poems,* 2006. Introduction by Sam Hamill.

Cassells, Cyrus. *Beautiful Signor,* 1997.

———. *The Crossed-Out Swastika,* 2012.

———. *More Than Peace and Cypresses,* 2004.

———. *Soul Make a Path Through Shouting,* 1994.

Centolella, Thomas. *Lights & Mysteries,* 1995.

———. *Terra Firma,* 1990.

———. *Views from Along the Middle Way,* 2002.

Chang, Victoria. *Barbie Chang,* 2017.

———. *Obit,* 2020.

———. *The Trees Witness Everything,* 2022.

Chatti, Leila. *Deluge,* 2020.

Clifton, Lucille. *The Book of Light,* 1993.

Cold Mountain (Han Shan). *The Collected Songs of Cold Mountain,* 1983, 2000. Translated from the Chinese by Red Pine.

Coleman, Elizabeth J. *HERE: Poems for the Planet,* 2019. Foreword by His Holiness the Dalai Lama.

Corn, Alfred. *Contradictions,* 2008.

———. *The Poem's Heartbeat: A Manual of Prosody,* 2008.

Costanzo, Gerald. *Badlands: First Poems,* 1973.

Csoori, Sandor. *Selected Poems of Sandor Csoori,* 1992. Translated from the Hungarian by Len Roberts.

Cuddihy, Michael. *Celebrations,* 1980.

D'Aquino, Alfonso. *fungus skull eye wing: Selected Poems of Alfonso D'Aquino,* 2013. Translated from the Spanish by Forrest Gander.

Darwish, Mahmoud. *The Butterfly's Burden,* 2006. Translated from the Arabic by Fady Joudah.

Davis, Jon. *Preliminary Report,* 2010.

Davis, Olena Kalytiak. *Late Summer Ode,* 2022.

———. *The Poem She Didn't Write and Other Poems,* 2014.

———. *shattered sonnets love cards and other off and back handed importunities,* 2014.

Dawes, Kwame. *Duppy Conqueror: New and Selected Poems,* 2013. Edited by Matthew Shenoda.

Daye, Tyree. *Cardinal,* 2020.

———. *River Hymns,* 2017.

DeFrees, Madeline. *Blue Dusk: New & Selected Poems, 1951–2001,* 2001.

———. *Magpie on the Gallows,* 1982.

—————. *Spectral Waves,* 2006.

Diaz, Natalie. *When My Brother Was an Aztec,* 2012.

Dickman, Matthew. *All-American Poem,* 2008.

Dickman, Matthew, and Michael Dickman. *50 American Plays (Poems),* 2012.

Dickman, Michael. *The End of the West,* 2009.

—————. *Flies,* 2011.

—————. *Green Migraine,* 2016.

Dimitrov, Alex. *Love and Other Poems,* 2021.

—————. *Together and By Ourselves,* 2017.

Dimkovska, Lidija. *pH Neutral History,* 2012. Translated from the Macedonian by Ljubica Arsovska
    and Peggy Reid.

Di Piero, W.S. *Nitro Nights,* 2011.

Dobyns, Stephen. *Winter's Journey,* 2010.

Doshi, Tishani. *Everything Begins Elsewhere,* 2013.

—————. *Girls Are Coming Out of the Woods,* 2018.

—————. *A God at the Door,* 2021.

Dubie, Norman. *Insomniac Liar of Topo,* 2007.

—————. *The Mercy Seat: Collected & New Poems 1967–2001,* 2001.

—————. *Ordinary Mornings of a Coliseum,* 2004.

—————. *The Quotations of Bone,* 2015.

—————. *Robert Schumann Is Mad Again,* 2019.

—————. *The Volcano,* 2010.

Ducey, Kevin. *Rhinoceros,* 2004. Introduction by Yusef Komunyakaa.

Ehret, Terry. *Lost Body,* 2000.

Eilbert, Natalie. *Overland,* 2023.

Elytis, Odysseas. *Eros, Eros, Eros: Selected & Last Poems,* 1997. Translated from the Greek by Olga
    Broumas.

—————. *Open Papers,* 1994. Translated from the Greek by Olga Broumas.

Emezi, Akwaeke. *Content Warning: Everything,* 2022.

Estes, Kathleen. *Omphalos,* 1979.

Evans, Kerry James. *Bangalore,* 2013.

Factor, Jenny. *Unraveling at the Name,* 2002.

Fang, Shangyang. *Burying the Mountain,* 2021.

Feinstein, Sascha. *Misterioso: Poems,* 2000.

Follain, Jean. *Transparence of the World,* 2003. Translated from the French by W.S. Merwin.

Forché, Carolyn. *The Country Between Us,* 1981.

Freeman, John. *Maps,* 2017.

—————. *The Park,* 2020.

—————. *Wind, Trees,* 2022.

Galvin, James. *As Is,* 2009.

—————. *Everything We Always Knew Was True,* 2016.

—————. *Lethal Frequencies,* 1994.

—————. *Resurrection Update: Collected Poems 1975–1997,* 1997.

—————. *X,* 2003.

Gammill, Billy Mack. *Prune,* 1979.

Gander, Forrest, and photographs by Jack Shear. *Knot*, 2022.

George, Jenny. *The Dream of Reason*, 2018.

Gerber, Dan. *The End of Michelangelo*, 2022.

———. *Particles: New and Selected Poems*, 2017.

———. *A Primer on Parallel Lives*, 2007.

———. *Sailing through Cassiopeia*, 2012.

Gerner, Ken. *House of Breath*, 1981.

———. *The Red Dreams*, 1978.

Gewirtz, Julian. *Your Face My Flag*, 2022.

Goedicke, Patricia. *As Earth Begins to End: New Poems*, 1999.

Goodly, Nicholas. *Black Swim*, 2022.

Graham, Jorie. *[To] The Last [Be] Human*, 2022. Introduction by Robert Macfarlane.

———. *To 2040*, 2023.

Griffin, Susan. *Bending Home: Selected & New Poems, 1967–1998*, 1998.

Gunn, Amanda. *Things I Didn't Do with This Body*, 2023.

Gustafsson, Lars. *A Time in Xanadu*, 2008. Translated from the Swedish by John Irons.

Haines, John. *At the End of This Summer: Poems, 1948–1953*, 1997.

Halperin, Mark. *A Place Made Fast*, 1982.

Hamill, Sam. *Animae*, 1980.

———. *The Calling Across Forever*, 1976.

———. *Heroes of the Teton Mythos*, 1973.

———. *The Loom*, 1975.

———. *Mid-Winter Break-Up*, 1977.

———. *October Frost*, 1982.

———. *Psalm*, 1977.

———. *Reading Seferis*, 1979.

———. *Triada*, 1978.

———. *Uintah Blue*, 1975.

———. *Yesterday's Faces*, 1979.

Hansen, Paul. *Before Ten Thousand Peaks: Poems from the Chinese*, 1980.

Harkness, Edward. *Long Eye Lost Wind Forgive Me*, 1975.

Harlan, Chelsea. *Bright Shade*, 2022. Introduction by Jericho Brown.

Harrison, Jim. *Dead Man's Float*, 2016.

———. *In Search of Small Gods*, 2010.

———. *Jim Harrison: Collected Ghazals*, 2020. Edited by Joseph Bednarik. Afterword by Denver Butson.

———. *Jim Harrison: Complete Poems*, 2022. Edited by Joseph Bednarik. Introduction by Terry Tempest Williams.

———. *Jim Harrison: The Essential Poems*, 2019. Edited by Joseph Bednarik.

———. *Letters to Yesenin*, 2007.

———. *Saving Daylight*, 2007.

———. *The Shape of the Journey: New and Collected Poems*, 1998.

———. *Songs of Unreason*, 2011.

Harrison, Jim, and Ted Kooser. *Braided Creek: A Conversation in Poetry*, 2003.

Hauge, Olav H. *The Dream We Carry: Selected and Last Poems of Olav H. Hauge,* 2008. Translated from the Norwegian by Robert Bly and Robert Hedin.

Hausman, Gerald. *Night Herding Song,* 1979.

Hecht, Jennifer Michael. *Who Said,* 2013.

Hedin, Robert. *At the Great Door of Morning: Selected Poems and Translations,* 2017.

———. *At the Home-Altar,* 1978.

———. *Snow Country,* 1975.

Hennen, Tom. *Darkness Sticks to Everything: Collected and New Poems,* 2013. Introduction by Jim Harrison.

Heynen, Jim. *A Suitable Church,* 1981.

Hicok, Bob. *Elegy Owed,* 2013.

———. *Hold,* 2018.

———. *Red Rover Red Rover,* 2020.

———. *Sex & Love &,* 2016.

Hightower, Scott. *Part of the Bargain,* 2005.

Hitchcock, George. *The Piano Beneath the Skin,* 1978.

Hồ, Xuân Hư'o'ng. *Spring Essence: The Poetry of Hồ Xuân Hư'o'ng,* 2000. Translated from the Nôm by John Balaban.

Holthaus, Gary. *Unexpected Manna,* 1978.

Hu, Tung-Hui. *Greenhouses, Lighthouses,* 2013.

Huerta, David. *Before Saying Any of the Great Words: Selected Poems,* 2009. Translated from the Spanish by Mark Schafer.

Hugo, Richard. *Duwamish Head,* 1976.

Hummel, Maria. *House and Fire,* 2013.

Hyde, Lewis, and paintings by Max Gimblett. *The Disappearing Ox: A Modern Version of a Classic Buddhist Tale,* 2020. Translated from the Chinese by Lewis Hyde.

Jacobsen, Rolf. *The Roads Have Come to an End Now: Selected and Last Poems of Rolf Jacobsen,* 2001. Translated from the Norwegian by Robert Bly, Roger Greenwald, and Robert Hedin.

Jay, T.E. *River Dogs,* 1976.

Jin, Ha. *A Distant Center,* 2018.

Johnson, Thomas. *The Ice Future,* 1977.

Jones, Patricia Spears. *The Beloved Community,* 2023.

Jones, Richard. *Apropos of Nothing,* 2006.

———. *At Last We Enter Paradise,* 1991.

———. *The Blessing: New & Selected Poems,* 2000.

———. *The Correct Spelling and Exact Meaning,* 2010.

———. *Stranger on Earth,* 2018.

Jordan, June. *Directed by Desire: The Collected Poems of June Jordan,* 2005. Edited by Jan Heller Levi and Sara Miles. Foreword by Adrienne Rich.

———. *The Essential June Jordan,* 2021. Edited by Jan Heller Levi and Christoph Keller. Afterword by Jericho Brown.

———. *Passion,* 2021. Foreword by Nicole Sealey.

Joubert, Jean. *Black Iris,* 1988. Translated from the French by Denise Levertov.

Joudah, Fady. *Alight,* 2013.

———. *Textu,* 2014.

Kaplinski, Jaan. *The Wandering Border,* 1987. Translated from the Estonian by the author with Sam Hamill and Riina Tamm.

Kasischke, Laura. *The Infinitesimals,* 2014.

———. *Lightning Falls in Love,* 2021.

———. *Space, in Chains,* 2011.

———. *Where Now: New and Selected Poems,* 2017.

Kaufman, Shirley. *Ezekiel's Wheels,* 2009.

———. *Rivers of Salt,* 1993.

———. *Roots in the Air: New & Selected Poems,* 1996.

———. *Threshold,* 2003.

Kido, Shuri. *Names and Rivers,* 2022. Translated from the Japanese by Tomoyuki Endo and Forrest Gander.

Kizer, Carolyn. *Carrying Over,* 1988.

———. *Cool, Calm & Collected: Poems 1960–2000,* 2002.

———. *Harping On: Poems, 1985–1995,* 1996.

———. *Mermaids in the Basement: Poems for Women,* 1984.

———. *The Nearness of You,* 1986.

———. *Proses: On Poems and Poets,* 1993.

Kloefkorn, William. *Not Such a Bad Place to Be,* 1980.

Knox, Jennifer L. *Crushing It,* 2020.

Kooser, Ted. *Delights & Shadows,* 2004.

———. *Kindest Regards: New and Selected,* 2018.

———. *Red Stilts,* 2020.

———. *Splitting an Order,* 2014.

Koriyama, Naoshi, and Edward Lueders, editors and translators from the Japanese. *Like Underground Water: The Poetry of Mid-Twentieth Century Japan,* 1995.

Kuusisto, Stephen. *Letters to Borges,* 2013.

———. *Only Bread, Only Light,* 2000.

Landau, Deborah. *The Last Usable Hour,* 2011.

———. *Skeletons,* 2023.

———. *Soft Targets,* 2019.

———. *The Uses of the Body,* 2015.

Lane, John. *Thin Creek,* 1978.

Lao-tzu. *Lao-tzu's Taoteching: With Selected Commentaries from the Past 2,000 Years,* 2009. Translated from the Chinese by Red Pine.

Laughlin, James. *The Bird of Endless Time,* 1989.

———. *The Owl of Minerva,* 1987.

Lee, David. *Driving and Drinking,* 1979, 1982, 2004. With drawings by Dana Wylder.

———. *A Legacy of Shadows: Selected Poems,* 1999.

———. *My Town,* 1995.

———. *News from Down to the Cafe: New Poems,* 1999.

———. *The Porcine Canticles,* 1984, 2004.

———. *The Porcine Legacy,* 1978.

———. *So Quietly the Earth,* 2004.

Lee, Sung-Il. *The Moonlit Pond: Korean Classical Poems in Chinese,* 1997. Translated from the Chinese.

Le Guin, Ursula K. *So Far So Good: Final Poems: 2014–2018,* 2018.

Lerner, Ben. *Angle of Yaw,* 2006.

———. *The Lichtenberg Figures,* 2004.

———. *Mean Free Path,* 2010.

Levertov, Denise. *Wanderer's Daysong,* 1981.

Levin, Dana. *Banana Palace,* 2016.

———. *In the Surgical Theatre,* 1999.

———. *Now Do You Know Where You Are,* 2022.

———. *Sky Burial,* 2011.

———. *Wedding Day,* 2005.

Lindsay, Sarah. *Debt to the Bone-Eating Snotflower,* 2013.

———. *Twigs & Knucklebones,* 2008.

Liu, Timothy. *Burnt Offerings,* 1995.

———. *Say Goodnight,* 1998.

Liu, Tsung-yuan. *Written in Exile: The Poetry of Liu Tsung-yuan,* 2019. Translated from the Chinese by Red Pine.

Lopez, Barry. *Desert Reservation,* 1980.

Macari, Anne Marie. *Ivory Cradle,* 2000.

Machado, Antonio. *Border of a Dream: Selected Poems of Antonio Machado,* 2003. Translated from the Spanish by Willis Barnstone.

Major, Clarence. *Configurations: New & Selected Poems 1958–1998,* 1998.

———. *Waiting for Sweet Betty,* 2002.

Maloney, Frank. *How to Eat a Slug,* 1976.

Mann, Randall. *Deal: New and Selected Poems,* 2023.

Manning, Maurice. *One Man's Dark,* 2017.

———. *Railsplitter,* 2019.

Martin, Chris. *American Music,* 2007.

Marvin, Cate. *Event Horizon,* 2022.

McCord, Howard. *The Old Beast,* 1975.

McCorkle, James. *Evidences,* 2003. Introduction by Jorie Graham.

McGrath, Thomas. *Death Song,* 1991.

———. *Letter to an Imaginary Friend,* 1997.

———. *Passages Toward the Dark,* 1982.

———. *Selected Poems: 1938–1988,* 1988. Edited and with an introduction by Sam Hamill.

———. *Trinc: Praises II,* 1979.

McGriff, Michael. *Early Hour,* 2017.

———. *Home Burial,* 2012.

McHugh, Heather. *Muddy Matterhorn,* 2020.

———. *Upgraded to Serious,* 2009.

McKee, Laura. *Uttermost Paradise Place,* 2009.

McKibbens, Rachel. *blud,* 2017.

McNulty, Tim. *At the Foot of Denali,* 1978.

———. *Pawtracks,* 1978.

Merwin, W.S. *The Book of Fables,* 2007.

———. *East Window: The Asian Translations,* 1998.

————. *The Essential W.S. Merwin*, 2017. Edited by Michael Wiegers.

————. *The First Four Books of Poems*, 2000.

————. *Flower & Hand: Poems, 1977–1983*, 1997.

————. *Garden Time*, 2016.

————. *The Lice*, 2017. Introduction by Matthew Zapruder.

————. *The Mays of Ventadorn*, 2019. Introduction by Maurice Manning.

————. *Migration: New & Selected Poems*, 2005.

————. *The Moon Before Morning*, 2014.

————. *Present Company*, 2007.

————. *The Second Four Books of Poems*, 1993.

————. *Selected Translations*, 2013.

————. *The Shadow of Sirius*, 2008.

————. *Spanish Ballads*, 2008.

Metres, Philip. *Shrapnel Maps*, 2020.

Miller, Jane. *August Zero*, 1993.

————. *Memory at These Speeds: New & Selected Poems*, 1996.

————. *A Palace of Pearls*, 2005.

————. *Paper Banners*, 2023.

————. *Thunderbird*, 2013.

————. *Wherever You Lay Your Head*, 1999.

————. *Who Is Trixie the Trasher? and Other Questions*, 2018.

Milosz, O.V. de L. *Fourteen Poems*, 1983. Translated from the French by Kenneth Rexroth.

Mitsui, James Masao. *Journal of the Sun*, 1974.

Morgan, Robin. *Death Benefits*, 1981.

Morín, Tomás Q. *A Larger Country*, 2012.

————. *Patient Zero*, 2017.

Mort, Valzhyna. *Collected Body*, 2011.

————. *Factory of Tears*, 2008. Translated from the Belarusian by the author with Elizabeth Oehlkers Wright and Franz Wright.

Musō, Soseki. *Sun at Midnight: Poems and Letters*, 2013. Translated from the Japanese by W.S. Merwin and Sōiku Shigematsu.

Neruda, Pablo. *The Book of Questions*, 1991, 2001. Translated from the Spanish by William O'Daly.

————. *Book of Twilight*, 2017. Translated from the Spanish by William O'Daly.

————. *The Hands of Day*, 2008. Translated from the Spanish by William O'Daly.

————. *The Heights of Macchu Picchu*, 2015. Translated from the Spanish by Tomás Q. Morín.

————. *The Sea and the Bells*, 1988, 2002. Translated from the Spanish by William O'Daly.

————. *The Separate Rose*, 1985, 2005. Translated from the Spanish by William O'Daly.

————. *Still Another Day*, 1984, 2005. Translated from the Spanish by William O'Daly.

————. *Stones of the Sky*, 1987, 2002. Translated from the Spanish by James Nolan.

————. *Then Come Back: The Lost Neruda*, 2016. Translated from the Spanish by Forrest Gander.

————. *Winter Garden*, 1986, 2002. Translated from the Spanish by William O'Daly.

————. *World's End*, 2009. Translated from the Spanish by William O'Daly.

————. *The Yellow Heart*, 1990, 2002. Translated from the Spanish by William O'Daly.

Nezhukumatathil, Aimee. *Oceanic*, 2018.

Nichols, Travis. *See Me Improving,* 2010.

Nickerson, Sheila. *Songs of the Pine-Wife,* 1980.

Normile, Chessy. *Great Exodus, Great Wall, Great Party,* 2020. Introduction by Li-Young Lee.

O'Daly, William. *The Whale in the Web,* 1979.

O'Driscoll, Dennis. *Dear Life,* 2013.

———. *Quote Poet Unquote: Contemporary Quotations on Poets and Poetry,* 2008.

———. *Reality Check,* 2008.

———. *Update: Poems 2011–2012,* 2015.

Olstein, Lisa. *Dream Apartment,* 2023.

———. *Late Empire,* 2017.

———. *Little Stranger,* 2013.

———. *Lost Alphabet,* 2009.

———. *Radio Crackling, Radio Gone,* 2006.

Orr, David. *Dangerous Household Items,* 2018.

Orr, Gregory. *The Caged Owl: New & Selected Poems,* 2002.

———. *Concerning the Book That Is the Body of the Beloved,* 2005.

———. *How Beautiful the Beloved,* 2009.

———. *Orpheus & Eurydice: A Lyric Sequence,* 2001.

———. *Selected Books of the Beloved,* 2022.

Ossip, Kathleen. *The Search Engine,* 2002. Introduction by Derek Walcott.

Pardlo, Gregory. *Totem,* 2007.

Pavese, Cesare. *Disaffections: Complete Poems 1930–1950,* 2002. Translated from the Italian by Geoffrey Brock.

Pavlić, Ed. *Paraph of Bone & Other Kinds of Blue,* 2001.

Pawlak, Mark. *The Buffalo Sequence,* 1977. Introduction by Denise Levertov.

Peñalosa, Javier. *What Comes Back,* 2023. Translated from the Spanish by Robin Myers.

Pereira, Peter. *Saying the World,* 2003.

———. *What's Written on the Body,* 2007.

Perillo, Lucia. *Inseminating the Elephant,* 2009.

———. *On the Spectrum of Possible Deaths,* 2012.

———. *Time Will Clean the Carcass Bones: Selected and New Poems,* 2016.

Perry, Nathaniel. *Nine Acres,* 2011.

Porchia, Antonio. *Voices,* 2003. Translated from the Spanish by W.S. Merwin.

Pound, Ezra. *From Syria: The Worksheets, Proofs, and Text,* 1981. Edited by Robin Skelton.

Prufer, Kevin. *The Fears,* 2023.

Rabins, Alicia Jo. *Divinity School,* 2015.

Rader, Dean. *Beyond the Borderless: Dialogues with the Art of Cy Twombly,* 2023.

———. *Self-Portrait as Wikipedia Entry,* 2017.

Randall, Belle. *The Orpheus Sedan,* 1980.

Rankine, Camille. *Incorrect Merciful Impulses,* 2016.

Ransom, W.M. *Finding True North,* 1972.

———. *Waving Arms at the Blind,* 1975.

Rao, Natasha. *Latitude,* 2021.

Rea, Tom. *Man in a Rowboat,* 1977.

Red Pine. *The Collected Songs of Cold Mountain*, 1983, 2000.

———. *Dancing with the Dead: The Essential Red Pine Translations*, 2023.

———. *Finding Them Gone: Visiting China's Poets of the Past*, 2016.

———. *Poems of the Masters: China's Classic Anthology of T'ang and Sung Dynasty Verse*, 2003.

Reeves, Roger. *King Me*, 2013.

Rekdal, Paisley. *Imaginary Vessels*, 2016. With photographs by Andrea Modica.

———. *Nightingale*, 2019.

———. *West: A Translation*, 2023.

Rexroth, Kenneth. *The Complete Poems of Kenneth Rexroth*, 2004.

———. *The Silver Swan: Poems Written in Kyoto, 1974–75*, 1976.

Richardson, James. *By the Numbers*, 2010.

———. *During*, 2016.

———. *For Now*, 2020.

Rilke, Rainer Maria. *Rilke: New Poems*, 2014. Translated from the German by Joseph Cadora.

Ríos, Alberto. *The Dangerous Shirt*, 2009.

———. *Not Go Away Is My Name*, 2020.

———. *The Smallest Muscle in the Human Body*, 2002.

———. *A Small Story about the Sky*, 2015.

———. *The Theater of Night*, 2006.

Roderick, David. *Blue Colonial*, 2006. Introduction by Robert Pinsky.

Roethke, Theodore. *On Poetry and Craft: Selected Prose*, 2001. Introduction by Carolyn Kizer.

———. *Straw for the Fire: From the Notebooks of Theodore Roethke, 1943–63*, 2006. Selected and arranged by David Wagoner.

Rollins, Alison C. *Library of Small Catastrophes*, 2019.

Romtvedt, David. *A Flower Whose Name I Do Not Know*, 1992.

Ruhl, Sarah. *44 Poems for You*, 2020.

———. *Love Poems in Quarantine*, 2022.

Sáenz, Benjamin Alire. *The Book of What Remains*, 2010.

———. *Dreaming the End of War*, 2006.

Saenz, Jacob. *Throwing the Crown*, 2018.

Scenters-Zapico, Natalie. *Lima :: Limón*, 2019.

Schmitz, Dennis. *Truth Squad*, 2002.

Seiferle, Rebecca. *Bitters*, 2001.

———. *Wild Tongue*, 2007.

Shapero, Natalie. *Hard Child*, 2017.

———. *Popular Longing*, 2021.

Shaughnessy, Brenda. *Human Dark with Sugar*, 2008.

———. *Our Andromeda*, 2012.

———. *So Much Synth*, 2016.

Shelton, Richard. *A Kind of Glory*, 1982.

Siken, Richard. *War of the Foxes*, 2015.

Simon, Maurya. *Days of Awe*, 1989.

———. *The Enchanted Room*, 1986.

Skoog, Ed. *Mister Skylight*, 2009.

———. *Rough Day*, 2013.

———. *Run the Red Lights*, 2016.

———. *Travelers Leaving for the City*, 2020.

Snyder, Gary. *Songs for Gaia*, 1979.

Sok, Monica. *A Nail the Evening Hangs On*, 2020.

Soto, Christopher. *Diaries of a Terrorist*, 2022.

Stafford, Kim Robert. *A Gypsy's History of the World*, 1976.

Stafford, William. *Sometimes Like a Legend*, 1981.

Stanford, Ann. *Holding Our Own: The Selected Poetry of Ann Stanford*, 2001. Edited by David Trinidad.

Stanford, Frank. *What About This: Collected Poems of Frank Stanford*, 2015. Edited by Michael Wiegers. Introduction by Dean Young.

Steele, Nancy. *Tracking*, 1977.

Stein, Melissa. *Rough Honey*, 2010.

———. *Terrible blooms*, 2018.

Stewart, Frank, editor. *The Poem Behind the Poem: Translating Asian Poetry*, 2004.

St. John, Primus. *Communion: Poems 1976–1998*, 1999.

———. *Skins on the Earth*, 1976.

Stone, Ruth. *The Essential Ruth Stone*, 2020. Edited by Bianca Stone.

———. *In the Dark*, 2004.

———. *In the Next Galaxy*, 2002.

———. *What Love Comes To: New & Selected Poems*, 2008. Foreword by Sharon Olds.

Stonehouse, *The Mountain Poems of Stonehouse*, 2014. Translated from the Chinese by Red Pine.

Stroud, Joseph. *Below Cold Mountain*, 1998.

———. *Country of Light*, 2004.

———. *Everything That Rises*, 2019.

———. *Of This World: New and Selected Poems*, 2008.

Su, Tung-p'o. *Selected Poems of Su Tung-p'o*, 1994. Translated from the Chinese by Burton Watson.

Sund, Robert. *The Hides of White Horses Shedding Rain*, 1981.

Sung, Po-jen. *Guide to Capturing a Plum Blossom*, 2012. Translated from the Chinese by Red Pine. Introduction by Lo Ch'ing.

Swenson, Karen. *A Daughter's Latitude: New & Selected Poems*, 1999.

———. *Landlady in Bangkok*, 1994.

Swir, Anna. *Talking to My Body*, 1996. Translated from the Polish by Czesław Miłosz and Leonard Nathan.

Sze, Arthur. *Archipelago*, 1995.

———. *Compass Rose*, 2014.

———. *The Ginkgo Light*, 2009.

———. *The Glass Constellation: New and Collected Poems*, 2021.

———. *Quipu*, 2005.

———. *The Redshifting Web: Poems 1970–1998*, 1998.

———. *Sight Lines*, 2019.

———. *Silk Dragon: Translations from the Chinese*, 2001.

Taggart, John. *Is Music: Selected Poems,* 2010. Edited by Peter O'Leary. Foreword by C.D. Wright.

Tagore, Rabindranath. *The Lover of God,* 2003. Translated from the Bengali by Tony K. Stewart and Chase Twichell.

T'ao, Ch'ien. *The Selected Poems of T'ao Ch'ien,* 1993. Translated from the Chinese by David Hinton.

Tao, Yuanming. *Enduring Poverty: The Complete Poems of Tao Yuanming,* 2023. Translated from the Chinese by Red Pine.

Terranova, Elaine. *Damages,* 1995.

Tone, Heather. *Likenesses,* 2016.

Torre, Mónica de la, and Michael Wiegers, editors. *Reversible Monuments: Contemporary Mexican Poetry,* 2001. Translated from the Spanish by several contributors.

Trakl, Georg. *Song of the Departed: Selected Poems of Georg Trakl,* 2012. Translated from the German by Robert Firmage.

Tranströmer, Tomas. *Iron Psalm: The Collected Works of Tomas Tranströmer,* 2023. Translated from the Swedish by Patty Crane.

Twichell, Chase. *Dog Language,* 2005.

———. *Horses Where the Answers Should Have Been: New and Selected Poems,* 2010.

———. *Things as It Is,* 2018.

Uyematsu, Amy. *Stone Bow Prayer,* 2005.

Valentine, Jean. *Break the Glass,* 2010.

———. *Shirt in Heaven,* 2015.

Vallejo, César. *The Black Heralds,* 2003. Translated from the Spanish by Rebecca Seiferle.

Valverde, Fernando. *America,* 2021. Translated from the Spanish and with an introduction by Carolyn Forché.

Van Dyke, Cheryl. *Cheat Grass,* 1975.

Vazirani, Reetika. *World Hotel,* 2002.

Villaurrutia, Xavier. *Nostalgia for Death & Hieroglyphs of Desire,* 1992. Translated from the Spanish by Eliot Weinberger.

Vuong, Ocean. *Night Sky with Exit Wounds,* 2016.

Wagoner, David. *After the Point of No Return,* 2012.

Wallschlaeger, Nikki. *Waterbaby,* 2021.

Wanek, Connie. *On Speaking Terms,* 2010.

Wang, Qingping, editor, with translation coeditors Sylvia Li-chun Lin and Howard Goldblatt. *Push Open the Window: Contemporary Poetry from China,* 2011.

Warn, Emily. *The Leaf Path,* 1982.

———. *The Novice Insomniac,* 1996.

———. *Shadow Architect,* 2008.

Warren, Noah. *The Complete Stories,* 2021.

Wasson, Michael. *Swallowed Light,* 2022.

Wee, Rebecca. *Uncertain Grace,* 2001.

Wei, Ying-wu. *In Such Hard Times: The Poetry of Wei Ying-wu,* 2009. Translated from the Chinese by Red Pine.

West, Kathleen. *Land Bound,* 1978.

White, Michael. *The Island,* 1992.

Wiegers, Michael, editor. *A House Called Tomorrow: Fifty Years of Poetry from Copper Canyon Press,* 2023.

———. *The Poet's Child: A Copper Canyon Anthology,* 2002.

———. *This Art: Poems about Poetry,* 2003.

Williams, Jonathan. *Jubilant Thicket: New & Selected Poems,* 2004. Introduction by Jim Cory.

Wilner, Eleanor Rand. *The Girl with Bees in Her Hair,* 2004.

———. *Reversing the Spell: New & Selected Poems,* 1997.

Wilson, Keith S. *Fieldnotes on Ordinary Love,* 2019.

Wiman, Christian. *Ambition and Survival: Becoming a Poet,* 2007.

———. *Hard Night,* 2005.

———. *The Long Home,* 2007.

Wolfe, Marianne. *The Berrypicker,* 1973.

Wright, C.D. *Casting Deep Shade: An Amble Inscribed to Beech Trees & Co.,* 2019. With photographs by Denny Moers.

———. *Cooling Time: An American Poetry Vigil,* 2005.

———. *Deepstep Come Shining,* 1998.

———. *One Big Self: An Investigation,* 2007.

———. *One With Others [a little book of her days],* 2010.

———. *The Poet, the Lion, Talking Pictures, El Farolito, a Wedding in St. Roch, the Big Box Store, the Warp in the Mirror, Spring, Midnights, Fire & All,* 2016.

———. *Rising, Falling, Hovering,* 2008.

———. *ShallCross,* 2016.

———. *Steal Away: Selected and New Poems,* 2002.

Wrigley, Robert. *The Sinking of Clay City,* 1979.

Wronsky, Gail. *Dying for Beauty,* 2000.

Yau, John. *Further Adventures in Monochrome,* 2012.

Yosa, Buson. *Collected Haiku of Yosa Buson,* 2013. Translated from the Japanese by W.S. Merwin and Takako Lento.

Young, Dean. *Bender: New & Selected Poems,* 2012.

———. *Fall Higher,* 2011.

———. *Shock by Shock,* 2015.

———. *Solar Perplexus,* 2019.

Yu, Han. *Growing Old Alive,* 1978.

Zamora, Javier. *Unaccompanied,* 2017.

Zapruder, Matthew. *Come On All You Ghosts,* 2010.

———. *Father's Day,* 2019.

———. *The Pajamaist,* 2006.

———. *Sun Bear,* 2014.

Zaqtan, Ghassan. *The Silence That Remains: Selected Poems,* 2017. Edited and translated from the Arabic by Fady Joudah.

Zurita, Raúl, and Forrest Gander, editors. *Pinholes in the Night: Essential Poems from Latin America,* 2014. Translated by several contributors.

Contributors

We are grateful to all the Copper Canyon community members who contributed a favorite poem to the making of this book:

Kelli Russell Agodon	Christie Collins
Zuhra Amini	Alfred Corn
Janeen Armstrong	Tyree Daye
James Arthur	Jackie Delaney
Elizabeth Ash	Martin Dent
Jenny Rae Bailey	Alex Dimitrov
John Balaban	Lidija Dimkovska
Ellen Bass	Tishani Doshi
Kris Becker	Cathy Edwards
Joseph Bednarik	Elaina Ellis
Erin Belieu	Laurie Eustis
Donna Bellew	Kerry James Evans
Emily Bennett	Shangyang Fang
Ruth Gila Berger	Sascha Feinstein
Linda Bierds	Rozlyn Anderson Flood
Jeffrey Bishop	Bob Francis
Ellie Black	Hailey Gaunt
Jacob Boles	Dan Gerber
Jaswinder Bolina	Sierra Golden
Marianne Boruch	Roger Greenwald
David Bottoms	James Gregorski
Geoff Bouvier	Josh Hamilton
Heather Brennan	Art Hanlon
Nellie Bridge	Clayton Haselwood
Traci Brimhall	Lilah Hegnauer
Joan Broughton	Jim Heynen
Olga Broumas	Scott Hightower
Jeffrey Brown	David Huerta
Josh Brown	Maria Hummel
Laura Buccieri	Mark Irwin
Vincent Buck	Julie Johnson
David Caligiuri	Patricia Spears Jones
Kayleb Rae Candrilli	Richard Jones
Cyrus Cassells	Asela Kemper
Sara Cavanaugh	Rick Kenney
Thomas Centolella	Mary Jane Knecht
Elizabeth J. Coleman	George Knotek

Phil Kovacevich
Randall Lane
Dylan Larson-Harsch
Dana Levin
Peter Lewis
Gary Lilly
Timothy Liu
Noah Lloyd
Alison Lockhart
Maurice Manning
Kelly McLennon
Hannah Messinger
Phil Metres
Jane Miller
Roger Mitchell
Tomás Q. Morín
Kate Morley
Valzhyna Mort
Justin Nash
Reuben Gelley Newman
Aimee Nezhukumatathil
Travis Nichols
Chessy Normile
Elizabeth O'Brien
William O'Daly
Kate O'Donoghue
Lisa Olstein
David Orr
Eric Pankey
Walter Parsons
Ed Pavlić
Peter Pereira
Nathaniel Perry
John Pierce
Melissa Pine
Kevin Prufer
Alicia Jo Rabins
Janna Rademacher
Dean Rader
Natasha Rao
Emily Raymond

Red Pine
James Richardson
Joseph Roberts
Sam Robison
David Romtvedt
Tonaya Rosenberg
Wesley Rothman
Larry Rouch
Elizabeth Rush
Lily Sadighmehr
Jacob Saenz
Tina Schumann
Kim Brown Seely
Nicolas Seow
Heidi Sewall
Natalie Shapero
Ira Silverberg
Ed Skoog
Monica Sok
Christopher Soto
Melissa Stein
Tree Swenson
Arthur Sze
Peter Szilagyi
Kaci Tavares
Elaine Terranova
Chase Twichell
Amy Uyematsu
Corey Van Landingham
Jeremy Voigt
Dan Waggoner
Connie Wanek
Sanna Wani
Emily Warn
Noah Warren
Michael Wasson
Rebecca Wee
Michael White
Cole Williams
Gail Wronsky
Matthew Zapruder

About the Editor

Michael Wiegers is the Executive Editor of Copper Canyon Press where, over the past three decades, he has edited and published more than five hundred titles. He additionally serves as poetry editor for *Narrative*. Wiegers edited two retrospective volumes of the poetry of Frank Stanford, *What About This* (a finalist for the 2015 National Book Critics Circle Award) and *Hidden Water* (with Chet Weise), and he is also the editor of *Reversible Monuments: Contemporary Mexican Poetry* (with Mónica de la Torre), *The Poet's Child*, and *This Art: Poems about Poetry*. He lives in Port Townsend, Washington, and is writing a book about W.S. Merwin.

Lannan Literary Selections

For two decades Lannan Foundation has supported the publication and distribution of exceptional literary works. Copper Canyon Press gratefully acknowledges their support.

LANNAN LITERARY SELECTIONS 2023

Jaswinder Bolina, *English as a Second Language*

Natalie Eilbert, *Overland*

Amanda Gunn, *Things I Didn't Do with This Body*

Paisley Rekdal, *West: A Translation*

Michael Wiegers (ed.), *A House Called Tomorrow: Fifty Years of Poetry from Copper Canyon Press*

RECENT LANNAN LITERARY SELECTIONS FROM
COPPER CANYON PRESS

Chris Abani, *Smoking the Bible*

Mark Bibbins, *13th Balloon*

Jericho Brown, *The Tradition*

Victoria Chang, *Obit*

Victoria Chang, *The Trees Witness Everything*

Leila Chatti, *Deluge*

Shangyang Fang, *Burying the Mountain*

Nicholas Goodly, *Black Swim*

June Jordan, *The Essential June Jordan*

Laura Kasischke, *Lightning Falls in Love*

Deborah Landau, *Soft Targets*

Dana Levin, *Now Do You Know Where You Are*

Philip Metres, *Shrapnel Maps*

Paisley Rekdal, *Nightingale*

Natalie Scenters-Zapico, *Lima :: Limón*

Natalie Shapero, *Popular Longing*

Arthur Sze, *The Glass Constellation: New and Collected Poems*

Fernando Valverde, *America* (translated by Carolyn Forché)

Michael Wasson, *Swallowed Light*

Matthew Zapruder, *Father's Day*

Poetry is vital to language and living. Since 1972, Copper Canyon Press has published extraordinary poetry from around the world to engage the imaginations and intellects of readers, writers, booksellers, librarians, teachers, students, and donors.

WE ARE GRATEFUL FOR THE MAJOR SUPPORT PROVIDED BY:

academy of
american poets

THE PAUL G. ALLEN
FAMILY FOUNDATION

4
CULTURE

Lannan

WASHINGTON STATE
ARTS COMMISSION

A&
OFFICE OF ARTS & CULTURE
—— SEATTLE ——

The Witter Bynner Foundation
for Poetry

TO LEARN MORE ABOUT UNDERWRITING
COPPER CANYON PRESS TITLES,
PLEASE CALL 360-385-4925 EXT. 103

WE ARE GRATEFUL FOR THE MAJOR SUPPORT PROVIDED BY:

Richard Andrews and Colleen
  Chartier

Anonymous

Jill Baker and Jeffrey Bishop

Anne and Geoffrey Barker

Donna Bellew

Matthew Bellew

Sarah Bird

Will Blythe

John Branch

Diana Broze

Sarah Cavanaugh

Keith Cowan and Linda Walsh

Stephanie Ellis-Smith and
  Douglas Smith

Mimi Gardner Gates

Gull Industries Inc. on behalf of
  William True

The Trust of Warren A. Gummow

William R. Hearst III

Carolyn and Robert Hedin

David and Jane Hibbard

Bruce S. Kahn

Phil Kovacevich and Eric Wechsler

Lakeside Industries Inc. on behalf
  of Jeanne Marie Lee

Maureen Lee and Mark Busto

Peter Lewis and Johanna Turiano

Ellie Mathews and Carl Youngmann
  as The North Press

Larry Mawby and Lois Bahle

Hank and Liesel Meijer

Jack Nicholson

Petunia Charitable Fund and
  adviser Elizabeth Hebert

Madelyn Pitts

Suzanne Rapp and Mark Hamilton

Adam and Lynn Rauch

Emily and Dan Raymond

Joseph C. Roberts

Jill and Bill Ruckelshaus

Cynthia Sears

Kim and Jeff Seely

Nora Hutton Shepard

D.D. Wigley

Joan F. Woods

Barbara and Charles Wright

In honor of C.D. Wright,
  from Forrest Gander

Caleb Young as C. Young Creative

The dedicated interns and faithful
  volunteers of Copper Canyon Press

A House Called Tomorrow: Fifty Years of Poetry from Copper Canyon Press features a new pressmark.

Inspired by Copper Canyon Press's legacy logo,
designer Phil Kovacevich has created a pressmark
that suggests entrance, connection, and interaction
while holding at its center
an attentive, dynamic space for poetry.

This book is set in Adobe Garamond Pro.
Book design by Phil Kovacevich.

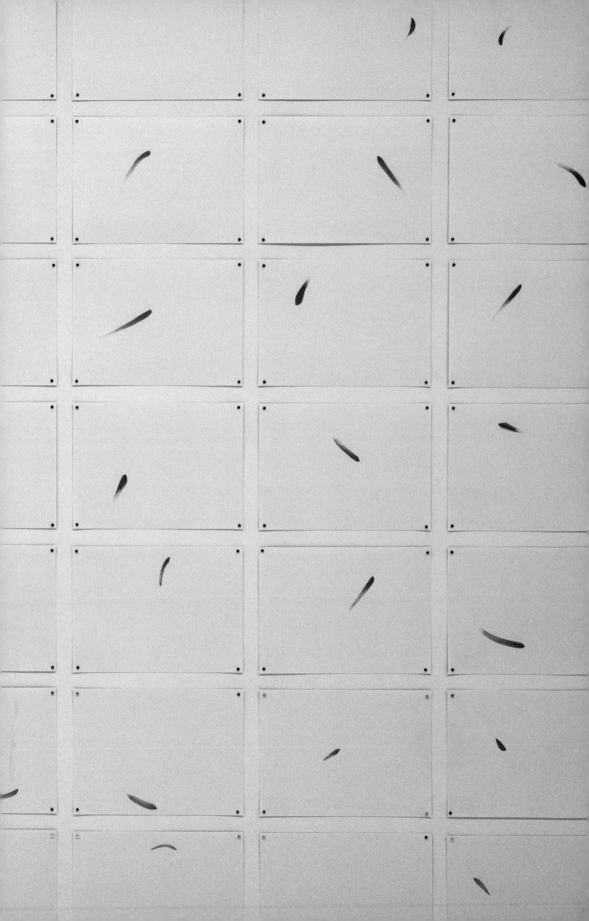